meditations
of a
holocaust
traveler

meditations
of a
holocaust
traveler

gerald e. markle

state university of
new york press

Cover illustration "Die Verdammten," used with permission of the Sammlung Felix Nussbaum der Niedersächsischen Sparkassenstiftung im Kulturgeschichtlichen Museum Osnabrück. Photograph: Foto Strenger, Osnabrück/Christian Grovermann.

Published by
State University of New York Press, Albany

For information, address the State University of New York Press, State University Plaza, Albany, NY 12246

Production by Bernadine Dawes • Marketing by Fran Keneston

Library of Congress Cataloging-in-Publication Data

Markle, Gerald E., 1942–
    Meditations of a Holocaust traveler / Gerald E. Markle.
        p. cm.
    ISBN 0-7914-2643-2. — ISBN 0-7914-2644-0 (pbk.)
        1. Holocaust, Jewish (1939–1945)—Influence.   2. Meditations.
    I. Title.
D804.3.M366 1995
940.53'18–dc20   94-42915
                                                                                        CIP

10 9 8 7 6 5 4 3 2

for sherman adelman
big brother
and
lifelong friend

contents

stone soup   xi

1. thinking   1
   snapshots / 2
   gray / 11
   approaches / 16
   meditation / 25

2. banality   31
   eichmann / 33
   ordinary killers / 42
   ordinary people / 45
   are we all nazis? / 53
   abraham's choice / 57

3. bureaucracy   63
   routine slaughter / 66
   two visions / 70
   blood and honor / 74
   functionalism / 84
   forgetting / 91
   krema / 96

4. modernity   99
   total domination / 101
   gardening / 108
   medical experiments / 115
   the american connection / 118
   enlightment? / 122
   a dialogue / 127

5. after   131

    in memoriam / 132
    collective memory / 135
    historiography / 137
    today / 142
    anamnesis / 146
    an ending? / 149
    another ending / 153

references   155

author index   169

subject index   173

We are so dazzled by power and prestige as to forget our essential fragility. Willingly or not we come to terms with power, forgetting that we are all in the ghetto, that the ghetto is walled in, that outside the ghetto reign the lords of death, and that close by the train is waiting.

—Primo Levi

stone soup
acknowledgments

Here is an old folk tale:

A stranger comes into a town and proclaims that he will cook an unusual and delicious soup. Even more, he will serve this fare to the entire population of the town. The recipe is simple: place two large stones in water, heat and simmer throughout the day. In the evening, with the townspeople gathered by the pot, the stranger tastes the soup. "Delicious," he pronounces. He pauses, then adds: "It would even be better if someone had just a bit of salt." "With such kindness, it's the least I can do," says one watcher. She leaves and returns with a handful of salt to add to the pot. "Wonderful," says the stranger. "Perhaps it would be perfect if we only had an onion." Soon, a man brings a few onions, and without being asked, several others bring a variety of root vegetables. The story repeats itself as a bone is added to the mixture, followed by a bit of cream, and finally, some bread and wine to serve with the soup. At the story's close, the people savor the tasty soup.

This book is stone soup.

The text which follows will indicate my great appreciation and debt to numerous scholars, writers and survivors. Without them, my book has no substance or seasoning.

Beyond this scholarly debt are personal ones. In particular, I thank the following:

Frances McCrea, my wife and colleague: My soul is hers. She shared her precious stories with me. She nourished and nurtured my intellect. I cannot imagine a world view, aesthetic or scholarly, without her at the center.

William Baum knows more about the Holocaust than anyone I know, and he has served as my kind mentor. When he first suggested that I teach a course on the Holocaust (as he does),

I said: "You must be crazy!" Everything has followed from that remark.

Mary Lagerwey's work on Auschwitz memoirs has greatly informed me. I am indebted to her for intelligent and thoughtful readings of many drafts of this book.

Christopher Browning guided my historiography and found numerous historical errors in earlier drafts. I hope that I have made all necessary corrections.

Many others added to the broth: David Isaacson, Allan Mazur, and Stanley Robin each gave the scholar's precious gift—a critical reading of the entire manuscript; Morton Wagenfeld and Barry Castro helped me solve problems with selected sections of the manuscript. Judith Hoover copyedited the manuscript with insight and also taught me some grammar in the process. Jennifer Boyers prepared the index with care and intelligence. Finally, my students in Honors 495 ("The Holocaust") at Western Michigan University suggested numerous changes, small and large, in this manuscript.

1   thinking

*At no other place or time has one seen a phenomenon so unexpected and
so complex: never have so many lives been extinguished in so short a
time, and with so lucid a combination of technological ingenuity,
fanaticism and cruelty.*
—Primo Levi, survivor of Auschwitz, 1988

Three propositions of a survivor:
*That hell is a denial of the ordinary; that nothing lasts; that clean white
paper waiting under a pen is the gift beyond history and hurt and heaven.*
—John Ciardi, American poet, 1959

*I had no clarity when I was writing this book, I do not have it today, and
I hope that I never will. Clarification would amount to disposal,
settlement of the case, which can then be placed in the files of history. My
book is meant to aid in preventing precisely this.*
—Jean Amery, survivor of Auschwitz, 1977

I am a generation removed from the Holocaust. As an American, I have lived a peaceful life, free from the curse of war and
destruction. None of my loved ones were killed in the cataclysm.
I, born in the early forties, did not even know of the Holocaust
as a child. My knowledge has come vicariously: I listened to survivors; I read memoirs and scholarly studies.

I have also been a tourist of the Holocaust. A half century
after the infamy, I have walked in Holocaust places.[1] On those

---

1. According to historian Michael Marrus, Auschwitz attracts seventy thousand visitors per year, a remarkable number given the location of the camp far
from the usual tourist route. These visitors have not left the site untouched. The
pile of inmate shoes and the mound of women's hair, are considerably smaller
now than they were a few years ago. One presumes that tourists, for whatever
reasons, treat these objects as memorabilia (or icons?) and take them home.

grounds, pondering the slaughter, I have felt the strangeness—the other-worldliness—that for me is so essential in approaching the Holocaust.

snapshots

I begin this book with three snapshots from my memory.[2]

a mountain top

Tourists often include mountain vistas in their itineraries. The Bavarian Alps are spectacular, and it would be hard to find a more beautiful place than the Eagle's Nest. Sitting on a mountaintop, this was Hitler's getaway, similar in function to an American president's Camp David. Here Hitler worked and here Hitler played.[3]

The day is foggy, drizzly, cold—and stunning. From what looks like the top of the world, life in the valleys below is hidden, then revealed through the gauze of fast-moving clouds. Such grandeur encourages one to meditate: not only about the meaning of the universe, but of the Eagle's Nest just a few decades ago. Hitler had undoubtedly gazed at the same view many times, perhaps musing about the Final Solution, perhaps dreaming of death.

The Bavarian government has converted Hitler's house into a tourist center and restaurant. We have lunch in what was the conference room, our table next to an impressive fireplace, a gift to Hitler from Mussolini. Eva Braun's bedroom is just to our left. We are cold and wet and shivering. The bockwurst, kraut, and beer, followed by hot spiced wine, then cake with

---

2. I keep a detailed journal when I travel, generally written each morning and evening. The "we" that follows refers to my wife and me.

3. The Eagle's Nest was built in 1937, for Hitler's fiftieth birthday. The approach road, four miles long and only thirteen feet wide, ascends almost 900 feet—a difficult engineering feat in the rugged mountain terrain. Today one must take a bus up a dizzying road. At its end, a luxurious elevator—with green leather and brass mirrors—whisks the visitor up through 330 feet of solid rock to the mountain top. According to some accounts, Hitler rarely used the place, preferring his villa on the lower slopes.

schlag—a good German meal—satisfy us. The fire and wine have warmed our bodies. We understand that we are not supposed to have a good time here. We buy a postcard or two to send home.

a music school

In Munich, one eats weisswurst, prepared fresh every morning, and washes it down with the finest beer in the world. The best place to have this meal is in a beer hall, perhaps one in which the unknown politician Adolf Hitler spoke, for this is the city where the Nazi Party was born.

Munich is a beautiful city—medieval gates, a gothic city hall, and flowers everywhere. Of the many buildings constructed in this city by the Nazis, only two remain. The designs for both were closely supervised by Hitler. In a city of lovely buildings, these were grim, bunkerlike blocks: long, low, square columns, flat; no trees, shrubs, or flowers.

We approach one, the former Nazi Party headquarters.[4] We look carefully and find neither sign nor plaque to mark the history of the building. Today it is a music academy. From the outside, we hear music and a hauntingly beautiful soprano voice singing a Mozart aria. I am transported into a surreal nightmare or perhaps an Ingmar Bergman movie. I feel like crying, and perhaps also like vomiting. Inside, we find marble floors, a grand stairway, and harsh light. Students walk to and fro, busy with the minutiae of their lives.

The Allies destroyed most of these Nazi buildings. I'm glad they saved this one; for better or worse, we should save and remember, never destroy, our history. But something is very wrong here. The memory has been badly twisted: Sweet music now emanates unknowingly from a place that produced the greatest cacophony. So the music, through no fault of the singer and players, is turned into something ugly.

---

4. At this site, Hitler and Neville Chamberlain signed the infamous Munich appeasement of 1938 which ceded the Sudetenland (part of the current Czech Republic) to the Nazis.

trees

At Dachau, a concentration camp near Munich, the Germans counted their victims; they carefully registered 31,591 murders.[5] Today Dachau is a tourist site for the curious. It is also a cemetery, though one without bodies. We walk the grounds of Dachau amidst the ashes. We cross ditches that once carried streams of blood. We stand in a barrack (a reconstruction, to be sure) of suffering. The barracks had stood in neat lines, each with a tree symmetrically placed.

Those trees still bother me. I have always seen beauty in trees, and these at Dachau were quite lovely. Yet for me the trees were obscene: for their roots, which entangled and sucked up the nutrient human ash, are to this day nurtured by ghosts.[6]

Dachau is clean, spotless. A half century ago, it was the same. If there is a symbol for the Holocaust, if any one image can capture both order and chaos, it is this: The Nazis starved their prisoners; they beat them; they degraded them in their own excrement.[7] But neatness, cleanliness, surrounded the filth, enveloped their deaths.

Not only neatness, but a certain beauty prevails. For the village of Dachau, from which the camp takes its name, is quite lovely.[8] According to its own brochure, replete with snapshots of the village past and present, "tranquility still graces the town."

---

5. The first concentration camp built by the Nazis, Dachau was initially used for political prisoners. It was never an extermination camp. Until the last days of the war, relatively few (by concentration camp standards) prisoners died there, though—as we will see in chapter 4—unspeakable things happened at that site. Just before the Russians liberated Auschwitz and other camps in the east, the Nazis force-marched prisoners to Dachau, and there murdered unknown tens of thousands.

6. Birkenau, the killing center at Auschwitz, is named for the trees in that area. The word means "birches" in German.

7. See Terrence Des Pres, *The Survivor: An Anatomy of Life in the Death Camps* (New York: Oxford University Press, 1976, p. 53ff). Sometimes emaciated people actually fell to their deaths through the latrine openings.

8. Claude Lanzmann's 1985 film *Shoah* quietly shocks the viewer with pacific scenery; a half century can transmogrify a killing ground into a scenic vista. Visiting Mauthausen, a concentration camp in Austria, I was disturbed and unsettled by the picture-postcard beauty of the site.

Visitors are urged to visit the palace, built in 1715, where "you can rest and feel at home on the terrace with its views of the gardens." The document also presents the years between 1933 and 1945 as the years of terror, but claims that its citizenry "didn't know the details of what was going on behind the walls of the camps." One more note: the brochure claims that in the years between 1573 and 1652, under the rule of Maximillian I, "Dachau experienced its worst time."[9]

The following snapshots were taken at Auschwitz: a fitting place—an inevitable place, a place that Primo Levi called "a ferocious sociological laboratory[10]—to begin thinking about the Holocaust. I found the snapshots in memoirs written by survivors.[11]

the bed-making ritual

Making a bed is perhaps a dull detail in the life of an ordinary person. For prisoners in concentration camps, Primo Levi tells us, bed-making was dangerous, a time of dark ritual. The beds (such as they were) were wooden planks; mattresses were thin and filled with wood shavings; pillows were torn and filled with straw; two men slept in each bed. After reveille, all beds had to be made "immediately" and "simultaneously" and "perfectly."

---

9. Today Dachau is home to one of the most active artistic communities in Germany, one that has explicitly and purposely explored Holocaust themes. "What the people of Dachau must come to understand," one artist asserted, "is that this great burden with which they have lived for 50 years can also be seen as a great opportunity." Quoted in Timothy Ryback, "Between Art and Atrocity," *Art News*, 92 December, 1993, p. 121. Though I respect the art, I have my doubts about the opportunity.

10. Primo Levi, survivor of Auschwitz, wrote numerous and brilliant works best described as memoirs. This quote is from *Other People's Trades* (New York: Summit Books, 1989, p. 104), a lovely collection of short essays, which says little directly about the Holocaust. Like all of Levi's books, one feels richer after the read.

11. For an analysis of survivors' memoirs, see Mary Lagerwey, *Gold-Encrusted Chaos: An Analysis of Auschwitz Memoirs* (Unpublished dissertation, Kalamazoo, MI: Western Michigan University, 1994). I gratefully acknowledge her help in preparing this section.

"It was therefore necessary for the occupants of the lower bunks to manage as best they could to fix mattress and blanket between the legs of the tenants of the upper levels."

Levi describes the "frantic moments" during *bettenbauen:* "The atmosphere filled with dust to the point of becoming opaque, with . . . curses exchanged in all languages." After this frenzy of activity, "each bed must look like a rectangular parallelepiped with well-smoothed edges, on which was placed the smaller parallelepiped of the pillow."[12]

There were, of course, consequences. Anyone who did not properly make the bed was "punished publicly and savagely." Reflecting on the Holocaust in his later years, Levi was puzzled by this strange activity. But this he knew: For the SS,[13] the bed-making ritual was a "sacral operation" of "prime and indecipherable" importance.[14] What the Germans wanted, and what they got, was order and control amidst chaos and death.

the orchestra

One image comes close to capturing my noncomprehension, my disbelief: the Auschwitz orchestra. This sounds like an oxymoron, but it is not. At Auschwitz, there was an orchestra (several

---

12. Levi, *The Drowned and the Saved* (New York: Vintage International Press, 1989), p. 117. Shortly before this book was published, Levi committed suicide.

13. Originally Hitler's elite bodyguards, the SS wore black uniforms, black caps with a death's-head emblem, a ring decorated with a death's-head, and for officers, a dagger bearing the motto: Loyalty is My Honor. Membership was contingent on Aryan appearance; officers and their wives supposedly had to prove their racial purity back to the year 1700. Under the leadership of Heinrich Himmler, who next to Hitler became the most powerful Nazi in Germany (see Richard Breitman, The Architect of Genocide: Himmler and the Final Solution [New York: Knopf, 1991]), the SS eventually developed into a large and complex institution. The SS was instrumental in all aspects of the Holocaust: from the creation of ghettos, to mass starvation, to the creation and operation of the death camps. By the end of the war, there were eight hundred thousand men in militarized SS units, known as the Waffen-SS.

14. Levi, *The Drowned and The Saved*, p. 117. I could just as well have chosen the "roll call" ritual, where "the dead and the dying had to show up . . . stretched out on the ground rather than on their feet." Such rituals had become "the very emblem of the Lager [concentration camp]" (p. 115).

orchestras, actually), whose musicians were prisoners. Our knowledge of these orchestras is considerable, for two surviving members, Syzmon Laks (who served as conductor) and Fania Fenelon, wrote their memoirs.[15]

For the musicians, the orchestra offered some protection from instant death. The music offered more. "I caressed the piano," Fenelon wrote; "it was my savior, my love, my life." And: "I played and played, oblivious of my surroundings, and totally happy."[16] For Laks, music transcended Auschwitz. As conductor of the men's orchestra, he was distressed by the quality of his music. "I was appalled," he wrote, "by the terrible playing out of tune of some of the wind instruments. The strings could not help, but fortunately the winds were drowned out by the powerful thumping of the bass drum and the simultaneous clashing of the brass cymbals."[17] Fenelon lamented: "Marches were taken in three-time, waltzes in two and four. What a mess." Then she added (curiously!): "I don't know how the SS put up with that din; you'd think they had no ears."[18] What's the world coming to, they seem to be saying, when classical music is played this badly!

Yet there was, most obviously, a darker—much darker—side. The orchestra played for visiting dignitaries and on special occasions. It regularly played for Josef Kramer, commandant at Birkenau. Fenelon recalled one occasion (perhaps I should say nightmare): Kramer, after a long day on the platform "selecting"

---

15. Syzmon Laks, *Music of Another World* (Evanston: Northwestern University Press, 1989), and Fania Fenelon, *Playing for Time* (New York: Atheneum, 1977). Vanessa Redgrave starred as Fenelon in a television movie based on Fenelon's memoirs.

16. Fenelon, pp. 27, 119.

17. Laks, p. 38.

18. Fenelon, p. 37. She often criticized the SS taste in music, referring to their favorite pieces as "Aryan schmaltz." Fenelon reported that the orchestra members occasionally played a "trick" (at life's risk) on the Nazis by playing the forbidden music of Jewish composers.

Levi remembered the orchestra with some irony: "Auschwitz was the only German place where Jewish musicians could, indeed were compelled, to play Aryan music." With his usual drollery, Levi concluded: "Necessity knows no rules" (*The Drowned and The Saved*, p. 116).

people for the crematoria, relaxed by listening to his orchestra play Mozart. "The commandant closed his eyes," she wrote years later, "letting the music wash over him." Listening to the orchestra, he became "tearful." Yet this Jewish witness saw more, far more, than tears: "Satisfied, he had relieved himself of his 'selection' by listening to music as others might do by masturbating. Relaxed, [he] shook his head and expressed his pleasure: 'How beautiful, how moving!' "[19]

On at least one occasion, the orchestra played as people walked to their deaths: "Behind the barbed wire . . . were the deportees. Suddenly, I saw one woman run up to the [electrified fence] and grip the metal. Violently shaken by the current, her body twisted and she hung there, her limbs twisted and she hung there."

"No one moved," Fenelon concluded, but "the music played on."[20]

The contradictions between the music and the surroundings were apparent to the memoirists: "Could people who love music to this extent, people who cry when they hear it, be at the same time capable of committing so many atrocities on the rest of humanity?"[21]

I listen to Ludwig von Beethoven's Ninth Symphony; its "Ode to Joy," written in 1785 by Friedrich Schiller, says: "All men become brothers under [nature's] wing." I am deeply moved by the power of this music, which is for me a celebration of humanity. Nazis also listened to this German music, with its German poetry, and then participated in mass murder. "Bestiality was at times enforced and refined by individuals educated in the culture of traditional humanism," George Steiner has written. Even more: "Knowledge of Goethe, a delight in the poetry of Rilke, seemed no bar to personal and institutionalized sadism. Literary values and the utmost of hideous inhumanity could coexist in the same community, in the same individual sensibility."[22] Note

---

19. Felenon, p. 93.
20. Fenelon, p. 192.
21. Laks, p. 70.
22. George Steiner, *Language and Silence* (New York: Atheneum, 1967), p. 61. That I find this image particularly awful probably says something important about me as an educator.

Steiner's phrases: "seemed no bar" and "coexist." Later in this book I will look for a deeper connection between high culture and mass murder.

a newborn

Auschwitz was first and foremost a place of death. You knew that you had adjusted, explained memoirist Sara Nomberg-Pryztyk, when you routinely and mindlessly stepped over dead bodies. "I got used to it. . . . I could look at the dead with indifference. When a corpse was lying across my path I did not go around it any more, I simply stepped over it."[23]

Imagine a birth at Auschwitz: improbable, seemingly impossible, surely remarkable, in this place of death. Now imagine the real life (and death) problems that result from this birth. For Josef Mengele[24] routinely killed not only the newborn, but also the mother. The newborn had no chance of survival. To save the mother's life, the women at Auschwitz routinely killed the infant before it took its first breath.

Nomberg-Przytyk, a Jew who worked in the Auschwitz hospital clinic, described the usual procedure: "It's very simple. We give the baby an injection. After that, the baby dies. The mother is told that the baby was born dead. After that, the baby is thrown on a pile of corpses, and in that manner we save the mother."

Nonetheless, one pregnant woman who knew the procedure protested the fate awaiting her baby: "What? A dead baby? I

---

23. Sara Nomberg-Przytyk, *Auschwitz: True Tales from a Grotesque Land* (Chapel Hill: University of North Carolina Press, 1985), p. 115.

24. Physician and SS captain, Mengele was in charge of "selections", the sorting of Jews as they were dumped off the trains, he sent all elderly and infirm, and all visibly pregnant women and children, to instant death—some two hundred thousand to four hundred thousand people in all. As one memoirist recalled: "He stood there like a charming, dapper dancing master directing a polonaise. Left and right and right and left his hands pointed with casual movements. He radiated an air of lightness and gracefulness . . . a master at his profession, a devil who took pleasure in his work (quoted in Gerald Astor, *The Last Nazi* [New York: Donald I. Fine, 1985], p. 2). I will discuss Mengele's medical experiments in chapter 4.

want to have a live baby. I am sure that when Mengele sees it he will let me raise it in the camp. It is going to be a beauty because my husband was very handsome. I want to have it in the infirmary."[25]

She bore her baby. With great pride, love and tenderness, she nursed him. Three days later, Mengele selected mother and child for death: "She went naked, and in her arms she held the baby. She held it up high as though she wanted to show them what a beautiful and healthy son she had." For it was not the fate of her baby that the new mother protested, but reality itself.[26]

In any album, each picture shows time stopped. The viewer can stare and ponder and reflect: that is the power of a picture. Yet the viewer is limited to the single perspective presented. One cannot start time, let alone control it. One is not permitted to turn the faces, ask for a smile, or stop an oncoming bullet.

My own pictures, in my mind at least, are in color; the memoirists' snapshots, black-and-white on the page, are not.[27] Perhaps that is fitting, for the dominant color in black-and-white pictures is gray. For gray—the color of prison drab, but also of ambiguity—seems to capture some essence of the discussion to follow.

---

25. Nomberg-Przytyk, pp. 69–71. Memoirist Isabella Leitner offered this poetic eulogy for an infant: "And so, dear baby, you are on your way to heaven to meet a recent arrival who is blowing a loving kiss to you through the smoke, a dear friend, your maker—your father" (*Fragments of Isabella* [New York: Crowell, 1978], p. 32). Leitner bore a son shortly after liberation. She revisited Auschwitz and rejoiced: "I stood in front of the crematorium, and now there is another heart beating within that very body that was condemned to ashes" (p. 96). For an analysis of Leitner, see my article (with Mary Lagerwey, Todd Clason, Jill Green, and Tricia Meade), "From Auschwitz to Americana: Texts of the Holocaust," *Sociological Focus* 25 (1992): 179–202.

26. In another protest against reality, some women on the trains hid their infants in suitcases, hoping against hope that their babies might survive. Nomberg-Przytyk reported: "Imagine. I unpack a valise, and find a dead girl in it. She must have been about two years old. The mothers hid the children in the hope that once they got them into the camp they and the children would remain together" (p.76).

27. *Night and Fog,* the superb 1955 French film of the concentration camps, was produced in black-and-white. Recently, however, it has been "colorized"! One can only hope that this new, high-technology version—somehow aesthetically obscene—does not replace the classic version.

Each of my snapshots is peaceful, at least on the surface; memoirists' pictures inevitably (and appropriately) show violence.

Finally, each snapshot—mine and the memoirists'—involves a profound contradiction of what we call progress or civilization. For amidst the massacre, there are—against all odds—the appurtenances of a modern world: a well-made bed, a symphony orchestra, the care of one human for another. Mountain views are still beautiful; sunflowers still blossom.[28] Perhaps we begin to grasp that to struggle with the Holocaust is to wrestle with the meaning of our own lives and times.

gray

I am compelled to write about violence. For when all is said and done, after all the recollection and all the intellectualization, the Holocaust was—and will always be—unspeakable, horrific violence.

Here is a 1942 entry from the diary of SS Sergeant Felix Landau: "We order the prisoners to dig their graves. Only two of them are crying, the others show courage. What can they be thinking? . . . I don't feel the slightest stir of pity. That's how it is, and has got to be. . . . The shooting goes on. Two heads have been shot off. Nearly all fall into the grave unconscious only to suffer a long while. The last group have to throw the corpses into the grave."[29] From the warmth of our homes, our loved ones nearby, these few lines challenge nothing less than our conventional view of what it means to be human.

Let us examine another diarist, Dr. Johann Kremer, a German physician at Auschwitz. At his trial after the war, he

---

28. Here I use Simon Wiesenthal's image, sunflowers blooming next to the gas chambers, from his fascinating 1970 book, *The Sunflower* (New York: Schochen Books, 1976).

29. This quotation and the one that follows are from Martin Gilbert, *The Holocaust: A History of the Jews of Europe During the Second World War* (New York: Henry Holt & Co., 1985), pp. 171, 472–73. This book is an invaluable historical account of the Holocaust, focusing almost entirely on firsthand accounts of suffering during those tragic times.

explained that in 1943: "I had been for an extensive period of time interested in investigating the changes developing in the human organism as a result of starvation. . . . The patient was put on the dissecting table while still alive. I then approached the table and put several questions to the man as to such details which pertained to my research. . . . When I had collected my information the orderly approached the patient and killed him with an injection. . . . I myself never made lethal injections." Kremer faithfully recorded in his diary: "First frost this night, afternoon sunny and warm. Fresh material of spleen, liver and pancreas taken from abnormal individual." Kremer's juxtaposition of the cool weather and the still-warm body parts chills me to the bone.

What are we to think? Landau was, after all, a member of the dreaded SS. It is perhaps easy to dismiss him as a barbarian. But Kremer? His "scientific" murder in cold blood is more difficult to explain. How are we to judge these human beings?

Primo Levi spent his life pondering such issues. Most of us think of concentration camps in simple terms, of evil as opposed to good. But for Levi, beaten and starved at Auschwitz, nothing involving human beings was simple. He wrote about a "gray zone" within a concentration camp. It was, he says, "an incredibly complicated internal structure which contains within itself enough to confuse our need to judge."[30]

I think of the entire Holocaust as a gray zone. The more I think about the Nazi genocide of the Jews, the more confused is my *need to judge*. But I live now near the turn of the twenty-first century, in America, not in the middle of the twentieth, in Europe. What might the Holocaust mean for me? The more I think about the general phenomena of racism, of obedience, of the alienation of modern life, of the hurt of history (to use Fredric Jameson's fine phrase), the more is my *ability to judge* confused.

I want to challenge the ways in which we typically think about the Holocaust: them versus us; then versus now; there ver-

---

30. Levi, *The Drowned and The Saved*, p. 42.

sus here. In considering the Holocaust, I hope to travel across time and place, and bridge those dichotomous, oppositional categories. Farthest from my intent is to blame any lineage of people. Hannah Arendt, the great German Jewish philosopher, caught the spirit of this argument. To friends who reported that Nazism made them ashamed to be Germans, she retorted: "I am ashamed of being human."[31]

Sad to say, genocide is a part (perhaps closer to the center than we would care to admit) of Western history. In this book, I focus on one particular genocide, the best documented of all. Jews left a remarkable and unprecedented record of their suffering: from ghetto diaries[32] found after the war, to memoirs and poetry written by survivors. Their compulsion to write was extraordinary. As poet Abraham Sutzkever wrote of the Vilna Ghetto:

Once hidden in a cellar
Beside a corpse laid out like a sheet of paper
Illuminated by phosphorous snow from the ceiling—
I wrote a poem with a piece of coal
On the paper body of my neighbor.[33]

Wondrous poetry notwithstanding, it is primarily from historical scholarship, a process which continues with great activity to

---

31. Quoted in Margaret Canovan, *Hannah Arendt: A Reinterpretation of Her Political Thought* (Cambridge: Cambridge University Press, 1992), p. 20. Arendt was educated in Germany where she studied with Karl Jaspers and Martin Heidegger. She escaped Germany with the onset of Nazism. For a fascinating biography, see Elisabeth Young-Bruehl, *Hannah Arendt: For Love of the World* (New Haven: Yale University Press, 1982).

In addition to her profoundly original work on the Holocaust, Arendt wrote as an academic philosopher. Unfortunately, her writings are mostly ignored by social scientists. I will return to Arendt's work in some detail in chapters 2 and 4.

32. In the Warsaw Ghetto, Nazis allowed each Jew only 185 calories per day. Nonetheless members of Oneg Shabbat, the Ghetto Archive, carefully recorded the details of their suffering. Ironically, Germans as well as Jews were careful recorders. For a fascinating collection of photographs of the Warsaw Ghetto, taken by German Army Sergeant Willy Georg, see *In the Warsaw Ghetto* (New York: Aperture Foundation, 1993).

33. Abraham Sutzkever, *Selected Poetry and Prose* (Berkeley: University of California Press, 1991), p. 232.

this day, that we have resurrected this particular infamy in such great detail.

Memories of other genocides are lost. Native Americans had an oral, rather than a written, tradition. When the whites slaughtered them, the stories of these indigenous peoples were destroyed. The same is true for Gypsies: their stories—and therefore a part of their history—perished amidst the Nazi slaughter.

I do not wish to engage in a contest of numbers—to say that one genocide was worse than another: more killed here than there; more infants and children now than then; more tortured there than here. Such discourse is obscene; such method disrespects all victims.

At the outset, I think that there are two reasons, two justifications, for focusing on this particular genocide. First: that it happened at the center of Western civilization was unexpected. This adjective, "unexpected," would seem to be a strange (and understated) choice of words. But "unexpectedness" goes to the heart of the issue. For me, the Holocaust is the central dilemma of the twentieth century. How could the government of the most scientifically and technologically advanced country in the world—and it was Germany, not America, which held this position—systematically kill five million[34] Jews and millions of other innocents? How could average citizens of a modern

---

34. Of course I am aware that the usual number reported is six million. Through careful historical reconstruction, Raul Hilberg, a noted historian of the Holocaust, concluded that the actual number was closer to 5.1 million. In the controversy which followed, some accused Hilberg of trivializing the Holocaust by diminishing the quantity of suffering, a charge which seems absurd to me.

According to Israel Gutman and Robert Rozett, Appendix 6, *Encyclopedia of the Holocaust* (New York: Macmillan, 1990), an excellent source for all the issues I consider in this book, the Nazis killed an estimated 5,860,000 Jews. Other estimates are slightly higher, depending on evidentiary criteria. The numbers are lower if one insists on forensic evidence, whereas administrative evidence will produce somewhat higher counts. I think that the debate is obscene. Not knowing the total death to the nearest tenth of a million underscores the extent to which individual lives lost all their meaning.

industrial state, many of them highly educated, commit or even be a party to such unspeakable acts? How could the perpetrators of the Holocaust be described as the people of "Poets and Thinkers?"[35]

Second: Nazi concentration camps were not only horrific; they were absolutely unique in world history. Imagine Auschwitz,[36] a concentration camp adjacent to a small town in southern Poland, thirty miles southwest of Kraków. An intricate rail system transported victims from all over Europe to that place; each day thousands of people were turned into ash: gold from teeth for the treasury; women's hair for stuffing pillows.

---

35. Jean Amery, *At the Mind's Limits* (New York: Schocken Press, 1990) p. xvii. A survivor of Auschwitz, Amery's hundred-page book is extraordinary. Amery never shades or compromises his analysis. He forgets nothing; he forgives no one, himself included. In 1978, he—like so many other survivors—committed suicide.

36. Five decades after the genocide, one can do more than imagine. An intrepid reader, especially one who does not suffer nightmres, might begin by looking at *Auschwitz: A History in Photographs*, edited by Teresa Świebocka (Bloomington: Indiana University Press, 1993), or reading Otto Friedrichs, *The End of the World* (New York: Fromm International Publishing Company, 1986, p. 279–334). For a more scholarly treatment, one could read the various articles in *Anatomy of the Auschwitz Death Camp*, eds. Israel Gutman and Michael Berenbaum (Bloomington: Indiana University Press, 1994), especially Robert-Jan Van Pelt, "A Site in Search of a Misson" (pp. 93–157) and Jean-Claude Pressac and Robert-Jan Van Pelt, "The Machinery of Mass Murder at Auschwitz" (pp. 183–245).

Auschwitz is the German name for the town, appropriately so because Auschwitz had long existed as a German border town at the edge of Slavic territories. Between the two world wars, then incorporated into Polish territory, its Polish name was Oświeceçim. (Birkenau, the killing center, is also Germanized; its Polish name is Brzezinka.) In 1939 the population of Oświeceçim was 12,000, of whom 5,000 were Jews. The Nazis had great ambitions for the city: a massive resettlement of ethnic Germans followed by a model medieval-style farming village—"a paradigm of the settlement in the East," according to SS leader Heinrich Himmler (quoted in Van Pelt, p. 106). To clear the site for ethnic Germans, all Jews and Poles were to be removed from the area. The transmogrification of Auschwitz into a huge death factory was complex and indirect, promoted by the I. G. Farben Company, which in 1941 located on site to take advantage of slave labor.

> There is no precedent for the almost endless march of millions of men, women and children into gas chambers. The systemization of this destruction process sets it aside from all else that has happened.[37]

Auschwitz attained its maximum efficiency in August 1944; in one day of that month—organized and refined as never before—the Nazis "processed" (that is to say, murdered) 24,000 Hungarian Jews in that place. In all, the Nazis murdered some 1.5 million people there.[38] Today it is the world's largest cemetery.

Perhaps we should not imagine such pictures, lest nightmares prevail.

approaches

Of all the snapshots in all the albums, which ones should I choose to consider the Holocaust? How do I crop the images? By what method do I adjust the light and shadow? Do I allow or hide the grain? What choices must I make even as I begin the analysis? How should one approach the Holocaust? I know that the answers to these questions reveal more about me—the fanciful photographer—than about the reader.

I want to consider briefly a number of approaches which scholars have used to study the Holocaust. I hope to show that each, within its own limitations, has been part of my education on the subject.

---

37. Raul Hilberg, "The Bureaucracy of Annihilation." In *Unanswered Questions,* edited by Francois Furet (New York: Schocken Books, 1989), p. 119.

38. Since most Jews were murdered immediately after they arrived at Auschwitz, the number of victims is unknown. Exactly 404,222 people were registered at Auschwitz with tatoo numbers. Rudolf Höss, commandant at Auschwitz claimed that 2.5 million people were murdered, but he was probably exaggerating. (Such embellishment strains sanity, but so does everything about Auschwitz!) Using forensic evidence, counting only those for whom "traces of established evidence remain" Uwe Dietrich Adam ("The Gas Chambers," in Furet, pp. 151 and 355, note 108) estimated that the Nazis murdered 1,323,000 Jews and 6,430 Gypsies at Auschwitz. These estimates do not include those who died of starvation, disease and abuse. Only 7,600 lived to see liberation.

victims and perpetrators

There are two types of snapshots which some have studied: those of victims and those of perpetrators.[39] From here on, I will have little to say about the victims, Jewish or otherwise. There is an impressive scholarship on victims, particularly the Jewish victims of the Holocaust. Yet it seems to me that in any political interaction between powerful and powerless, one learns more (or at least one learns differently) by studying the former. For it is not slaves[40] but their masters who design and effect the policies of their captivity and death.

The ultimate perpetrator explanation focuses on one individual: Hitler. The name is all one needs to say, for the word *Hitler* has become an icon of evil.[41] Hitler, according to biographer Joachim Fest, "demonstrated the stupendous power of a solitary person over the historical process. . . . No one else produced, in a solitary course lasting only a few years, such incredible acceleration in the pace of history."[42] For historian John Lukacs, Hitler was the most significant revolutionary of the twentieth century: "Much of the twentieth century before 1940 led up to Hitler. And so much of the century . . . was a consequence of the Second

39. A third choice of some scholars has been to study bystanders. See, for example, Raul Hilberg, *Perpetrators, Victims, Bystanders: The Jewish Catastrophe 1933–1945*. New York: Harper Collins, 1992.

40. For an argument to the contrary, see Richard Rubenstein, *After Auschwitz*, 2d ed. (Baltimore: Johns Hopkins University Press, 1990). Rubenstein, whose work I will consider in some detail in chapter 4, argues that explanations of the Holocaust which depict Jews as completely passive, "as objects of action, rather than parties of conflict" (p. 88), are inadequate. Rubenstein most certainly does not wish to blame the victims. Nonetheless, he maintains, "[t]he Holocaust can be understood with least mystification if we do not ignore the abiding elements of conflict characterizing the relations between Jews and their neighbors throughout the entire period of their domicile in the European-Christian world" (p. 90). Perhaps the point is that Jews were not slaves. Many held important intellectual, cultural, and financial positions. Had they been slaves, no one would have bothered to exterminate them.

41. See Alvin Rosenfeld, *Imagining Hitler* (Bloomington: University of Indiana Press, 1985), for a discussion of Hitler's evil in contemporary literature.

42. Joachim Fest, *Hitler* (New York: Harecourt, Brace & Jovanovich, 1974), p. 7. Of all the biographies written of Adolf Hitler, Fest's is perhaps the best.

World War that he alone had begun and that was dominated by his presence."[43]

I am extremely suspicious of so-called "great man" theories of history.[44] Such explanations lead us away from understanding, for in focusing on one individual, we focus blame on one person. As Fest maintains, this argument ultimately serves as a "justification felt by millions of one-time followers who can easily see themselves as victims of so much 'greatness.' " The one-man theory of history makes it too easy to put the Holocaust aside as an aberration caused by one demented person. Such an explanation, then, "amounts to a surreptitious maneuver in the course of a broad campaign of exculpation."[45]

My snapshots have revealed details about people and places, but photographic metaphor takes us only so far. For the Holocaust cannot be reduced to individual people or places. To focus on victims or perpetrators is to study individuals, to say (in effect) that the Holocaust might be understood in terms of individual action or choice. Throughout this book, my focus will not be on individual perpetrators, even one as significant as Hitler.

germany

If not Hitler, or a small group of Nazis, we might reasonably focus on the German people as perpetrators of the Holocaust. Some scholars have thus sought to identify unique traits in German culture or history as an explanation of that infamy.[46]

In his 1941 book, *Escape from Freedom*, Erich Fromm argued that Nazism was the ultimate expression of the German authori-

---

43. John Lukacs, *The End of the Twentieth Century and the End of Progress* (New York: Ticknor & Fields, 1993), pp. 287–88; 9.

44. For background on this concept, see Jacob Burckhardt, *Force and Freedom: Reflections on History* (New York: Pantheon Books, 1943), p. 313ff.

45. Fest, p. 6.

46. We do not typically ask: Why Austria? Yet many top Nazis were Austrian, and at every level, Austrians participated in the Holocaust. Historians, perhaps seeing Austria as an unwilling ally of Germany, have been kinder in their evaluation of that country. In retrospect, correctly or not, Austrian history is far less tainted than is German history by the Holocaust.

tarian personality. This personality defect resulted from child-rearing practices which were reinforced by a rigorous and strict educational system. At the root of authoritarianism was a psychically degraded personality, usually characterized as sadomasochistic. Authoritarianism was thus a psychic defensive mechanism, a method of "escaping" from freedom.

I find this type of explanation generally unhelpful.[47] I am not convinced that the German personality and German child rearing—to cite two common explanations of the Holocaust—are particularly authoritarian, especially in comparison to other modern societies.[48]

To focus on the "Germanness" of the crime is far too narrow. In the words of Zygmunt Bauman, such an effort is "an exercise in exonerating everyone else, and particularly *everything else*." Rather than closing the subject within a particular place (Germany) and time (say, 1932–1945), we need to open the Holocaust dialogue. The Holocaust, Bauman continues, should serve as "a window, rather than a picture on the wall. Looking through that window, one can catch a glimpse of many things otherwise invisible."[49]

anti-semitism

Hitler and other Nazis made the most virulent anti-Semitic statements. Listen to a passage in *Mein Kampf* written in 1925, seven

---

47. To accept the thesis, we must assume that German children were reared (more or less) similarly. I would ask: Did variance in child rearing predict eventual adherence to Nazism? Even more: What historical and social conditions led to such authoritarianism? Perhaps most importantly, we would need to demonstrate that *only* in Nazi Germany were such child-rearing patterns extant.

48. Others sought to vindicate the greatness of German culture from the presumably temporary blight of Nazism. In 1930, Sigmund Freud maintained: "A nation that produced Goethe could not possibly go to the bad." Ernst Cassirer, German Jewish philosopher and author of *Philosophy of Symbolic Forms*, developed this exculpation to its extreme. Shortly before his death in 1945, in the United States, he claimed: "This Hitler is an error of history. He does not belong in German History at all. And therefore he will perish" (quoted in Frederic Grunfeld, *Prophets Without Honor* [New York: Holt, Rinehart & Winston, 1979], pp. 61, 17).

49. Zygmunt Bauman, *Modernity and the Holocaust* (Ithaca: Cornell University Press, 1990), p. viii. I will elaborate Bauman's analysis in chapter 4.

years before Hitler seized power: "The black-haired Jewish youth lies in wait for hours on end, satanically glaring at and spying on the unsuspicious girl whom he plans to seduce, adulterating her blood and removing her from the bosom of her own people." And, perhaps more ominously: "If at the beginning of [World War I] and during the war, twelve or fifteen thousand of these Hebraic corruptors of the nation had been subjected to poison gas . . . then the sacrifice at the front would not have been in vain."[50]

No doubt: Hitler had dreams of blood. No doubt: Hitler was virulently anti-Semitic. But Hitler's anti-Semitism was not only heavy-fisted, it was also subtle and complex. In a letter written in 1919, *before* he joined the Nazi Party,[51] Hitler made an important analytic distinction between "emotional" and "rational" anti-Semitism: "Anti-Semitism on purely emotional grounds will find its ultimate expression in the form of pogroms. Anti-Semitism of reason, however, must lead to a systematic and legal struggle."

Hitler understood that random, unplanned, and uncoordinated attacks against Jews were not only troublesome, but exceedingly inefficient. It was his genius (dare I use the word?) to see that the world accepted discriminatory laws and statutes more readily than it acquiesced to sporadic violence. "The only way to deal with the [Jewish] problem," Hitler said in 1939, "is that of legislative action."[52] Emotional anti-Semitism might be used to incite crowds, and Hitler was not above that practice. But only rational anti-Semitism could be used to achieve practical goals.

Most contemporary historians de-emphasize emotional anti-Semitism—a popular explanation a few decades ago—as *the* cause of the Holocaust. Even rational anti-Semitism (I use Hitler's terminology to avoid confusion) is problematic as a primary and indepen-

---

50. Quoted in Gilbert, p. 27.
51. The "German Workers' Party," one of many insignificant, right-wing political parties active in the years after World War I, was founded in 1919 by Anton Drexler. In 1920, under Hitler's influence, the Party changed its name to Socialist German Workers' Party. For a history, see Charles Flood, *Hitler: The Path to Power* (Boston: Houghton Mifflin, 1989).
52. Quoted in Leni Yahil, *The Holocaust: The Fate of European Jewry* (New York: Oxford University Press, 1990), p. 70, from a speech made to celebrate the Nuremberg laws of blood and honor which I discuss in chapter 3.

dent causal factor of the Holocaust.[53] "If German anti-Semitism is to *explain* the unequaled case of Auschwitz," Shulamit Volkov has summarized, "then it must itself be perceived as unique—both in relation to previous anti-Jewish manifestations and in comparison with contemporary anti-Semitism elsewhere."[54] Yet historians have shown that anti-Semitism was not uniquely German. The most anti-Semitic country in Europe was Poland; among developed countries, France—generally thought of as the quintessence of Western culture—had a more virulent history of anti-Semitism than did Germany.[55] During World War I, anti-Semitism was not a significant factor in German life. In the Great War, Jews fought as Germans; of six-hundred-thousand German Jews, fully one-hundred-thousand served in the German army, and twelve-thousand were killed in the war.[56]

For Hitler, anti-Semitism was not simply an ideology; it was also the basis for tactics in the political arena. Hitler needed a political target around which his quest for power would evolve and expand. Jews (and Gypsies, to a degree) met his needs. "Without the Jews in our midst," Hitler wrote, "we should have to invent them. It is essential to have a tangible enemy, not merely an abstract one."[57]

---

53. In Raul Hilberg's magnum opus, *The Destruction of European Jews*, 3 vols. (New York: Holmes & Meier, 1985), the term "anti-Semitism" does not appear in the subject index.

54. Shulamit Volkov, "The Written Matter and the Spoken Word," in Furet, p. 38.

55. Here I follow George Mosse, *The Crisis of German Ideology: Intellectual Origins of the Third Reich* (New York: Grosset and Dunlop, 1964), p. 294ff.

56. In World War I, Corporal Adolf Hitler received an Iron Cross, First Class, for bravery; the medal was proposed and awarded by his Jewish commander, Lieutenant Hugo Guttman.

57. Quoted in Leni Yahill, pp. 42–43. In his essay *Anti-Semite and Jew* (New York: Schocken Books, 1948 [1946]), p. 13, Jean-Paul Sartre, presumably unaware of Hitler's words, wrote: "If the Jew did not exist, the anti-Semite would invent him." In postwar Europe, there are many historical examples of Jews serving as targets of convenience. In 1967, for example, the Polish government conducted anti-Zionist purges throughout the country, this despite the fact that there were only twenty-five thousand Jews (0.2 percent of the population) in the entire nation. In fact, most people who suffered loss of job or worse were not Jewish (Paul Lendavi, *Anti-Semitism Without Jews* [New York: Doubleday, 1971], p. 21ff.). See also Randolf Braham, "Antisemitism and the Treatment of the Holocaust in Post-Communist East Central Europe," *Holocaust and Genocide Studies* 8 (1994): 142–63.

Anti-Semitism, it seems to me, is a piece of the puzzle, not the whole picture. For anti-Semitism rarely manifests itself in isolation. Nationalism, misogyny, hatred for all minorities—these are almost inevitably expressed alongside anti-Semitism. Thus, to use Volkov's phrase, anti-Semitism would seem to be a "cultural code," a convenient abbreviation for a broad "cluster of ideas, values and norms."[58]

fascism

The term *Fascism* evokes in us a powerful set of images: "Jackboots, barbed wire and corpses"; and then a bit more abstractly: "irrational, anti-Semitic, totalitarian and genocidal."[59] Despite its common usage, fascism is a remarkably difficult term to define.[60] It cannot be viewed as the single cause of the Holocaust. For in Italy, where fascism was founded—which was fascist by definition!—there was no Holocaust. Even more: there was little anti-Semitism in Italy; in the 1920s, Jews often supported, and were even members of, the Italian Fascist Party. And during the Holocaust itself, Italian officials often protected Jews. Indeed, Italy treated Jews better than any other continental European state, including Denmark, generally considered the exemplar. [61]

---

58. Volkov, in Michael Marrus, pp. 12–13.

59. Gilbert Allardyce, "What Fascism Is Not: Thoughts on the Deflation of a Concept," *American Historical Review* 84 (1979): p. 370. The term *fascismo* ("union" or "bundle" in Italian) describes various political parties, including Mussolini's Blackshirts and later the Nazis, which sought political power between the two World Wars.

60. Fascism is "anti-parliamentary, anti-liberal, anti-communist, anti-proletarian, partly anti-capitalist and anti-bourgeois and anti-clerical" (Stanley G. Pane, "Fascism in Western Europe," in Walter Laqueur, *Fascism: A Reader's Guide* [Berkeley: University of California Press, 1976], p. 12). Defining fascism as an ideology of what-is-not is reminiscent of anti-Semitism as a "cultural code."

61. For the remarkable treatment of Jews by the Italians, see Susan Zuccotti, *The Italians and the Holocaust: Persecution, Rescue and Survival* (New York: Basic Books, 1987).

the great war

Rather than focusing on Germany, I would open the camera's aperture to include a violent event—World War I—which immediately preceded the Holocaust. The Versailles Treaty which ended that war was, as many have pointed out, unfair. Germany lost 13 percent of its land, and economic penalties forced great hardships on German citizens.[62] But perhaps we should linger not so much on the treaty, but the Great War itself.

Ten million soldiers and civilians were killed between 1914 and 1918. At the battle of Verdun in 1916, each side lost about a half million (mostly young) men; at the Somme, in the same year, there was slaughter of the same magnitude. As one theologian summarized: "Both the British and the German generals made the same decision: their country's young men were expendable."[63]

And let us not forget that under the cover of World War I, the Turks massacred one million Armenians. Though the killing was primitive by later standards—no railway system, no gas, no ovens—it was nonetheless organized from the top down. The central authorities were, in the words of Arnold Toynbee, "directly and personally responsible without exception, from the beginning to the end, for the gigantic crime which devastated the

---

62. Unfair and unjust treaties are well known in European history. In the Franco-Prussian war, the Germans had forced extremely difficult terms on the French. The treaty of Brest-Litovsk, which marked the 1917 Russian surrender to Germany, was most harsh: the Russians were required to pay huge reparations and fifty-six million Russians, one-third of the entire population, came under German rule.

Neither France nor Russia perpetrated a holocaust, though in the 1930s, Stalin murdered some twenty million Soviet citizens, one of the greatest mass murders of history. I will return to the Nazi-Soviet comparison in chapter 4. For now, it is worth pondering the effect of the Brest-Litovsk treaty on the later Soviet infamy.

63. Richard Rubenstein, *The Cunning of History: Mass Death and the American Future* (New York: Harper & Row, 1975), p. 9. In *Twentieth Century Book of the Dead* (New York: Scribner, 1972), Gil Elliot concluded that 110 million people had died as the result of war in the twentieth century. And remember: Eliot's book was published before the final quarter, and a violent one it has been, of that hundred years.

Near East in 1915."[64] For the Holocaust that was to follow, the significance of the Turkish action cannot be overstated. For it was "the first full-fledged attempt by a modern state to practice disciplined, methodically organized genocide."[65]

Even for a civilization (and I use that term advisedly) that had a most violent history, the deaths from and associated with World War I were unprecedented. Mass death was now an acceptable part of the experience and values of European culture.[66] It would be ridiculous to claim that World War I led in some direct way to the Holocaust. Other nations have lost wars and not perpetrated genocide. But it is difficult to imagine the fifty million deaths of the Second World War, and the Holocaust that it encased, without the "Great War" that preceded it.

We wish to say: The Holocaust happened because of Hitler's personality, or flaws in the German character, or because of some historical movement acting like a runaway engine.[67] But such comforting answers elude us.

At a minimum, we might agree on the following: The perpetrators—of whom the most significant were German and Austrian—were guilty of the most heinous crimes; victims suffered immensely; anti-Semitism, especially combined with fascism, especially within an international climate of state-sponsored violence, was invoked to slaughter countless innocents. My own thinking about the Holocaust is based, at least in part, on these traditional understandings.

---

64. Quoted in Marrus, p. 22.

65. Rubenstein, *The Cunning of History*, p. 11. For comparisons of the Turkish- and German-perpetrated genocides, see Robert Melson, *Revolution and Genocide* (Chicago: University of Chicago Press, 1992).

66. Stefan Zweig, well-known humanist and author, could imagine nothing worse than World War I. In his memoirs, he wrote: "Hell lay behind us. What was there to frighten us after that" (*The World of Yesterday* [London: Cassell and Company, 1953], p. 26). Zweig, who lived in Salzburg, fled the Nazis for Brazil, where he and his wife committed suicide in 1942.

67. One of my students attributes the Holocaust to Hitler's undescended testicle (a condition he did not have); another hypothesizes that the lack of olive oil in the German diet produced a constipation that led to genocide. Though I'm aware that humor is inappropriate here, there is something in the simplicity of these explanations—so different from the complex intellectual arguments I now present—that appeals to me.

meditation

When we examine the Holocaust, we inevitably—perhaps painfully—examine ourselves. This "reflexivity" is not really a choice, but an inevitable part of thinking and writing. For this book, two of my identities are most important: I am a Jew and a sociologist. My vision of the Holocaust, be it clouded or clarified, appears by necessity through these lenses.

What is my Jewishness? This I can say: I reject the theology of Judaism. I find the Mosaic God petty, vengeful, and morally immature—a poor guide for ethical behavior. The notion that Jews are a chosen people seems to me at best arrogant, at worst racist. The rituals of orthodoxy do not move me; I find no merit in following the dietary laws. Nor does the Reform Jewish movement, with its effort to "modernize" the religion, appeal to me. I do not think that sacred and secular do—or even should—mix. I am an atheist, but at least I am an orthodox atheist!

For me, Judaism is more an ethnic than religious identity. I am an American Jew in the same sense that one might be an American Irish or an American Greek. It is a nondebatable part of who I am. My preference for the word, written or oral; my combined assertiveness and aversion toward violence, or even sustained physical activity; my antipathy for the mechanical (are all inanimate objects anti-Semitic?)—these in some way are derived from the Jewish culture of which I am a part.

Perhaps there is one additional way to describe my Jewish identity: as, in the fine phrase of the sociologist Georg Simmel, a "stranger."[68] American Jews are mostly—but not completely—assimilated. We are, at least to a degree, culturally marginal.

---

68. Kurt Wolff, *The Sociology of Georg Simmel* (New York: Free Press, 1950), p. 404. Simmel (1858–1918) was born in Berlin, the son of a Jewish family that had converted to Christianity. Simmel wrote "The Stranger" (his quintessential example being the European Jew) in 1908, partly in an attempt to understand his own marginal status. I am impressed with Simmel's sociology.

Simmel, or the tradition in which he wrote, has shaped my entire intellectual approach. "Simmel often appears as though in the midst of writing he were overwhelmed by an idea, by an avalanche of ideas, and as if he incorporated them without interrupting himself, digesting and assimilating only the extent granted him by the onrush" (Wolff, p. xix).

Christmas (candy canes as well as crèches) is not our holiday. Simmel's stranger is not "radically committed to the unique ingredients and particular tendencies of the group"—the *dominant ideology*, in today's jargon. This does not imply "passivity and detachment," but rather a "particular structure composed of distance and nearness, indifference and involvement." It is from this stranger's position of cultural ambivalence that I examine the Holocaust.

Perhaps the stranger is also attracted to sociology. Did I become a sociogist to save the world? Did I hope to contribute to the science of society? Perhaps—less prosaically, but more realistically —I needed a student draft deferment to avoid the Vietnam War. The reasons vary with the telling of the story. I have given up on the first two goals: messianic sociology is way beyond my grasp and belief, and I no longer believe in the creed of positivism. Vietnam is history. Nonetheless, I have found a pleasant living as a sociologist, even as the search for patterns devolved into an appreciation of chaos.

As a sociologist, I study what happens to most people most of the time: the normal, not the abnormal; the everyday, not the unique. When we think of the Holocaust, we think of something uniquely horrific and horrifyingly unique. Yet I believe that we cannot understand the Holocaust without appreciating its normalcy, its everydayness.

This book is a sociological meditation on the Holocaust.[69] These two words—*sociology* and *meditation*—do not usually go

---

69. American sociologists have written remarkably little about the Holocaust, an intellectual hiatus addressed by R. Ruth Linden and Helen Fein. In *Making Stories, Making Selves: Feminist Reflections on the Holocaust* (Columbus: Ohio State University Press, 1993), Linden advocates a "phenomenology of surviving" (p. 95 ff.), a complementary (but different) sociological analysis to the one I am pursuing here. She also presents a thorough and sensitive exploration of the reflexive method, though Linden seems more interested in studying the Holocaust to understand herself, whereas my approach is to use autobiography to more clearly see the Holocaust. Fein's *Genocide: A Sociological Perspective* (Newbury Park, CA: Sage Publications, 1993) is positivistic rather than reflexive, thus quite different from my effort.

together; the former is analytical and rigorous, the latter speculative and subjective. But I believe that a sociological meditation might help us see the Holocaust from a different perspective. I ask difficult sociological questions: How are given societies put together in ways that permit or promote (the verb is crucial here) or prevent state-sponsored genocide? Why did the Holocaust happen—unexpectedly—at the center of Western civilization? What kind of civilization produces Auschwitz and Beethoven? or more pointedly: an orchestra of slaves that plays Beethoven as thousands are incinerated? My goal is not any particular set of answers, but an appreciation of what it means—for better and for worse—to live in the modern world after the Holocaust.

I write this book not so much to wrestle with the Holocaust (let alone the angel), but rather to wrestle with myself. I write, therefore I am. As another scholar of the Holocaust has justified his book (and his intellectual life): "Writing becomes itself the means of vision or comprehension, not a mirror of something independent, but an act and commitment—a doing rather than a reflection or description."[70]

Perhaps there is an echo of Franz Kafka in me. For Kafka, writing was a form of prayer: "the strange, mysterious, perhaps dangerous, perhaps saving comfort that there is in writing." It is, he concluded, "a leap out of murderer's row."[71]

As someone who did not suffer through the Holocaust, I write with a certain amount of (to use the Yiddish phrase) chutzpah. Some survivors maintain that only they, with their

---

70. Berel Lang, *Act and Idea in the Nazi Genocide* (Chicago: University of Chicago Press, 1990), p. xii. I am also aware that the very act of writing conceals as well as reveals. Primo Levi wrote just before his death: "I will tell just one more story, the most secret, and I will tell it with the humility and restraint of him who knows from the start that this theme is desperate, the means feeble, and the trade of clothing facts in words is bound by its very nature to fail."

71. In the same letter, however, Kafka despaired that writing was at best a temporary expedient: "as though for someone writing his last will and testament, just before he hangs himself" (quoted in Robert Alter, *Necessary Angels: Tradition and Modernity in Kafka, Benjamin and Scholem* [Cambridge: Harvard University Press], 1991), p. 93. I will say more about Kafka in chapter 3.

firsthand, direct—privileged—knowledge, should write.[72] But others, poets as well as scholars, have written. Perhaps the best I can hope for—and just as importantly, the problems I have— are summarized by another survivor: "Let others not be pre- vented from empathizing. Let them contemplate a fate that yesterday could have been and tomorrow can be theirs."[73]

My reflexivity would be incomplete and dishonest without one more story. For I became involved with Holocaust Studies (only academics could invent such a phrase) vicariously. This story begins with a man who was not Jewish. Marko Banjac was a Bosnian Serb. In the mid-1990s, Americans read with horror about the ethnic war and massacre in Bosnia. Marko's story is a different Bosnian—and Holocaust—tragedy.

In 1942, at age thirty-two, Marko's life began a downward spiral. Drafted into the Yugoslav Army, he was—with the defeat of his country by the Nazis—deported to Austria. There he la- bored as a slave. If Jews were nonhuman, Slavs were (in Nazi lexicography) subhuman.

Marko worked on a small farm in a little village between Salzburg and Linz in Upper Austria. Whereas jagged rocks erupted from the mountains of his native land, here the rolling hills sprouted wildflowers. The scene might have been pacific, but life was not: he knew nothing about the safety of his family back home; he feared the capricious Nazi murderers, let alone death from the sky as American bombers blasted everything in sight.

---

72. See Elie Wiesel, "Trivializing the Holocaust: Semi-Fact and Semi- Fiction," *New York Times* (16 April 1978), Section II, pp. 1, 29. In a slightly dif- ferent position, Bruno Bettelheim, prisoner for a short time at Dachau and re- nowned psychoanalyst, has written: "there are acts so vile that our task is to reject and prevent them, not to try to understand them empathetically." Bettelheim eventually wrote as an authority on autism, suggesting that autis- tic children lived in environments similar to Auschwitz. As the parent of an autistic child, I find Bettelheim's position not only insulting, but an unfortu- nate example of the trivialization of the Holocaust.

73. Amery, p. 93. However, he continues: "Their intellectual effort will meet with our respect, but it will be a skeptical one, and in conversation with them we will soon grow silent and say to ourselves: go ahead, good people, trouble your heads as much as you want; you still sound like a blind man talk- ing about color."

Small solace: the family for whom he worked treated him well. In this collapsed world, Marko met a young Austrian woman. From that union—who is to know about love in times such as these?—came in 1944 the miracle of life in the midst of death. During the birth, Marko approached the bedroom window from the field outside, awaiting the news: a girl was born. He must have pondered the sheer impossibility of the situation.

The baby's Austrian grandfather, at grave risk to himself, signed the birth certificate as father. But the Nazis, ever vigilant about race laws, discovered the identity of the real father. One night in May 1945, about a month before the end of the war, the mayor of the town and several others marched Marko to a nearby rail bridge. There they murdered him with a gunshot to the head.

Mother and daughter were to be sent to death at the Mauthausen concentration camp, a few miles east of Linz. But Nazi justice followed due process. The documents needed to be just so. Fortunately, the chief of police understood the futility of killing more people—even just two more. With the war almost over, he sat on the paperwork. His delaying tactics, it turns out, saved these two lives.

My wife is Marko's daughter.

1983: She and I visit the Mauthausen concentration camp. It is my first experience as a tourist of the Holocaust. Mauthausen, located at the confluence of the Enns and Danube Rivers, is in a picture-postcard beautiful setting. I had expected an ugly place, one that conjured death, and this beauty is oddly disorienting.

Some 200,000—162,000 of whom were not Jewish—were murdered at Mauthausen. By order of the commandant, Franz "Babyface" Ziereis, prisoners were starved, gassed, shot, beaten, sprayed with cold water until they died, and thrown over the cliff into the quarry. By the spring of 1945, it is almost certain that any new arrival—my wife, her mother—would have been gassed and cremated within a day.

We walk the grounds almost four decades later. We see the gas chamber and the crematorium. We stand at the so-called Wall of Lamentations, where prisoners were tortured before the camp assembly. We walk down the infamous "186 steps" to the rock quarry. Prisoners were forced to carry stones weighing over one hundred pounds up these stairs. Many fell to their death, or were murdered for failing the task.

We ponder the accidents of history: a half-Slav who escaped death here by a hair's breadth, accompanied by her Jewish husband, visiting this haunted place. What is one to do? What is one to think? at a place such as this, amidst the ghost ashes, wildflowers and flowing rivers.

I have begun this book with some very general ways of thinking about the Holocaust. In the middle three chapters, I look at the Holocaust from what sociologists call "micro" (focus on individuals), "meso" (focus on social organizations and bureaucracies), and "macro" (focus on whole societies) perspectives. Chapter 2 looks at individuals—Nazis and others—and asks: "Are we all Nazis?" Chapter 3 examines the Holocaust as a product of two components of Nazi Germany—its organization and its chaos—which are also characteristics of all modern societies. Chapter 4 examines the Holocaust in light of, and as a continuing part of, the modern, scientific world. In chapter 5, I meditate on memory and history. While most of us think that the future is derived from the past, I think that the opposite is true as well. What we think about the Holocaust, its meaning for our times, says as much about us as about the mass murder itself.

2 banality

May 1993: I am in Berlin at the Staatsoper, a beautifully restored fin-de-siècle opera house, in the former East Berlin. I
listen to *Lohengrin*, written by Richard Wagner in 1850. Wagner:
who said "I am the most German of beings, I am the German
spirit"; who claimed that Jews —"former cannibals, educated to
be business leaders of society"—had stolen the godhead from
Aryans; who wrote that Christ himself was an Aryan.

Under huge crystal chandeliers, the music is brilliant and
wild; the voices strong and passionate. Lohengrin's story—of
myth, mystery, and idealized romance—discomforts and transports me. I am astounded to hear the "Wedding March"—had
I forgotten, repressed, or never known that this music was
Wagner's? I have heard this piece at so many American weddings, Jewish included. The sweetness and näiveté of weddings,
the dark boldness of Wagner: I feel confused and disjointed, two
different histories pulling my thoughts asunder.

I think of Adolf Hitler, who surely saw this opera in this very place. He called Wagner "the greatest prophetic figure the German people have had"; more ominously (for me, tonight), he said: "Whoever wants to understand National Socialism must know Wagner." The charged emotionality of these operas, one of which now entrances me, brought Hitler—in the words of one Nazi —"to bright flames." With all of this I struggle, but to no avail or conclusion.

Earlier that day, I visited the remnants of the Berlin Wall, was unmoved (perhaps antimoved) by Checkpoint Charlie, its silly military lingo name, its museum faithfully showing the various elaborate escape schemes over the wall, as if the wall were the most onerous symbol of German history. My mind is on events from a few decades earlier.

After the opera (Pommeray and caviar during intermission!), we walk past Humbolt University, where Karl Marx was a student; a few blocks further is the Oranien district. A half century ago, this was the center of Jewish life in Berlin. The heart of that neighborhood was the beautiful Moorish-style synagogue. "The fact that Jews could build a synagogue that was as visually impressive as a church, located in central Berlin and on a street rather than a lane, marked a significant victory," wrote Carol Krinsky in *Synagogues of Europe*. This synagogue, the largest in the world when it was completed in 1866, represented the highest "achievements of technology and civilization." It was partly destroyed on 11 November 1938 during the infamous Kristallnacht, then completely destroyed by Allied bombers in 1943; it is now after all these years almost rebuilt. Next door is the Beth Café, the first Jewish business to open in this area since the Nazi era. We consider a restful coffee, but are turned off by all the German yuppies in the place. A block away is the grave of the great German Jewish philosopher, Moses Mendelssohn, and the site (irony intended by the Nazis) from which fifty thousand Berlin Jews were deported to their deaths.

The Oranien district looks strange, as though it were caught in a weird time warp. Many buildings are in severe disrepair, some still bombed out from the war. In these building shells now reside various itinerant artists. Here it seems difficult to imagine Kristallnacht (I don't like this Nazi term, but don't know what else to call it!), during which storm troopers destroyed 191 synagogues and tens of thousands of shops. Forgotten in these statistics are ninety-one killed and thirty thousand arrested, of whom about one thousand would die within a few weeks.

Outside, the graffiti says "Nazi Raus [get out]." But inside in the Tachele, a bar thick with people and smoke (peculiarly sweet smoke!), we rub elbows with spiky-haired punkers. The rock music is so loud that I can't really hear it as much as feel it. I am reminded of Josef Goebbels, Nazi propaganda minister, who in 1939 said: "National Socialism has understood how to take the soulless framework of technology and fill it with the rhythm and hot impulses of our time."

My mind is filled with Wagner and wine. Present and past meld: Where is the spirit of Mendelssohn and the countless Jews of but a few decades ago? What beautiful and horrendous things have happened within shouting distance of this place? Who among these punkers (and others) is a neo-Nazi? But particularly, I wonder: What kind of people were the Nazis of a half century ago?

In this chapter I take a trip across time and space in an attempt to understand how individual human beings—perhaps the fathers and mothers of the people in the Tachele—might participate in genocide. The trip begins in Solingen, a German town in the Rhineland famous for its knives, scissors, and surgical instruments—the birthplace of Adolf Eichmann; it ends in an American city: New Haven, Connecticut. Along the way I ask the most difficult and troubling questions about who the Nazis were—and who we are.

—   eichmann

As head of Section IV-B-4, the Gestapo section for Jewish Affairs, Adolf Eichmann played a major role in "administering" the Holocaust. He was in charge of the initial stages of the entire operation: his office promulgated anti-Jewish laws, seized Jewish property, organized the shipment of Jews from their homes to the concentration camps, and worked out the complicated train schedules to ship human cargo. His job, in other words, was to organize the departure; arrival was someone else's worry. Nonetheless, departure involved a variety of complex operations, and Eichmann carried out these tasks with considerable administrative skill and originality.

Eichmann was one of fifteen invitees who, on 20 January 1942, attended the infamous Wannsee Conference. At this lake resort, in a suburb of Berlin, Nazi officials[1] planned what they called the Final Solution—the extermination of European Jewry. Conferees discussed extermination and liquidation of the entire Jewish population; they openly referred to various methods by which they might most efficiently murder Jews.[2]

In May of 1960, Israeli agents kidnapped Eichmann from Argentina, where he was then living, and brought him back to Israel to face trial. The trial, held in 1961 and 1962, aroused great attention around the world. This was the first time that the Nazi genocide was presented in great detail to a worldwide audience.

At stake at the trial was not only Eichmann's fate, a foregone conclusion,[3] but also through this trial an attempt to understand the infamy. Adolf Eichmann stood accused on fifteen counts: the Israeli prosecution charged that he had committed crimes against the Jewish people, crimes against humanity, and war crimes during the whole period of the Nazi regime, and especially during World War II.

To the formal charges against him, Eichmann's plea was strangely ambiguous: "Not guilty in the sense of the indictment."

---

1. The conference was planned and chaired by Reinhard Heydrich, head of the SD, the intelligence branch of the SS. Heydrich, in charge of the Einsatzgruppen—the mobile killing squads that brutally murdered hundreds of thousands of Eastern European Jews—was assassinated in Prague in 1942.

2. As Yehuda Bauer summarized in *A History of the Holocaust* (New York: Franklin Watts, 1982), p. 206, "The importance of Wannsee lies in the fact that at that place and at that time the entire German bureaucracy became involved in the conscious effort to murder a nation."

3. A country without capital punishment, Israel had—in preparation for Eichmann's trial—passed special legislation that permitted the death penalty for Holocaust-related crimes.

His defense was the same one that had been used previously at the Nuremberg trials[4]—that he was a small cog in the machinery of murder, an underling who had no choice but to carry out orders given by his superiors.

Covering the trial for the *New Yorker* magazine was Hannah Arendt. My concern here is not so much with Eichmann's guilt, about which much has been written. Rather I want to consider Arendt's interpretation of Eichmann and his deeds, published in 1963 as *Eichmann in Jerusalem*. In this book, Arendt recounts the career of Eichmann and considers various legal and moral issues surrounding the trial. But now I want to explore the controversial thesis of her book, expressed by the subtitle, *A Report on the Banality of Evil*.[5]

At the time of the trial, most analysts invoked the idea of evil, or some sort of collective insanity, to account for Nazism. They used terms such as *madman* and *monster* to describe Eichmann and other Nazis, and cited psychopathy, sex perversion, fanaticism, and xenophobia (especially focused on Jews) as causes of Nazi behavior. "The gathering chaos of German life after World War I," wrote political scientist Florence Miale and

---

4. After the war, the victorious allies conducted criminal trials in the city of Nuremberg. There an international military tribunal convicted Nazi leaders, including Hermann Göring and Rudolf Hess, of war crimes.

5. Hannah Arendt, *Eichmann in Jerusalem: A Report on the Banality of Evil* (New York: Viking Press, 1963). In addition to her interpretation of the nature of the defendant and his crime, Arendt also raised controversy by criticizing the Israeli conduct of the trial, and also—and this is a sore point—the passive behavior of the Jewish victims during the Holocaust. But her most controversial claim was neither of these, nor the one I am developing in the text. Arendt received a storm of criticism over her claim that the Jewish leadership, the Judenrat, had by their actions actually increased the Jewish death toll (see, for example, the bitter attack by Jacob Robinson, *And the Crooked Shall Be Made Straight* [New York: Macmillan, 1965]).

Substance aside, Arendt invited criticism by the tone of her book, which reviewers found to be unfriendly, cold, distant, and even malicious. Eichmann and his trial are frequently described in comedic terms. Gershom Scholem, the great Jewish theologian, wrote to Arendt: "It is that heartless, frequently almost sneering and malicious tone with which these matters, touching the very quick of our life, are treated in your book to which I take exception" (Gershom Scholem, "Letter to Hannah Arendt," *On Jews and Judaism in Crisis* [New York: Schocken Press, 1976], p. 302).

psychologist Michael Seltzer, "provided a handful of psychopaths with the opportunity to rally to their banner a large proportion of the psychopathic population of Germany."[6]

Arendt's thesis (really an antithesis) was simple. She rejected out of hand this admixture of explanations based on psychology. Nor did theological explanations seem adequate, for Eichmann's evil did not seem to result from any sort of temptation. She insisted that Eichmann's deeds must be understood within an entirely secular framework.

What kind of man was this persecutor of Jews? Arendt starts with what he was *not*. He did not seem particularly evil, neither in the Wagnerian epic sense, nor in the ordinary theological usage of the word. Nor was he (in any psychiatric sense) abnormal. Such terrible deeds, she concluded, were in fact committed by an ordinary, insubstantial person—thus this ironic phrase: "the banality of evil."

Let us consider the evidence for this rather remarkable conclusion. Eichmann's early life was unremarkable. Born in 1906, he was a poor student, finally dropping out of vocational school, where he studied mechanics. He eventually became a traveling salesman for Vacuum Oil, an American company, where he made a decent living during the terrible depression years. The company folded, Eichmann lost his job and, in 1932, he turned to the Nazis. We might think that he was attracted to Nazi evil. But apparently not. "He did not enter the Nazi Party out of conviction, nor was he ever convinced by it. . . . He did not know the Party program, he never read *Mein Kampf*."[7] He was ambitious, and he hoped to carve out a successful career within this new organization that was taking over Germany.

For Jews he showed no personal dislike. A distant relative, married to a Jewish woman, had helped Eichmann get his job at Vacuum Oil. Eichmann reported that he was grateful for this fa-

---

6. Florence Miale and Michael Seltzer, *The Nuremberg Mind: The Psychology of the Nazi Leaders* (New York: Quadrangle, 1975), p. 283. In the 1930s, Albert Einstein characterized Nazism as a "state of psychic distemper in the masses" (quoted in Grunfeld, p. 149).

7. Arendt, p. 29.

vor. "I had no hatred for the Jews," he testified remarkably at his trial, "for my whole education through my mother and father had been strictly Christian."[8] In Vienna, where he was extraordinarily successful in arranging the forced emigration of Jews in 1939, he had a Jewish mistress.

Nor did Eichmann have any taste for killing. He had a desk job far from the blood and gore. On two occasions, however, he was a witness to the slaughter that was under his command. In 1941 he visited an execution site at Minsk. "There were piles of dead people. They were shooting into the pit," Eichmann testified that he told the local SS commander: "Well, it is horrible what is being done around here. . . . How can one do that? Simply bang away at women and children? That is impossible. Our people will go mad or become insane."

At the Chelmno concentration camp, he saw people being gassed in a van.

> I couldn't even look at it. All the time I was trying to avert my sight from what was going on. It was quite enough for me what I saw. The screaming and shrieking—I was too excited to have a look at the van. . . . The van was making for an open pit. The doors were flung open and corpses were cast out as if they were some animals—some beasts. They were hurled into the ditch. I also saw how the teeth were being extracted. And then I disappeared; I entered my car and didn't want to look at this heinous act of turpitude. Then I took the car; for hours I was sitting at the side of the driver without exchanging a word with him. Then I knew I was washed up.[9]

---

8. Arendt, p. 26. Prudence and skepticism (let alone cynicism, which seems so appropriate here) suggest that we be suspicious of the veracity of Eichmann's testimony at his own trial. Yet Arendt and other commentators seem to accept the excerpts presented in this section as generally accurate. Eichmann's reportage seems consistent with other testimony and historical documentation.

9. Arendt, pp. 82–83. After seeing carnage at Minsk, Eichmann took a train ride. "I came to Lvov," he testified, "and for the first time saw a charming picture—the railway station which was built in honor of the sixtieth year of the reign of Franz Joseph; and I always found pleasure in that period, maybe because I heard so many nice things about it in my parents' home. . . . It was painted yellow and I remember it, and I remember that the date was inscribed on the wall. This for the first time drove away these terrible thoughts which had never left me since Minsk, this was the first time I could forget" (p. 44).

Whatever Eichmann meant by "washed up," it did not stop him from returning to his desk and, from that vantage point, supervising the killings of millions more.

Eichmann was not insane, at least by the generally accepted usage of that term. Six psychiatrists had certified him as "normal," "more normal at any rate," said one, "than I am after having examined him."[10] Another psychiatrist found that his whole outlook, his attitude toward his wife and children, mother and father, brothers, sisters, and friends was "not only normal, but most desirable." In prison he was given the book *Lolita* for reading relaxation. Two days later, Eichmann returned it: "Quite an unwholesome book," he indignantly judged. Finally, the minister who visited him regularly declared him to be "a man of very positive ideas."[11]

What Eichmann wanted was to follow—and be rewarded for following—orders. What Eichmann wanted to be was the proverbial (but in this case, most frightening) cog in the machine. When Germany lost the war, for Eichmann it meant: "I would have to live a leaderless and difficult individual life. I would receive no directives from anybody, no orders or commands would any longer be issued to me, no pertinent ordinances would be there to consult—in brief, a life never known before lay before me."[12]

"The trouble with Eichmann," Arendt concluded, "was precisely that there were so many like him" who were, and still are,

---

10. In "A Devout Meditation in Memory of Adolf Eichmann," Catholic theologian Thomas Merton wrote: "A man can be 'sane' in the limited sense that he is not impeded by his disordered emotions from acting in a cool, orderly manner, according to the needs and dictates of the social situation in which he finds himself." From Eichmann, we learn that it is our definition of *normal* that needs examination: "The sanity of Eichmann is disturbing. We equate sanity with a sense of justice, with humaneness, with prudence, with the capacity to love and understand other people. We rely on the sane people of the world to preserve it from barbarism, madness, destruction. And now it begins to dawn on us that it is precisely the *sane* ones who are the most dangerous." *Raids on the Unspeakable* (New York: New Directions, 1966) pp. 45, 44.
11. Arendt, pp. 22, 44.
12. Arendt, p. 28.

"terribly and terrifyingly normal." This normalcy was "more ter-
rifying than all the atrocities put together." The judges missed
the greatest moral and legal challenge of the whole case, Arendt
asserted. They failed to realize that "an average, 'normal' person, neither feeble-minded nor indoctrinated, nor cynical, could
be perfectly incapable of telling right from wrong." Or, as Arendt
asserted: "there is a new type of criminal who commits his crimes
under circumstances that make it well-nigh impossible for him
to know or to feel that he is doing wrong."[13]

Eichmann's perfidy arose, in Arendt's argument, from an
extreme version of an unthinking life. Such lives are characterized by an unthinking use of language, by cliché rather than
thought. The longer one listened to him, Arendt reported, the
clearer it became that he had an "inability to think," particularly
to "think from the standpoint of somebody else."[14] It would seem
as though Eichmann had lost the ability, or had a severely diminished capacity, to do what sociologists claim is necessary for any
significant social interaction: to take the role of the other.

Thus does Arendt throw down the gauntlet, a gauntlet that
I think has real insight. It seems obvious in retrospect, but nev-
ertheless we must begin with this simple notion: that Eichmann
existed in, was a part of, and cannot be understood outside of,
the context of Nazi Germany.

In any society, we ask: How free are individuals to stand up
for their beliefs? or even—here is a more basic question—to have
beliefs independent of the mass? All of us wish to think that we
have an autonomous center with which we control our destiny,
or at least our daily environment. Yet we know that our ability
to act morally (whatever that might mean) has been compromised, even severely compromised, in twentieth-century mass
society.

And what of autonomous behavior in Nazi society? Here,
wrote Dagme Barnouw in a friendly and perceptive critique of

---

13. Arendt, pp. 253, 23.
14. Arendt, p. 44. On this point, see Berel Lang, "Hannah Arendt and the
Politics of Evil." Pp. 41–57 in *Hannah Arendt; Critical Essays*, eds. Lewis
Hinchman and Sandra Hinchman (Albany: State University of New York Press,
1994).

Arendt, the relationship between the individual and society became perverted. It is extraordinarily difficult for the individual to arrive at an independent, moral judgment without being able to rely on a general code established by social agreement at large. Is autonomous judgment of the particular possible, asks Barnouw, without reference to a general rule? "In a totalitarian society, only an extraordinary person retains such ability." "The needs of the social organism," she concluded, "have been perverted in their total turn against the other; the individual, swept up by the energy of this turn, is totally isolated."[15]

A student of Arendt's, Michael Denneny, developed these ideas further. Eichmann was certainly sane in that he was able to exercise what the German philosopher Immanuel Kant called "determinative judgment," the ability to subsume the particular under the general concept or rule. But he was apparently incapable of what Kant called "reflective judgment." He never looked at a particular case in front of him and tried to judge it without a rule. "And the rules society gave him to work with were criminal." Eichmann's conscience and morality, Denneny quoted Arendt as saying, "were working exactly in reverse. This reversal is precisely the moral collapse that took place in Europe."[16]

How was it possible that these morals and ethics, derived from the very basis of Western culture, dissolved so quickly, so completely? Here Arendt came to the sociological heart of the matter: The Holocaust shows, she asserted, that Western morals and ethics "had suddenly revealed themselves for what they were—that is, customs or behavior patterns which could be changed as easily as table manners."[17]

What are we to make of Arendt's ideas?[18] Survivors have said: She was not there, not hurt, not starved, not tortured—so

---

15. Dagme Barnouw, "The Secularity of Evil: Hannah Arendt and the Eichmann Controversy," *Modern Judaism* 3 (1983): 76.

16. Michael Denneny, "The Privilege of Ourselves: Hannah Arendt on Judgment." In Melvin Hill (ed.), *Hannah Arendt: The Recovery of the Public World* (New York: St. Martins 1979), pp. 254–55. In Kant's analysis the term *reflective* is restricted to aesthetic analysis. Arendt has considerably widened its use.

17. Denneny, p. 254

18. A thorough evaluation must await chapter 4, where I develop Arendt's concept of totalitarianism in which "banality" is nested.

how could she understand? "There is no banality of evil," Jean Amery wrote, "and Hannah Arendt, who wrote about it in her Eichmann book, knew the enemy of mankind only from hearsay, saw him only through the glass cage."[19] One can understand this sort of criticism, for Auschwitz was nothing if not humiliation, pain, and death. Nonetheless, while survivors do have a privileged voice, they do not have the only voice. Any intellectual analysis of the Holocaust is an attempt to look for insight that transcends an individual experience.

Most critics, intellectuals like Arendt, have pointed toward the polemical nature of her analysis. Of course most Nazis were not pathological monsters, they agree; but can one really claim that they were ordinary? "The 'banality of evil' is the catchword of our generation," claims Cynthia Ozick.[20] To say the word *banality*, is to dismiss a complex analysis.

Mr. Arthur Sammler, survivor and protagonist in Saul Bellow's novel, *Mr. Sammler's Planet*, voices a scathing critique of Arendt. "The idea of making the century's great crime look dull is not banal," he says. "Politically, psychologically, the Germans had an idea of genius. The banality was only camouflage. What better way to get the curse out of murder than to make it look ordinary, boring or trite." "With horrible political insight," he continues, "they found a way to disguise the thing."[21] Thus Bellow accuses the Nazis not of pathology, but of spectacular pretense, not of dullness, but genius. I think Bellow gives the Germans too much credit.

Eichmann recognized that he had participated in what was perhaps the greatest crime in history. He insisted, however, that

---

19. Amery, p. 25.

20. Cynthia Ozick, "On Christian Heroism," *Partisan Review* 49 (1992): 44. In today's jargon, some would say that both "evil" and "banality" resist deconstruction which might expose opposite, but hidden, ideological presumptions.

21. Saul Bellow, *Mr. Sammler's Planet* (New York: Viking Press, 1969), p. 12. Sammler (through Bellow) continues: "This woman professor's enemy is modern civilization itself. She is only using the Germans to attack the twentieth century—to denounce it in terms invented by Germans. Making use of a tragic history to promote the foolish ideas of Weimar intellectuals." I will return to this insightful observation in chapter 4.

he had no choice. Sartre wrote about "bad faith," to pretend something is necessary when in fact it is voluntary. Arendt goes much further, for it is her contention that Eichmann was not "pretending," that in fact he was caught in, and part of, a totalitarian thought warp. He is mediocre; he is ludicrous; therefore he is horribly dangerous. And here is, of course, the ultimate irony, and also a real insight: that his ordinariness, his banality is exactly what makes him so very frightening and dangerous.

ordinary killers[22]

Adolf Eichmann was a member of the dreaded SS, soldiers who were highly trained, motivated, and rewarded for their role in the Holocaust. But most of the actual killing was not done by such people. Rather, the killers were ordinary men of no rank or training who were caught up in extraordinary times. I now consider one case of mass murder which occurred in Józefów, a small town in southeastern Poland.

The date is 12 July 1942.

Early on that morning, Major William Trapp, affectionately referred to as "Papa Trapp" by the men of German Reserve Police Battalion 101, gave the orders for the day: the Battalion was to select all young males for a work camp in Lublin. The remaining Jews of Józefów, about fifteen hundred women, children, and elderly, were to be shot.

Major Trapp hardly fits our image of a mass murderer. A fifty-three-year-old career policeman, Trapp had joined the Nazi Party in 1932; but he was not a member of the SS, nor did he have SS-equivalent rank.[23] Nor did he relish his own command that day: "Oh God, why did I have to be given these orders," he said to one man. While Jews were murdered at his command, Trapp

---

22. This section is drawn from Christopher Browning, *Ordinary Men* (New York: Harper Collins, 1992). Browning's sources for all quoted material are judicial records in the Stattsanwalschaft Hamburg, from an investigation conducted from 1962 to 1972.

23. His two captains, by contrast, were Party members and SS officers. In testimony twenty years later, they made no attempt to conceal their contempt for their commander as both weak and unmilitary.

did not visit the killing field. Throughout the day, according to one policeman, he "wept like a child."[24]

Nonetheless, orders were orders. The men of his command rounded up the Jews. Then, in the words of one of the policemen, the battalion doctor "outlined the contour of a human body, at least from the shoulders upwards, and then indicated precisely the point on which the fixed bayonet was to be placed as an aiming guide."[25]

Reservists transported the Jews in trucks to the edge of the forest; there, the squad members paired off face-to-face with individual Jews. They forced the Jews to lie face down in a row and shot them point-blank. Soon the forest was filled with bodies; it was a problem to find places to make the Jews lie down so that they might be shot. The men in Reserve Police Battalion 101 shot Jews throughout the day, finally, numbingly, losing count as the piles of bodies mounted. The killing, begun at dawn, was not complete until dusk, by which time the dead numbered some fifteen hundred.

The action was not planned too carefully: the Germans did not bury the dead—there was no time—nor did they engage in systematic plunder; the pile of the Jews' luggage, left in the marketplace, was burned. Just before the battalion left the village, a young girl appeared, bleeding from the head. Trapp took her in his arms and said: "You shall remain alive."[26]

I want to leave this grisly scene for a moment to seek some perspective. In mid-March of 1942, some three-quarters of all victims of the Holocaust were still alive; eleven months later, by February 1943, the situation was exactly the reverse: three-quarters were dead. Many of the victims were killed in the infamous concentration camps of Poland; many died concentrated in ghettos; many were killed by the Einsatzgruppen.

---

24. Browning, p. 58. After the war, however, he was convicted of war crimes and executed in Poland. Without making any judgments about Trapp, it seems to me that his death did little to advance the cause of justice for that unfortunate country.

25. Browning, p. 60. According to this witness, who played the violin, the physician played "a wonderful accordion."

26. Browning, p. 69.

But the Jews of Józefów were not in a ghetto; nor were they shipped to a concentration camp; nor were they killed by SS. The perpetrators of the Józefów massacre, and countless other village massacres, were members of the Order Police. Similar to the National Guard, the men from Battalion 101 were civilian draftees considered too old for frontline service. Prior to the war, about 60 percent held semiskilled jobs, such as dock workers and truck drivers; most of the remainder were salesmen and office workers, but three were professionals—two druggists and one teacher. Their average age was thirty-nine, and half were between ages thirty-seven and forty-two.

Age is important here; most of these men had gone through their formative years in the pre-Nazi era. Thus, unlike younger men, they had not experienced lifelong immersion in Nazi propaganda. Geography was important, too. Most of the men of Battalion 101 came from Hamburg, one of the least "Nazified" cities in Germany. Few of the perpetrators expressed any sort of anti-Semitism.

Like their commander Trapp, the soldiers, it would seem, were poorly cast in their roles as mass murderers. One, a former cigarette sales representative, was in great turmoil and "shot too high." As a result, the entire back of the skull of "my Jew" was torn off and flew into the sergeant's face. "I became so sick that I simply couldn't [kill Jews] anymore." Another, a tailor, discovered that his victims were Jews from Germany, a mother and daughter, and also quit the killing. Yet another policeman "ran deep into the forest and vomited" after killing his fourth victim.[27] These reports, and others like them, hardly suggest that the perpetrators of the Józefów massacre were sadists.

At the time Trapp gave the orders for the massacre, he also made an extraordinary offer to his men: Any who did not feel up to the task could decline the duty! After some hesitation, some dozen men were dismissed from the forthcoming action. We know that the men who declined participation were not punished in any significant way.[28] Yet it is hard to imagine the men perceiving

---

27 Browning, pp. 66–67.

28. Lieutenant Hans Buchmann, a member of the Nazi Party, head of a family lumber business in Hamburg, had learned the day before of the planned massacre. He refused—and was not reprimanded for his refusal—to participate in an action in which defenseless women and children were to be shot.

Trapp's offer as a real existential choice. Perhaps we should ask: Did such choices even exist in Nazi Germany? Many must have assumed, and with some historical justification, that not declining Trapp's offer might have serious consequences.

Why did ordinary men massacre helpless Jews? Let us listen to the men, as they talked about their motives in testimony twenty years later. Several said that they did not want to be considered cowards by their fellow soldiers; others cited their careers back home: they were afraid that they would not receive promotions or do well after the war. But perhaps we err in listening to motives, for such a discussion implies thoughtfulness and reflexivity. "I must say," one policeman reported, "that at the time we did not reflect about it at all."[29]

Browning concludes that two factors, crushing conformity and careerism, combined as the most important factors to explain how the men of Battalion 101 became mass murderers. "If the men of Reserve Police Battalion 101 could become killers," Browning asks, "what group of men cannot?"[30]

ordinary people

Let us for the moment leave war-torn Europe, the agony of Poland, with its unbelievable pain and suffering, and cross the Atlantic Ocean. Our destination is New Haven, Connecticut, where citizens live in (comparative) safety, warmth, and good stead. I want to consider a number of experiments conducted in the early 1960s by a social psychologist, J. Stanley Milgram.[31] These experiments, called the "Eichmann experiments" by the noted American psychologist Gordon Allport, have challenged the way we think about the Nazis, which means that they have challenged the way that we think about human nature.

Milgram's story is so dramatic, so filled with emotion and tension, that a number of authors have chosen to portray his

---

29. Browning, p. 73.
30. Browning, p. 189.
31. J. Stanley Milgram, *Obedience to Authority* (New York: Harper & Row, 1974).

work phenomenologically—that is to say, not from Milgram's point of view, but from the subject's own experience.[32] I will begin with the same dramatic license.

Suppose you see an ad in your local newspaper, "WE WILL PAY YOU $4.00 FOR ONE HOUR OF YOUR TIME," which then asks for volunteers for a study of memory being conducted at Yale University. "No special training, education, or experience is needed." Sounds like good money,[33] you say to yourself, and you follow directions and make arrangements to participate.

Arriving at the psychology building at Yale, you meet two people: Mr. Smith, a rotund, rather jolly looking man about fifty years old, who, like you, has responded to the ad; and Mr. Williams, younger, more severe in appearance, who is conducting the experiment. Williams begins right away by paying you and Smith. "From this point, no matter what happens, the money is yours," he says. He explains that in the forthcoming experiment, one of you will be the teacher and one will be the learner. You draw lots and it turns out that you are the teacher.

Williams explains the experiment, which sounds very complicated. But the essence is this: Smith will be wired up to a shock machine and you will give him a test. Every time he misses, you will give him a shock, beginning with low levels and increasing in intensity for every mistake Smith makes. Williams asks for your help in strapping Smith into the chair, particularly in attaching the leather thongs and a metal bracelet to Smith's arm. Williams puts electrode paste on Smith's arm "to avoid burns and blisters." Smith seems a little scared, and says: "I hope this doesn't hurt too much, because I have a heart condition." "Although the shocks can be painful," Williams replies, "they cause no permanent damage."

Next Williams shows you the shock machine. It has thirty lever-type switches in a left-to-right row; toward the right, you

---

32. See, for example, Alan C. Elms, *Social Psychology and Social Relevance* (Boston: Little, Brown, 1972), p. 111ff.

33 Let me remind the reader that the dollar has become quite inflated since 1963, the year in which this experiment took place. At that time, $4.00 per hour was good money.

note the labels "Very Strong Shock," "Extreme Intensity Shock," and "Danger: Severe Shock." The last two switches are marked only with "XXX." "Let me give you a sample shock," Williams says. He pulls the third switch, 45 volts; it hurts, and you wince.

You begin the experiment. At first, Smith answers correctly, but as the task becomes more complicated he begins to make frequent errors. For each mistake, you shock him. At 90 volts, Smith grunts. At 120 volts, he shouts that the shocks are becoming painful. You turn to Williams for guidance, but he is working on his notes and does not acknowledge you. At 135 volts, Smith shouts: "Get me out of here! I won't be in this experiment anymore! I refuse to go on!" You turn to Williams: "He won't go on," you say. "Please continue," says Williams. "But he says he doesn't want to go on," you plead. "Whether the learner likes it or not, you must go on until the experiment is completed," Williams says.

Let us pause at this point and ask what would appear to be a simple question: What would each of us do if we were in this situation? Most of us, certainly I included, would answer unambiguously: We would quit the experiment! But before I continue with Milgram's most disturbing findings and conclusions, let us pause once again. It turns out that Milgram's experiment was a setup: Smith was a confederate, an actor—his agonized responses were carefully scripted. The real subject of the experiment was not Smith, but you—the object being to determine how you would follow orders, even orders that you believed would cause great physical pain, and perhaps even endanger the life of Smith.

Having exposed Milgram's ruse,[34] let us return to our story. Smith's script becomes more agitated and desperate: at 180 volts

---

34. Milgram's experiments aroused a storm of protest. Most commentators labeled his work unethical on the principle that he not only deceived his subjects, but as well took great advantage of them. This is not the place to detail such criticism, much of which I agree with. But I should note that Milgram's defense against ethical violations, just like the experiment itself, is quite interesting. In a 1971 book, *The Individual in a Social World* (Reading, MA: Addison-Wesley), he maintained that criticism of the experiment came not from ethical considerations, but from the radical nature of his findings: "If everyone had broken off at light or moderate shock," and thus disobeyed the experimenter, "this would be a very reassuring finding, and who would protest?" (p. 78).

he cries out: "I can't stand the pain"; at 270 volts he screams, as if in agony. After 330 volts he screams intermittently, but never gives a correct—or even a coherent—answer. After 400 volts he kicks at the wall and then, for the last few levers, only silence!

Now we are even more certain: We (which is to say, people like us) would never do violence to Smith in this way.[35] But we are wrong. Not one of forty subjects stopped the shocks prior to 135 volts. One subject stopped at that level and five stopped at 150 volts. But twenty-five (63 percent) shocked all the way to 450 volts. And the mean maximum shock level was the twenty-fourth (labeled "Extreme Intensity Shock") lever, or 360 volts, at which time the victim is screaming, demanding his freedom, and giving rather incoherent answers.[36]

How can this be? How do we account for the apparent brutality of these Americans? In Experiment 4, the victim is in "touch proximity" with the subject. Here the subject must use his own hand to force Smith's hand on the shock plate. It is one thing to deliver pain to a remote victim, but quite another to hurt someone sitting next to you. Yet even under the most dramatic circumstances of Experiment 4, not one of forty subjects stopped before 135 volts; the mean maximum shock delivered was 270 volts (which the machine labels "Intense Shock"); and twelve subjects (30 percent) shocked Smith all the way to 450 volts.

Milgram was disturbed and perplexed: "Subjects have learned from childhood that it is a fundamental breach of moral

---

35. We are not alone in this assessment. Milgram described the experimental condition to three groups of people: thirty-nine psychiatrists (including some who were quite prominent), thirty-one college students, and forty middle-class adults. Not one of these individuals predicted that an experimental subject would shock all the way to 450 volts. In fact, the highest prediction was for a shock level of 300. The mean maximum shock levels predicted by the three groups were between 120 and 135 volts. So Milgram showed what we guessed about ourselves: Most people do not think that subjects would inflict significant pain on Smith.

36. Milgram, *Obedience to Authority*, p. 35. I have described Experiment 2. Experiment 1 is similar except that the subject cannot hear Smith's voice. In those circumstances, twenty-six of forty subjects (65 percent) shocked all the way to 450 volts, and not one subject stopped before administering a shock of 300 volts. In other words, hearing Smith had an effect, but a rather small one, on the subjects' behavior. In all there were eighteen experimental variations, each rich in imagination and import.

conduct to hurt another person against his will. Yet almost half of the subjects abandon this tenet in following the instructions of an authority who has no special powers to enforce his commands."[37]

He thought that perhaps the setting of the experiment, the psychology department at Yale University, had a strong effect on subject compliance. In postexperimental interviews, several subjects claimed that the locale and sponsorship of the study gave them confidence in its integrity, competence, and benign purposes of the personnel. So Milgram moved the setting to a shabby building in downtown Bridgeport, and conducted the experiment under the auspices of "Research Associates of Bridgeport." Here, two subjects refused to administer even the lowest shock, the only initial disobedience shown by more than one thousand subjects studied by Milgram. Despite them, the findings were grim: nineteen of forty (48 percent) subjects shocked all the way to 450 volts, and the mean maximum shock was level 20, some 300 volts. So: Experimental setting does ameliorate behavior, but only to a small degree.[38]

How am I to explain this behavior? Social psychologists, on whose academic turf this battle was first fought, initially asked questions about personality. They expected—but failed—to find a personality flaw in the obeyers that was absent in others. Milgram's student Alan Elms found no differences whatever between obeyers and disobeyers on the Minnesota Multiphasic Personality Inventory (MMPI), nor on a host of other personality inventories.[39]

---

37. Milgram, *Obedience to Authority*, p. 41. Milgram's use of "half" refers to Experiments 1 through 4 combined.

38. So far all the experiments had been done on men. But what about women? On the one hand, women are socialized to be more compliant and yielding than men—so they should shock more; on the other, they are socialized to be less aggressive and more humane than men—so they should shock less. In Experiment 8, Milgram repeated his basic Bridgeport protocol on forty female subjects. No woman stopped shocks prior to 150 volts, and the mean maximum shock level was identical to that of male counterparts, as was the proportion (65 percent) who shocked all the way to 450 volts.

39. "However I analyzed the answers to this questionnaire, forward, backward, upside down and sideways, the obedients and the defiants just weren't much different." Elms, 135–136.

Milgram had found small differences between obeyers and others: Catholics were a bit more obedient than other religious groups; the better educated were more defiant; those in humanistic professions were more defiant than those in technical professions; and the longer one's military service, the more obedient, except that former officers were less obedient than enlisted men.

Those who obeyed did not seem particularly sadistic. Let us examine an actual transcript from a subject, Fred Prozi.[40] After 180 volts:

SUBJECT: I can't stand it. I'm not going to kill that man in there. You hear him hollering?
EXPERIMENTER: As I told you before, the shocks may be painful, but—
SUBJECT: But he's hollering. He can't stand it. What's going to happen to him?
EXPERIMENTER: The experiment requires that you continue, teacher.
SUBJECT: Aaah, but unh, I'm going to get that man sick in there . . . know what I mean?
EXPERIMENTER: Whether the learner likes it or not, we must go on.

I will return to this particular transcript in a moment. But it would appear that this subject got no pleasure out of inflicting pain on Smith. According to Milgram, most subjects were anything but sadists. They were observed: "to sweat, tremble, stutter, bite their lips, groan, and dig their fingernails into their flesh. These were characteristic rather than exceptional responses to the experiment." After the maximum shock had been delivered, "many obedient subjects heaved sighs of relief, mopped their brows, rubbed their fingers over their eyes, or nervously fumbled cigarettes." One subject "pushed his fist into his forehead and muttered: 'Oh, God, let's stop it.' "[41] Yet this subject, too, obeyed to the end and shocked Smith with 450 volts.

If obeyers were not sadists, perhaps disobeyers were heroes. Let us again quote from an actual transcript, this text coming after 315 volts: "He's banging in there. I'm going to chicken out. I'd like to continue, but I can't do that to a man." This is not a John Wayne-Hollywood scenario. Note the apologetic nature of the defiance: he asserts not a Judeo-Christian ethic, but rather,

---

40. Milgram, *Obedience to Authority*, p. 74. The name is fictitious, of course.
41. J. Stanley Milgram, "Behavioral Study of Obedience," *Journal of Abnormal and Social Psychology* 67 (1963): 375; Milgram, *Obedience to Authority*, p. 377.

in his own words, a weakness[42] of character in "chickening out."
Hardly the actions or language of a heroic figure!

Let us return to the transcript of Fred Prozi, still at 180 volts:

LEARNER: Let me out of here. My heart's bothering me! (Subject looks at experimenter.)
EXPERIMENTER: Continue please.
LEARNER: Let me out of here. You have no right to keep me here. Let me out of here, my heart's bothering me. Let me out.
SUBJECT: (Shakes his head, pats the table nervously) I refuse to take responsibility. He's in there hollering! . . . I mean, who's going to take responsibility if anything happens to that gentlemen?
EXPERIMENTER: I'm responsible for anything that happens to him.
SUBJECT: All right.

The transcript slaps us in the face! The subject does not wish to hurt Smith. He does not degrade Smith; in fact, he refers to him in parlor language, as a gentleman. He derives no psychic pleasure from inflicting pain. He does it because he is told to do it, because someone else takes responsibility. He complains about the order; he struggles against the order. Let us return to the same transcript, except now all the way up to 375 volts:

SUBJECT: (Stands up) I think something's happened to that fellow in there. I don't get no answer. He was hollering at less voltage. Can't you check in and see if he is all right, please?
TEACHER: Please continue, teacher.
SUBJECT: Something has happened to that man in there. You better check on him, sir. He won't answer or nothing.
TEACHER: Continue. Go on, please.
SUBJECT: You accept all responsibility?
TEACHER: The responsibility is mine.

Indeed: he complains; he struggles. But ultimately he caves in. He deems himself non-responsible and therefore behaves wrongly.

---

42. The nonshooters of Reserve Police Battalion 101 also consistently cited "weakness" as the reason they gave to their officers for not participating in the killings.

Milgram's own conclusions are deeply pessimistic. In the laboratory, he was able with little effort to create an environment that manipulated people in the most frightening ways. "With numbing regularity," he wrote in an often quoted conclusion, "good people were seen to knuckle under to the demands of authority and perform actions that were callous and severe. Men who are in everyday life responsible and decent were seduced by the trappings of authority, by the control of their perceptions, and by the uncritical definition of the situation into performing harsh acts."[43] But Milgram is not just worried about laboratory behavior. The results of the experiment, he wrote, "raise the possibility that human nature, or—more specifically—the kind of character produced in American democratic society, cannot be counted on to insulate its citizens from brutality and inhumane treatment at the direction of malevolent authority."[44]

His conclusion ought to send a deep chill down our spines. Recall Arendt's assertion that Western morals and ethics were not etched in the sinew of human nature, but rather could be changed as easily as table manners. Milgram similarly asserts the ephemeral nature of morals. "Though such prescriptions as 'Thou Shalt Not Kill' occupy a preeminent place in the moral order, they do not occupy a correspondingly intractable position in the human psychic structure." In times of war, men are led to kill with little difficulty. Even in the laboratory, he maintains, "Moral factors can be shunted aside with relative ease by a calculated restructuring of the informational and social field."[45]

---

43. Milgram, *Obedience to Authority*, p. 123.
44. Milgram, *Obedience to Authority*, p. 189.
45. Milgram, *Obedience to Authority*, p. 7. I have not considered the famous (or infamous) experiment of the social psychologist Philip Zimbardo. He set up a mock "prison," in which "normal, intelligent, emotionally stable" students were randomly assigned the roles of inmates and guards. Zimbardo had to break off the experiment after only six days. "In less than a week the experience of imprisonment undid (temporarily) a lifetime of learning; human values were suspended, self-concepts were challenged and the ugliest, most base, pathological side of human nature surfaced. We were horrified because we saw some boys (guards) treat others as if they were animals, taking pleasure in cruelty, while other boys (prisoners) became servile, dehumanized robots" ("Pathology of Imprisonment," *Society* 9 [April, 1972]: p. 4).

In some ways the Zimbardo experiment supports my argument better than do the Milgram experiments. Yet I am suspicious of Zimbardo's work. The method is certainly not as rigorous or convincing as Milgram's, and for obvious reasons the mock prison has never been repeated. But perhaps I just cannot believe—though I know better—that people would really do such things as Zimbardo described.

are we all nazis?

Even if we believe Milgram, and I do, we face a logical problem. Granted, frightening behaviors happened in the laboratory. What does that tell us about Nazi Germany? and about us? Milgram faced this question head-on in the preface to his book. Of course, he wrote, the differences between the laboratory and the Holocaust are "enormous." Yet differences in "scale, number and political context may turn out to be relatively unimportant." The question of generality is not resolved by enumerating the patently obvious differences between the two settings, but, "by carefully constructing a situation which captures the essence of obedience—that is, a situation in which a person gives himself over to authority and no longer views himself as the efficient cause of his own actions."[46]

So: Are we all Nazis? The question is insulting. Of course we are not Nazis! We were not there; we did not shoot innocents;[47] we did not gas and incinerate babies. The question is obviously analogical,[48] and a mean analogy it is! Yet the question will not go away: in its meanness there is an urgency.

How different were Milgram's subjects (which is to say, you and I) from the average, typical Nazi? Milgram's subjects were dealing with possible harm, Nazis with certain death; Milgram's with ephemeral authority, Nazis with legal and ideological authority; Milgram's with cooperation, Nazis with occupational obligation; Milgram's with an isolated incident; Nazis with

---

46. Milgram, *Obedience to Authority,* p. xii.

47. Of course it is not only Nazis who have killed innocent people. History is full of horrible massacres. In a particularly thorough analysis of the American war crime at My Lai in 1968, Herbert Kelman and V. Lee Hamilton in *Crimes of Obedience: Toward a Social Psychology of Authority and Obedience* (New Haven: Yale University Press, 1989), identify three "prevailing conditions," dehumanization, routinization and authorization, necessary for all crimes of obedience.

48. Note that I am not considering a homology, in which a fundamental similarity is posited, but rather an analogy, a correspondence of certain characteristics. Analogies have long been used as an analytic tool in social research, especially as a way of relating events across time or space. An analogy never proves anything in a formal sense, but rather may give us some insight hitherto unseen.

continuous, daily behavior. Despite these differences, we should not take comfort too quickly.

I want to review and meditate on several studies that ponder the relation between Nazis and us. This consideration will bring us full circle, for it involves an analysis of the Nazi psyche in light of Arendt's thesis and Milgram's empirical work.

After the war, several psychiatric studies assessed Nazi personality and character by using Rorschach "ink blot" tests. Miale and Seltzer, whom I quoted earlier in this chapter, concluded that Nazis demonstrated severe pathology. The lesson to be learned, they claimed, "is not that in a wicked world decent people will act in a wicked way but that in a wicked world people with a penchant for wickedness will freely indulge it, justifying themselves . . . on the ground that they were merely obeying orders."[49]

Henry Dicks, a psychiatrist, concluded the opposite. He conducted extensive interviews with eight former SS, and in addition reviewed numerous case studies of other SS officers and men. These were men who had committed the most horrible of acts. Dicks described one warrant officer: "He had used the method of inserting a fire hose into a victim's mouth and running water in under pressure until the man literally burst; he had flung people into cesspits and watched them drown there." He made elderly, frail or starving people: "cross the camp parade ground loaded with very heavy sacks of cement, and then kicking or whipping them if they collapsed—and all of this to the blare of . . . gypsy music."[50]

This is the most terrible infamy, no doubt about that. Yet Dicks asserted that it is a mistake to consider these SS insane or uncontrollable people, or to see their terrorism as the result of narrowly focused anti-Semitism. Under normal conditions, few

---

49. Miale and Seltzer, p. 11. The authors claim that "Milgram's experiments are almost irrelevant to an understanding of the Nazi phenomenon." For comparability with the Nazis, they claim, he would have needed subjects such as "the Ku Klux Klan as teachers and black persons as learners." This criticism misses the point: Milgram's sample of ordinary citizens, about whom one can generalize to larger populations, is a strength of his study.

50. Henry V. Dicks, *Licensed Mass Murder: A Socio-Psychological Study of Some SS Killers* (New York: Basic Books, 1972), p. 96.

if any of these killers would have become "common" (whatever that might mean! I have my doubts that such a species exists) murderers.

Dicks outlines the transmogrification of a common person into a mass murderer. His key to understanding is not an Oedipal complex, or death wishes, or some regression or repression—all of which are considered in his presentation. Rather, the key is conformity. "By colluding with those early elements of terror, in the shape of 'authentic' representatives of the new and required group ethos," conformity "replaced individual rational criticism and moral judgments."[51]

Nazi evil is not pathological; rather, it is (in Dicks's words) "banal." In form, if not content, Nazi activities are homologous to Milgram's subjects. New Haven subjects and Dicks's SS subjects use the "same ego defenses" as justifications for their behaviors; Milgram's experiments have exposed the "all too human propensity to conformity and obedience to group authority."

The analogy between Nazis and us has been presented most forcefully by a clinical psychologist, Hans Askenasy, whose book title I have borrowed to head this section. Askenasy is not timid. Of high SS officials, he concludes: "They were above all ordinary—banal in Hannah Arendt's term. And banal were their most inconceivable crimes." Even more: Nazis were "as normal and ordinary as those good citizens who walked the streets in New Haven."[52]

---

51. Dicks, p. 255. First, a person with an "averagely humane conscience" would condemn himself for lack of moral courage. But this is an intolerable position, so next comes denial: surely there must be some truth to the ideals of Nazism. The idea that "Fate is tragic" follows along with the notion that murderous behavior is part of a "great happening of history." Finally the individual spirals into complete dehumanization, when the "hitherto respected human being is replaced by the dehumanized stereotype."

I think that Dicks's explanation has merit, yet I mistrust any system that posits stages of development. To the extent that they capture a process, they at the same time miss the dialectic between actor and society. I am impressed with the importance of unanticipated consequences and irony which seem to defy any mechanical explanations. Nazi behavior, like all behavior, is complex and idiosyncratic.

52. Hans Askenasy, *Are We All Nazis?* (Secaucus, NJ: Lyle Stuart, 1978), pp. 191, 49.

Remember that both Arendt and Milgram depicted ethics and morals not as bedrocks of the human soul, but as something more ephemeral. This position, which some have called "radical situationalism,"[53] leads to Askenasy's most frightening conclusion: "And so we now know that those Nazis and these Americans —which is to say you and I—for all our superficial differences such as time and place, are, psychologically speaking, interchangeable."[54]

This conclusion, which I think is worthy of our deepest consideration, does not in any way diminish the Nazi crime. Quite the opposite: For if Nazis are demonic then they can be dismissed as aberrations, freak mutants of the world's cultures; but, if they are essentially like you and me, then we must make some frightening conclusions about the potentials of human nature and culture.

Which is right? Miale and Selzer's "pathology" thesis, or Dicks's and Askenasy's "normalcy" thesis?[55] Rorschach tests tell us little. For every researcher that found pathology, another found that variance in Nazi personality profiles was not too different from what one would find in any society. This should not surprise us: Rorschach and other projective tests probably "project" more about the analyst than they tell us about the subject. Proponents of the pathology model purport a world of dichotomy: of wickedness and goodness, of right and wrong, of Nazi and us. This world, in short, contains no gray zone. Perhaps it is my own limitation, but the concept of "wickedness"—a quasi-religious idea—gives me little insight into Nazism and the Holocaust.

My interpretation of the data and my view of human nature (or more precisely, my view of human behavior within the cultural context of modern society) lead me to reject pathology as an explanation of the Holocaust. I am more sympathetic toward Dicks's and Askenasy's thinking. Their view of humans is

---

53. Arthur Miller, *The Obedience Experiments* (New York: Praeger, 1986), p. 191.

54. Askenasy, p. 49.

55. These terms were coined by Arthur Miller, whose scholarship guided me through this literature.

more complex: Individuals live not in isolation, but in culture; situations, as well as character, influence behavior; personality changes as the world changes.

Nonetheless, I do not want to accept Dicks's and Askenasy's conclusions without reservation. I want to avoid choosing between the normalcy and pathology hypotheses. I find it unhelpful to use psychiatric criteria to distinguish between Nazis and us. I would choose rather to reject the entire dichotomy. Psychiatric criteria are of limited utility for assessing complex social and cultural phenomena. Their locus of explanation is improperly the individual, when it should be the social structure.

We do better to treat the relation between Nazis and us not as clinical, but as analogical. By now we should understand that the very asking of the question that heads this section—the consideration of this outrageous possibility—is more important than a particular answer.

abraham's choice

I read Genesis 22. God commands Abraham: "Take your son, Isaac, your only one, whom you love, and go to the land of Moriah. There you shall offer him up as a holocaust."[56] Abraham follows these commands and prepares Isaac for sacrifice, taking "the knife to slaughter his son." Only at the last moment, God's messenger stops the sacrifice, explaining that the whole incident was designed as a test of Abraham's faith.[57]

---

56 In chapter 5, I will explain how this biblical word *holocaust* came to signify (perhaps inappropriately) the Nazi genocide of the Jews.

57. For a fascinating (and critical) account of Abraham's travail, see Soren Kierkegaard, *Fear and Trembling* (Princeton: Princeton University Press, 1983). For a less respectful account of this same story, see Woody Allen's "The Scrolls": As Abraham is ready to sacrifice Isaac, the Lord said: "'Does thou listen to every crazy idea that comes thy way?' And Abraham fell to his knees, 'See, I never know when you're kidding.' And the Lord thundered: 'No sense of humor. I can't believe it'....And the Lord said: 'It proves that men will follow any order as long as it comes from a resonant, well-modulated voice.'"(*Without Feathers*, [New York: Random House, 1972], p. 24).

I am troubled by this fable. Perhaps God's words should not be interpreted as an order. Listen to the following dialogue, from a novel set in Berlin, 1947. The protagonist is a German police officer. An American army officer asks for his help:

> "Who knows—if enough Germans do the same then maybe the account can be settled," the American says.
> "What are you talking about? . . . What account?"
> "God's account," he said.
> I laughed and shook my head in disbelief.
> "What's the matter? Don't you believe in God?"
> "I don't believe in trying to make deals with him. You speak about God as if he sells secondhand cars. I've misjudged you. You're much more of an American than I thought you were."
> "Now that's where you're wrong. God likes making deals. Look at the covenant he made with Abraham, and with Noah. God's a huckster. Only a German could mistake a deal for a direct order."[58]

In the gray zone of our lives, perhaps much of what we interpret as direct orders are really deals.

Here is another version of Isaac's story, but one with feminist variation. Here Sarah, not Abraham, is the recipient of God's command. "No," said Sarah to the Voice. "I will not be chosen, nor shall my son." For Sarah, the moral issue is clear though terrible: "Either this sacrifice is a sham or it is a sin," she says. To the omniscient God, she remonstrates: "You must have known I would choose Isaac." A mother would never sacrifice a child for some abstract principle, even one with the weight of history behind it. "What use," Sarah concludes, "have I for History—an arrow already bent when it is fired from the bow?"[59]

Sarah's behavior is exemplary. For nowhere in our Judeo-Christian tradition are we commanded to disobey a wrongful order. We celebrate Abraham for preparing to follow an order to kill his son. The Third Commandment of Moses would seem to be a decoration, rather than a foundation, of our civilized home. I wish

---

58. Philip Kerr, *Berlin Noir* (London: Penguin Books, 1993), p. 728.
59. Eleanor Wilner, *Sarah's Choice* (Chicago: University of Chicago Press, 1989), pp. 21–22.

the story had a different ending. Abraham should have cried No! No command, he should have shouted, could make me kill my beloved son. Anyone who so orders, he should have concluded, is not worthy of my faith. Imagine the lessons of such a story for Western civilization.

But let us put the Abraham allegory aside. In the all-too-real world of the Holocaust, not every German followed orders; not every German obeyed. At Józefów several Order Police took advantage of an opportunity not to slaughter Jews. And more: There were people, ordinary people, who risked their own lives—and the lives of their kin—to save Jews.[60] Their motives, by their own tellings, were various; but most were unable to articulate any general notion of why they had saved Jews. Some, most interestingly, were anti-Semitic. I am impressed and deeply moved by their stories of bravery.[61]

Milgram also played with the calculus of obedience and disobedience. In Experiment 7 the teacher is called away from the laboratory and gives his orders by telephone; "only" (if I dare use that adverb) one-fifth of the subjects shocked all the way. In Experiment 15, two authorities give contradictory orders after 135 volts. One subject had previously stopped, eighteen stopped at the point of this disagreement, while one subject gave one more shock and then stopped: "in no instance did individual aggressive motives latch on to the authoritative sanction provided by the malevolent authority."[62] Finally, in Experiment 17 there is a second teacher, a confederate, who rebels after 210 volts. Under these conditions twelve subjects stopped immediately and only

---

60. Perhaps the best historical example of altruism en masse happened in the small French village of Le Chambon where thousands of Jews were saved, primarily through the moral leadership and organizational efforts of a clergyman. Philip Hallie, *Lest Innocent Blood Be Shed* (New York: Harper & Row, 1979).

61. See Samuel Oliner and Pearl Oliner, *The Altruistic Personality: Rescuers of Jews in Nazi Germany* (New York: Free Press, 1968), and Nechama Tec, *When Light Pierced the Darkness* (New York: Oxford University Press, 1986). These scholars have attempted to isolate personality factors that might differentiate "altruists" from ordinary people, and they have attempted to develop theoretical and empirical models, which might identify such individuals. I find the stories uncovered by these scholars incredible. I am less convinced by their social psychological models, which fail, I think, to capture the richness and essence of these remarkable deeds.

62. Milgram, *Obedience to Authority*, p. 107.

four shocked all the way. In other words, the provision of peer support undercut the experimenter's authority.

We ask: Who obeys and who does not? "The story of ordinary men," Christopher Browning concludes, is not the choice of all men. "Some refused to kill and others stopped killing. Human responsibility is ultimately an individual matter."[63] Browning's psychological analysis is appealing; it strokes our senses of autonomy, freedom, and self. Yet while I do not disagree with his answer, I think his question, "Who obeys?" is unhelpful. It is a mistake, I believe, to focus too much attention on the personality of the obedient versus the disobedient person. "Why do you have to ask why the concentration camp commandants did what they did or how they could have done it?" asked Hannah Arendt. "They simply did it and that is all there is to it."[64] Arendt's reply, it seems to me, shows her usual wisdom.

For sociologist Barrington Moore, obedience exists not only as individual choice, but as an expression of culture. His historical study of injustice and obedience attempts (as it were) to turn Milgram on his head: "The more one thinks about [Milgram] . . . the more surprising it becomes that disobedience did occur at all, and even more that it occurred on such a large scale. Evidently empathy under the right conditions can break through some very powerful obstacles."[65]

The impediments to a more just society come not from the perversion of personality, but rather from an inequitable society. Moore concludes: "The obstacles to moral autonomy come rather from the fact the opportunities to control this atmosphere are

---

63. Browning, p. 188.

64. Tom Segev, *Soldiers of Evil: The Commandants of the Nazi Concentration Camps* (New York: McGraw Hill, 1987), p. 214. Curiously, Segev characterizes Arendt's thesis as a "faith, a philosophy, maybe only a mood, but not historical research."

65. Barrington Moore, *Injustice: The Social Basis of Obedience and Revolt* (White Plains, NY: M. E. Sharpe, 1978), p. 98. Disobedience can also be created artificially. See William Gamson, B. Fireman and S. Rytina, *Encounters With Unjust Authority* (Homewood, Ill.: Dorsey, 1982). In a rather complex experiment, these sociologists showed that experimental conditions may encourage small groups to disobey what is perceived to be an unjust authority.

unequally distributed in hierarchically organized societies."[66] I think this is a wise conclusion.

Ordinary people do obey apparently malevolent authority, as Milgram showed. And ordinary people surrounded by Nazi culture did indeed commit the most heinous crimes. Milgram's evaluation of Arendt's thesis is pertinent: "I must conclude that Arendt's conception of the 'banality of evil' comes closer to the truth than one might dare imagine."[67] For me, it is useful (though not necessarily true) to think of Nazi evil—perhaps all evil—as banal. I think that this banality has deep historical and cultural roots.

So we see, finally, that human beings are ultimately social. Individual freedom and autonomy, to the extent that they exist, or to the extent that they are suppressed, are inherently properties of the group, the collectivity, the culture. It is to these groupings, these hierarchies, that we now turn in our effort to understand how the Holocaust happened.

66. Moore, p. 100.
67. Milgram, *Obedience to Authority*, p. 6.

3 bureaucracy

Most of you know what it means when 100 corpses lie there, or 500 lie there, or 1000 lie there. To have gone through this and—apart from the exceptions caused by human weakness—to have remained decent, that has hardened us.
—Heinrich Himmler in a speech to SS commanders, 1943

Most bureaucrats composed memoranda, drew up blueprints, talked on the telephone, and participated in conferences. They could destroy a whole people by sitting at their desks.
—Raul Hilberg

There is an absolutely unforgettable scene (one of many) in Claude Lanzmann's film, *Shoah*. We are on a train, heading down the tracks. Through the camera's eye, we see the tracks in front, receding rapidly, the train's engineer in the foreground. For several moments, nothing happens as the tracks disappear before the speeding train. There is much repetition, much silence, in this film. Then the train stops and we see a sign: Treblinka. The conductor draws his hand ominously across his throat.

The train is one of the most powerful images of the entire Holocaust. For it was on trains, most typically, that victims were transported to their deaths; that most ghastly trip: no sunlight, food, or water, no sanitation, so little air to breathe amidst the press of bodies. Countless thousands died on the train; for millions, the train trip was the journey to death.

The Reichsbahn, the German rail system, was one of the largest organizations in the Third Reich. In 1942 it employed approximately 1.4 million Germans: 900,000 employees and 500,000 civil servants; an additional 400,000 worked for the system in occupied Poland and Russia.

Writing from the University of Vermont, Raul Hilberg (whose work I will discuss shortly) had a crucial insight: one cannot understand the Holocaust without understanding the role of the Reichsbahn. The railroads, he wrote, were not on the fringe of the Holocaust, but were "indispensable at its core." "Year after year, they transported millions of Jews to the mysterious 'east' where they could be annihilated quietly, out of the range of peering bystanders, and prying cameras."[1] This task Reichsbahn bureaucrats carried out—with perseverance and creativity—under increasingly difficult conditions of war.

The Reichsbahn operated as a business. It charged the SS set rates, for one-way trips, for each Jew transported: for adults, 4 Pfenning per track kilometer, half of that for children under age ten; those under age four traveled free. The SS negotiated group rates: for over four hundred per transport, all charges would be halved.[2] In the event of "exceptional filth" or damage to the cars, there was a surcharge.

The SS would often pack up to four thousand Jews into a train. Some trains in Poland contained five thousand Jews, which figures to less than two square feet per person. The very weight of these trains slowed them. There was no rush: Military trains had priority, and whether Jews died in transit or in gas chambers was of little concern to the Nazis.

To finance the deportations, the SS had to be creative. Unlike most SS programs, the finance ministry had provided no line item in their budget for the Jewish problem. Their solution? The SS seized Jewish capital so that Jews, in effect, financed their own deportations. The SS had to launder its money carefully because finance ministry officials opposed this policy. More complications arose because of multiple currencies as trains crossed national borders. The Reichsbahn calculated total trip costs in partial payments in each local currency. These monies had to be changed to German Marks at favorable rates, a complex administrative task.

---

1. Raul Hilberg, "German Railroads, Jewish Souls," *Society* (April 1986): 60–61.

2. For trips with fewer than four hundred passengers, the SS would still pay for that number, in order to maintain the discount.

Reichsbahn bureaucrats were experts not in policy, but in timetables; not in labeling people, but in moving them from place to place. It mattered not who they were: military, or passengers, or Jews. They allocated equipment; they planned the efficient schedules. For Reichsbahn officials, transporting Jews was a job like any other. In the years that the Reichsbahn transported 2.5 million and countless others to their deaths, "no one resigned, no one protested and hardly anyone asked for a transfer."[3]

Five decades later I ride these trains. Today they are called the DB, the Deutsche Bundesbahn in the West; the former East, still public-relations deficient, has kept the old Reichsbahn name.

I like the German trains. I can set my watch by their arrival and departure. Despite my skepticism based on limited experience with Amtrak, I routinely make three-minute connections. And more, I find this mode of travel quite civilized: no compressed time here, with suns rising and setting at odd times; I have the pleasure of watching the countryside go by at a speed that I can understand.

I am reminded of Paul Theroux' charming book, *The Great Railway Bazaar*, in which the point of the trip is the train, not the destination. The whistle of the train, he writes, "sings bewitchment." And more: "The train can reassure you in awful places." I particularly enjoy the dining car. To have a fine meal with good wine while I gaze at a picturesque village, a mountain vista, or at nothing in particular, seems to me the quintessence of civilization.

Yet other images of trains, far darker, discombobulate me, roiling the sediments of my mind. Writer Norma Rosen reports similar disquiet. As her train arrives at the suburban station in a burst of power and noise, "there is a moment of hideous hallucination, and then one steps into the train and opens the newspaper."

For survivors of the Holocaust, there are no mixed images. The memory is horrific, the train a transit to nightmare. Listen to Primo Levi: "Almost always, at the beginning of the memory

---

3. Hilberg, "German Railroads, Jewish Souls," p. 70.

sequence, stands the train, which marked the departure toward the unknown, not only for chronological reasons, but also for the gratuitous cruelty." In his memoir, *Night*, Elie Wiesel wrote: "A prolonged whistle split the air. . . . The doors were closed. We were caught in a trap, right up to our necks. The doors were nailed up; the way back was finally cut off. The world was a cattle wagon hermetically sealed.

I look at the drawings of György Kádár, survivor and artist. Shortly after liberation, he drew a crayon picture of his train trip to Auschwitz. Harsh and darkly expressionist, in a style that reminds me of Käthe Kollwitz, the picture shows half-dead, dispirited people huddled in a boxcar. Above the suffering is a window, but few look toward the barbed-wire scene which awaits them. I read Kádár's straight-forward explanation: "Many people died on the trains to the camp. There was no food or water; no sanitation or privacy. They treated us like livestock. The dead remained among the living until the train arrived as Auschwitz."

Remember the epigraph to this book from Primo Levi's great work, *The Drowned and the Saved*. We are dazzled by power; we are fragile; our world is a ghetto; outside is death. And finally, Levi concludes with an image so frequently used by survivors: "close by the train is waiting." Ask not for whom the train waits, laments my colleague Mary Lagerwey, it waits for thee.

I, too, know that there is another side to these DB trains, a side filled with death. But this I make an effort to forget, lest the sweet ease of a civilized trip be violated.

routine slaughter

Here are two images of the Holocaust: In the first, psychopathic killers murder one Jew after another; in the second, Reichsbahn bureaucrats design and maintain a system of transportation that was used (I use the passive purposely, for those bureaucrats never actually committed murder) to slaughter millions. The numbers are all wrong for the first (more popular of the two) image. The German state annihilated between five and six million Jews. As with so many huge numbers, this one is difficult to comprehend in everyday terms. But a bit of arithmetic shows that our conceptualization of the Holocaust needs a qualitative, as well as a quantitative, reconsideration.

John Sabini and Maury Silver have done the calculation and the thinking. At the rate of one-hundred murders per day, a day's work for a mob, the Holocaust would have required nearly two-hundred years. Mob violence rests on violent emotion, an impossible psychological basis for the Holocaust. "People can be manipulated into fury, but fury cannot be maintained for 200 years." A lynch mob is brutal but unreliable and unpredictable. The mob might kill, but it might also on any given day spare the child. "To eradicate a race it is essential to kill children."[4]

The Holocaust was murder, to be sure. But it was thorough, comprehensive, and exhaustive murder. To commit a Holocaust, bureaucracy must replace the mob; routinized behavior must supplant rage; emotional anti-Semitism must be transmogrified into rational anti-Semitism. All distinctions among Jews are irrelevant: children as well as adults, scholars as well as thieves, rich as well as poor—all are murdered with an equivalent proficiency.

Let us leave the Holocaust for a moment and open our daily newspaper. We find on page one reports of brutal murder, and perhaps of a heroic act, the rescue of a small child from danger. This is not history in the making, but rather the random events of a day's life. It is not individuals acting alone who shape history or even shape the day. Each act is isolated; the murderer's deed, no matter how terrible, seldom affects many of us. Heroic acts, no matter how brave or fearless, rarely escape their immediate context. History-making behavior, for better or worse, most often occurs—and is most significant—as a part of bureaucratic behavior. Seldom do such actions make headlines.

Mass murder, genocide—these, so sad to say, have always been part of our world. In this chapter I consider what is unique

---

4. John Sabini and Maury Silver, "Destroying the Innocent with a Clear Conscience: A Sociopsychology of the Holocaust." In Joel Dimsdale (ed.), *Survivors, Victims and Perpetrators: Essays in the Nazi Holocaust* (Washington, D.C.: Hemisphere Publishing, 1980), pp. 329–30.

about the Nazi genocide. First: its careful planning, its organization, its due process. The writings of three diverse intellectuals—Max Weber, Franz Kafka, and Raul Hilberg—help us understand how the Holocaust happened. Second, and opposite to bureaucracy: anarchy and chaos prevail. Only through these two opposites might we gain perspective to understand the Holocaust.

To set the stage for this argument, however, I first return to Milgram's experiments. For in his work, there is still more to be learned. To understand Milgram, Sabini and Silver assert, one must see Milgram's experiments not as a totality, but rather as a process, a sequence of events. It is not a question of *whether* to obey or disobey, but a question of *when* to become disobedient. The first part of the experiment is easy: show up, take money, walk into a room, sit down—each a trivial act. The first shock is 15 volts: almost imperceptible, harmless. It could be said: There is no moral issue here. But the subject begins to slide, as it were, into moral quicksand. As one struggles, one sinks deeper: "The quality of the subject's action changes from something entirely blameless to something unconscionable, but by degrees. Where exactly should the subject stop? How is the subject to know? It is easy to see that there must be a line, it is not so easy to see where that line ought to be."[5]

Here is an important insight: If you wish to promote obedience, then you break the task into discreet steps, and you arrange those so that one follows closely upon the other. This leads, to use the clever phrase of Zygmunt Bauman, to the paradox of sequential action.[6] Back to Milgram's experiments, we note the subject's problem: "To deny the propriety of the step he is about to take is to undercut the propriety of the step he just took, and this undercuts the subject's own moral position. The subject is trapped by his own moral commitment to the experiment."[7]

If sequencing (the functional division of labor, in sociological jargon) is one key to obedience, then hierarchy is surely another. Obedience to authority rests on the simple fact that people occupy roles of varying power or status, Barrington Moore

---

5. Sabini and Silver, p. 342.
6. Bauman, p. 158. My reading of Milgram has been informed by chapter 6, "The Ethics of Obedience."
7. Sabini and Silver, p. 342.

stressed, and that there are rules and expectations that define appropriate behaviors at different positions in the hierarchy.

Two social psychologists, Kilham and Mann, attempted to study obedience by creating a microcosm of bureaucracy. They created two separate but interdependent roles for their experiment: The first, a "transmitter," performs most of the duties of Milgram's teacher, with one crucial exception—the transmitter does not shock the victim; the second person, called the "executant," presses the switches at the command of the transmitter. Their findings? Forty percent of male executants, but 68 percent of male transmitters, were fully obedient. "The individual in the transmitter role, because he is one step removed from the act, is more obedient to destructive commands than the subject in the executant role." In "real organizations," note Kilham and Mann, "the transmitter role is often regarded as a minor one that entails little or no responsibility." The transmitter becomes a cog in the larger bureaucratic machine. But with the passage of time, such individuals "often begin to respond as machines, dehumanizing themselves and others."[8]

"Would workers in the chemical plants that produce Napalm accept responsibility for burned babies?" ask historian George Kren and psychologist Leon Rappoport. "Would such workers even be aware that others might reasonably think they were responsible?"[9] By itself, each piece of divided labor is without meaning: everything one does is in principle "multifinal." It will be "the others," who are anonymous and beyond our control, Zygmunt Bauman concludes, "who will sometime, somewhere, decide that meaning."[10]

In modern society there is a great distance between a decision and its accomplishment. This social space is filled with

---

8. W. Kilham and L. Mann, "Level of Destructive Obedience as a Function of Transmitter and Executant Roles in the Milgram Obedience Paradigm," *Journal of Personality and Social Psychology* 29 (1974): 697, 701. Female transmitters and executants paired together were less obedient: 40 percent of the former, and 16 percent of the latter, shocked all the way.

9. George Kren and Leon Rappoport, *The Holocaust and the Crisis in Human Behavior* (New York: Holmes & Meier, 1980), p. 141. This book was one of my first and most rewarding forays into the scholarly literature on the Holocaust. Kren and Rappoport raised many of the issues which I pursue in this book.

10. Bauman, p. 100.

inconsequential actors and trivial acts. The increase of physical or psychic distance between the act and its consequences suspends moral judgment. Even more, it destroys, or at least muddies, the moral significance of the act: "It is difficult to accept that often there is no person and no group that planned or caused [cruelty]. It is even more difficult to see how our own actions, through their remote effects, contributed to causing misery."[11]

And so we see that individual actions are sensible only within a context of organizational behavior. Even the most heinous acts are possible once the linear hierarchy of command is supplemented by functional division and separation of tasks. In Zygmunt Bauman's sharp phrase: "Morality boils down to the commandment to be a good, efficient and diligent expert and worker."[12]

two visions

Would that these ideas were new, that they had been developed to explain the horrors of the Holocaust. Yet this line of thinking existed many decades before the Holocaust. For example: "the more bureaucracy is 'dehumanized,' the more completely it succeeds in eliminating from official business love, hatred and all purely personal irrational and emotional elements which escape calculation. This is its 'special virtue.' "[13] And: "The fully developed bureaucratic mechanism compares with other organizations exactly as does the machine with the non-mechanical modes of organization." And: "Precision, speed, unambiguity, knowledge of files . . . strict subordination . . . these are raised to the optimum point in the strictly bureaucratic organization."

---

11. John Lachs, *Responsibility of the Individual in Modern Society* (Brighton: Harvester, 1981), p. 58.

12. Bauman, p. 102.

13. This and the next two quotes are from Max Weber, in *From Max Weber: Essays in Sociology*, trans. and ed. by Hans H. Gerth and C. Wright Mills (New York: Oxford University Press, 1946), pp. 215–16, 214. Richard Rubenstein's *The Cunning of History* helped me appreciate Weber's work in this context.

In the context of this book, these quotations seem to characterize in a rather dry and abstract way the Nazi killing machine. Yet they were not written about the Holocaust, nor were they even written after World War II. The year was 1916, the writer, Max Weber.[14]

Weber was particularly interested in how modern societies develop from traditional ones. For him, the problem of rationalization was the key to understanding: the way in which older, spontaneous methods of social organization are replaced by abstract, explicit, carefully calculated rules and procedures. The world, Weber felt, was becoming dull, drab, and "disenchanted." Humans, he feared, would soon live in an "iron cage" of rationality. The mechanism of this rationalism was the bureaucracy, in which human beings were subordinated to the interests of impersonal, technical goals.[15]

According to Weber, a bureaucracy establishes a set of relations between authorities and their subordinates. These relations are characterized by a division of labor in which each worker has a specialized job and concentrates on a specific task; a hierarchy of authority in which each takes orders from those directly above, and in turn gives orders to those directly below; an elaborate system of regulations that governs day-to-day behavior; and impersonality, in which personal feelings are excluded from the decision-making process.[16]

How do these ideas help us understand the Holocaust? In traditional societies, power was based originally on land, and

---

14. Weber was born in 1864, grew up in Germany during the Bismarckian era, and died in 1920. He played a role in writing the constitution for the Weimar Republic after World War I. His writings, ranging from works on Chinese religion to methods of scientific analysis, have profoundly shaped contemporary sociology.

15. For contemporary implications of Weber's iron cage, see George Ritzer, *The McDonaldization of Society* (Newbury Park, CA: Pine Forge Press, 1993).

16. For a discussion of Weber on bureaucracy, see Reinhard Bendix, *Max Weber: An Intellectual Portrait* (Garden City, NY: Doubleday, 1960), p. 423ff. Weber wrote of three other characteristics of bureaucracies relevant to this discussion: careful record-keeping, in which information is kept in standardized formats; an administrative staff whose work is not substantive, but rather organizational; and a career structure that allows—and rewards—employees with incremental advance.

later on capital. In modern societies, domination would come with the control of the bureaucratic apparatus.[17] Bureaucracy becomes not only a mode of organization, but more importantly, an exercise of power. "The honor of the civil servant is vested in his ability to execute conscientiously the order of superior authorities, exactly as if the order agreed with his own conviction," Weber wrote. This holds, he continued, "even if the order seems wrong to him and if, despite the civil servant's remonstrances, the authority insists on the order." For a civil servant, this is "moral discipline and self-denial in the highest sense."[18]

Here is an important point: moral responsibility, once thought to be primary, now takes a back seat. Through bureaucratic obligation—honor, in Weber's terms—discipline is substituted for moral responsibility. As Bauman summarizes: Rules internal to the bureaucracy transcend and "delegitimize" the rules of the outer world. The authority of the private conscience is diminished; concomitantly, organizational rules become the basis for the highest moral virtue, the source and guarantee of propriety.

A nightmarish twist on Weber's insights came from the pen of his contemporary, Franz Kafka.[19] Kafka was "condemned" to forsee our "post-Auschwitz world," in the words of his biographer Ernst Pawel, "with such blinding clarity that he found it unbearable."[20] Much of Kafka's work depicts individuals lost

---

17. This does not mean, of course, that bureaucracies will not be controlled by the traditional class advantages which are based on land and capital. Rather it leaves the possibility—born out in the twentieth century by the Nazis and the Soviets—that these traditional sources of power can be bypassed to a degree.

18. Quoted in Gerth and Mills, p. 95. Weber's term *civil servant* is probably a bit archaic. Today we refer to such people as "experts." Bureaucratic experts most typically have administrative skills (financial, personnel, etc.) without which the organization could not function.

19. Kafka, a German Jew, was born in Prague in 1883 and lived there his whole life. Trained in law, he worked his entire adult life as a technical expert for the Workers' Accident Insurance Institute for the Kingdom of Bohemia. He died in 1924, survived by three sisters, two of whom died in the Lodz ghetto; the third perished at Auschwitz.

20. Ernst Pawel, *The Nightmare of Reason: A Life of Franz Kafka* (New York: Farrar, Straus & Giroux, 1984), p. 328. Of all the biographies on Kafka, this is the best I have read.

within bureaucratic mazes. *The Trial*, for example, begins with Joseph K's arrest: "Someone must have denounced Joseph K, for without his having done anything wrong, he was arrested one fine morning." K never discovers (nor does the reader) the charges against him; the only certainty of the book is the orderly process by which K's fate—an anticlimactic death on the final page of the book—is adjudicated.

Most prescient for this meditation is Kafka's *The Penal Colony*,[21] a truly modern story of torture. On a remote island, a military officer punishes a soldier. The punishment? An elaborate machine inscribes a message, the prisoner's penalty, which slowly ruptures the skin on his chest; prior to death, the prisoner (who does not know that he was found guilty or even sentenced) realizes his fate and understands (for the first time, as an epiphany, just before death) the machine's logic. As the prisoner dies, the officer explains the entire process—from the complex workings of the machine to the victim's contortions—in precise and technical language, to a third character, an explorer: "As soon as the man is strapped down, the Bed is set in motion. It quivers in minute, very rapid vibrations, both from side to side and up and down. You will have seen similar apparatus in hospitals."[22] The explorer watches and listens without passion. He claims to disapprove, but does nothing to intervene.

In a review of the story, written in 1920, Kurt Tucholsky[23] characterized the officer as neither "crude nor cruel," but something much worse: he is amoral. "The officer is no torturer, let alone a sadist. His delight in the manifestations of the victim's . . . agony merely demonstrates his boundless, slavish worship of the machine, which he calls justice and which in fact is power."[24]

---

21. Written in 1901 and published in 1919.

22. Franz Kafka, *The Penal Colony* (New York: Schocken Books, 1961), p. 197.

23. Tucholsky was a brilliant satirist. Like so many Weimar intellectuals, he committed suicide—in 1935 in Sweden. Shortly before his death, at age forty-five, he wrote: "If I had to die now, I would say: 'Was that all?' And: 'I don't quite understand it properly.' And: 'It was rather loud' " (quoted in Grunfeld, p. 219).

24. Quoted in Pawel, p. 328.

The officer might represent any technical expert. But according to Pawel, the officer is "a prescient portrait of Adolf Eichmann." I think not. Eichmann planned and administered, but never supervised, the murders. The officer is excited, his life turned alive by the process; he is above all passionate. Eichmann signed papers; he is dull. I wonder about the explorer, who watched with intelligence and curiosity. He disapproved but did nothing. Perhaps he is the model for the social scientist.

Let me return to Tucholsky's review, which showed amazing insight. *The Penal Colony* showed, he asserted, the "exercise of power without constraints," the "dream" of being able "to impose one's will without limits."[25] "Don't ask what it means," Tucholsky concluded of *The Penal Colony* (but we might also say: of the Holocaust). "It means nothing."[26]

blood and honor

In chapter 1, I searched for a key that might open the door to our understanding of the Holocaust. What was the one best explanation? I asked, but did not answer. Raul Hilberg, perhaps the best known of all scholars of the Holocaust, has taken a very different approach. "In all my work," he has written, "I have never begun by asking the big questions, because I was always afraid that I would come up with small answers."[27]

With this pithy remark, Hilberg suggests a different approach to Holocaust scholarship. Rather than thinking deductively, as though the Holocaust were the result of some grand scheme of history, Hilberg built his understanding inductively, from the details of what happened. Rather than asking why, Hilberg asked how. "From the start," Hilberg wrote in his three-volume *Destruction of the European Jews*, "I wanted to know how

---

25. I return to this point, developed by Hannah Arendt, in chapter 4.
26. Quoted in Pawel, p. 329.
27. Quoted in Claude Lanzmann, *Shoah: An Oral History of the Holocaust. The Complete Text of the Film* (New York: Pantheon, 1985), p. 70. I should add that in my opinion, this film—which lasts eight hours—is a masterpiece, a great work of pain and art.

the Jews of Europe were destroyed. I wanted to explore the sheer mechanism of destruction."[28] "I sought," he said, the "minutiae or details" to construct "a picture which, if not an explanation, is at least a description, a more full description of what transpired."[29]

Let me attempt to summarize Hilberg's vision and its implications for my thinking. First, he conceptualizes the Holocaust as a machine; the parts all work together and smoothly, to be sure, but it is the whole machine—indivisible—that is responsible for the Holocaust.[30] His leitmotif is its gigantic scale. In three volumes of documentation, he describes the intricate workings of this fearful machine all across Europe. Ultimately, it is the machinery itself—not individuals, not some master plan—that is the driving force. In the final analysis, Hilberg wrote, the Holocaust was "not so much a product of laws and commands as it was a matter of spirit, of shared comprehension, of consonance and synchronization; each step is important in and of itself, but cannot be understood without the prior and next step."[31]

Second, though he never mentions the work of Max Weber, Hilberg saw the Nazi machine as fundamentally bureaucratic: "Jews were destroyed as a consequence of a multitude of acts performed by a phalanx of functionaries in public offices and private enterprises." Taken one by one, he continues, these measures "turn out to be bureaucratic, embedded in habit, routine and tradition."[32]

"Habit, routine and tradition?" This is really a different way—an especially frightening way, I might add—of thinking about mass murder, very different from our common notion of

---

28. Raul Hilberg, *The Destruction of the European Jews*, p. ix.

29. Quoted in Lanzmann, p. 71.

30. For an interesting discussion of this point, see Michael Marrus, "The History of the Holocaust: A Survey of Recent Literature," *Journal of Modern History* 59 (1987): 114–60.

31. Hilberg, *The Destruction of the European Jews*, p. 55. At other times Hilberg seems to emphasize the Holocaust as process. The destruction of the Jews appeared "indivisible, monolithic, and impenetrable"; but it was not: it had a "logic of development" (p. 53).

32. Hilberg, "The Bureaucracy of Annihilation," in Furet, p. 119.

the Holocaust as a runaway serial murder. Never before, Hilberg concluded, "had the total experience of a modern bureaucracy been applied to such an undertaking. Never before had it produced such results."[33]

Hilberg's understanding of the Holocaust rests upon two seemingly contradictory premises. First, it was unique: "There is no precedent for the almost endless march of millions of men, women and children into the gas chamber," he writes. "The systemization of the destruction process sets it apart from all else that has ever happened." Second, it was—and here Hilberg sounds like Arendt—ordinary. If we examine the Holocaust in step-by-step detail, we see much in the destruction that is "familiar and even commonplace in the context of contemporary institutions and practices."[34] Amazingly little was newly invented by Nazi bureaucrats. The millions were killed not with some high-technology weapon, but by the most dangerous of all modern inventions: a bureaucracy of destruction that operated with its own dynamics—speed and efficiency.

I now illustrate Hilberg's thesis—and then show its limitations—by describing in detail one of his examples: the Nazi's law of blood and honor.[35]

After the Nazi takeover in 1933, there were myriad discriminations against the Jews: they were dismissed without exception from certain positions; various bureaucracies, schools for instance, were Aryanized; huge taxes, property taxes for example, were levied selectively on Jews; Jewish bank assets were blocked; and in selected jobs, Jewish wages were reduced.

Germany was a modern industrial country that prided itself on its institutions of government and, in particular, on its due process of law. Therefore, the Nazi bureaucracy had to tackle a difficult conceptual problem: Who is a Jew? This seemingly simple question is really quite complicated. In a Polish village, one might define by sight: Jews dressed differently, acted differ-

---

33. Hilberg, "The Bureaucracy of Annihilation," p. 119.
34. Hilberg, "The Bureaucracy of Annihilation," p. 119.
35. In this section I draw heavily from Hilberg, *The Destruction of the European Jews*, vol. 1, p. 71ff., 160ff.

ently, and even spoke a different language. In modern Germany, none of these criteria worked. Even more, there was substantial intermarriage in modern Germany: How were the progeny of these unions to be defined?

At the simplest level, one might think of Jews as people who practiced some variant of the ancient Hebraic religion. But if this were the definition of a Jew—that is, the practice of a belief—then the Nazi genocide could not have been perpetrated. In the religious violence between European Catholics and Protestants, one could (at least sometimes) escape death by the renunciation of belief: swear allegiance to, or disclaim, the Pope.[36] Not so with the Nazis. They gave the Jew no choice.

The Germans understood the vagaries of belief. They chose genetics, for reasons that will become obvious in the next chapter, as the defining criterion of Judaism. On 7 April 1933 (shortly after they took power)[37] Nazis defined the terms *Aryan* and *non-Aryan*. Aryans were people of "pure German blood"; non-Aryans (Jewish or Christian) were those who had at least one Jewish parent or grandparent. This definition is not really a definition at all, for it defines its two key concepts—Aryan and Jew—tautologically, and moreover does not distinguish between Jew and non-Aryan.

The new set of definitions, promulgated by the interior ministry, immediately caused problems for officials in the foreign ministry: its geopolitical implications (e.g., that all non-Germans were inferior—including Japanese allies) were embarrassing. Moreover, the term "non-Aryan" included many thousands of German citizens who, presumably, had little or no idea of their "Jewishness."

---

36. I do not mean to trivialize belief. That many thousands did not renounce their beliefs and consequently sacrificed their lives attests to the strength of religiosity. During the Spanish Inquisition, Jews were often given a similar choice, and many saved themselves through conversion.

37. A month later, on 10 May, the Nazis organized book burnings at all major universities. A century earlier, Heinrich Heine, a German Jewish poet, wrote: "Whenever books will be burned, men also, in the end, are burned." How terribly correct this dictum was to be.

Another two years were to pass before the Germans did better. On 15 September 1935, the Nuremberg laws, particularly the Law for the Protection of Blood and Honor, were designed to overcome previous difficulties. They were drafted by Bernhard Lösener, who had recently transferred from the customs administration. He was later to draft twenty-seven different decrees about definitions of Jewishness.

Here is Lösener's definition of a Jew: (1) someone who is descended from three Jewish grandparents (meaning the grandparents were full Jews or at least three-quarter Jews; or (2) descended from two Jewish grandparents (half-Jewish), and (a) belonged to the Jewish religious community on 15 September 1935, or (b) was married to a Jewish person before that date, or (c) was the offspring of a marriage contracted with a three-quarter or full Jew, born after that date, or (d) was the offspring of an extramarital relationship with a three-quarter or full Jew and was born out of wedlock after 31 July 1936—some ten and one-half months after the promulgation of the law!

At this point, most of us think: This is absurd! This is not rule of law, but chaos! But in understanding the logic (and I use that word on purpose, for the Nuremberg laws had their own internal logic) that follows, I hope to gain some insight into the bureaucratic processes that drove—let us use Hilberg's imagery—the killing machine. For the bureaucratic distinctions, upon which depended life and death, had just begun!

The most serious issue Lösener faced was the problem of the progeny of mixed marriages. In other words, what was to be done with half Jews? Previously, half and full Jews had been treated equivalently. But this was seen as problematic. "In principle half-Jews should be regarded as a more serious enemy than a full Jew," Lösener wrote. German "goodness" and Jewish "badness"—if you will—were a dangerous combination: "in addition to Jewish characteristics, [the mixed Jew] possesses so many Germanic ones which the full Jew lacks."[38]

Should the half Jew be subject to the full set of discriminations of the Third Reich? The issue was vexing various due pro-

---

38. Hilberg, *The Destruction of the European Jews*, vol. 1, p. 71.

cesses: Could they emigrate? Could they be employed? Could they serve in the armed forces? At stake in this last issue were some forty-five-thousand men. What about the economic boycott? It would be financially disastrous to blacklist all half-Jewish businesses. And finally, and most importantly: What was to be the legal status of marriages of various combinations of mixed partners?

The core of Lösener's solution was to divide the category of half Jew into a hierarchy of different groups. The Reich Citizenship Law separated non-Aryans into two categories: Jews and *Mischlinge*, persons of mixed Jewish blood.

A Mischlinge was defined as (1) a person who descended from two Jewish grandparents, but who (a) did not adhere to the Jewish religion on 15 September 1935, *and* (b) was not married—or no longer married—to a Jewish person on that date. Such a person was termed a "Mischlinge of the first degree." A "Mischlinge of the second degree" had a simple definition: any person descended from one Jewish grandparent.[39]

To distinguish between first- and second-degree Mischlinge, and indeed to establish Aryan status, it was thus necessary to prove descent. Such proof required various documents, including birth or baptismal certificates of person, parents, and grandparents. Prior to 1875 births were registered only in churches. Thus crucial, lifesaving or life-threatening, data were held by religious institutions. Most Germans were Lutheran; a minority (particularly in Bavaria) were Roman Catholic. Sadly, these institutions cooperated with the Nazis in implementing and administering racial policy.

Once begun, the bureaucratic process spins its own logic and (as it were) its own enforcement stepchildren. To use the above scheme, it is necessary to know one's family history. But, of course, there is a major problem yet unaddressed: What is to be done when the father is unknown? The family research office, founded to implement the Nuremberg laws, offered a solution. For a Jewish woman, a child born before 1918 was presumed to

---

39. This distinction, between first and second degree, was not contained in the original Nuremberg law, but was added in a later decree by the ministry of the interior.

have a Jewish father; after 1918, the baby was presumed to have a Christian father!

The reason for this seemingly bizarre ruling was based on a Nazi idea called Emancipation Theory. Before the founding of the Weimar Republic in 1918, Jews had little opportunity—according to Nazi doctrine—for sexual intercourse with Germans; after 1918, the theory purported, Jews pursued the systematic "disintegration" of the German people through elicit sex. Here is the reasoning: Jewish men would surely attempt to defile German women; though the Jewess would obviously choose a German over a Jew, it could hardly be assumed that she would become pregnant to harm a German man.

These designations—not only Aryan and Jew, but first- and second-degree Mischlinge—stigmatized in the extreme: one's life depended on one's status.

Yet, as important as these statuses were, they were not absolutely fixed. As early as 1935 procedures were established to allow one to "up" a category in the racial schemata. This procedure was known as "liberation," and as we might guess (and fear), there were two different categories: "pseudo-liberation" and "genuine liberation." The former was based on law: showing, for example, that a grandparent really was not Jewish, or that assumed adherence to Jewish religion was mistaken; the latter, however, was based on "merit." Here it had to be shown that an applicant, through exceptional service, deserved to be reclassified. Nor were such actions taken lightly. All civilian applicants had to be approved by Adolf Hitler himself.[40]

The concept of liberation offers insight into Nazi behavior and the Holocaust that was soon to follow. It shows that Nazi Germany was not a simple or monolithic place; its bureaucracy was not only complex and intricate, it was also inventive. Later

---

40. One example should suffice: Herr Killy of the Reich chancellory performed significant functions in the destruction of Jews. He was a Mischlinge of the second degree; worse, his wife was a Mischlinge of the first degree. After the 1933 law, he offered to resign, but his superiors interceded for him. Under the Christmas tree in 1936 was a special gift from Adolf Hitler: genuine liberation for him, his wife, and all their children. Hereafter, he and his family were Aryan!

in this chapter I will return to the idea—at first glance, a contradiction—of an inventive bureaucracy.

The Nuremberg laws of blood and honor not only defined the races, as we have seen, but additionally defined who could marry whom. Approved were all marriages where both parties were German or both were Jewish.[41] Also approved were marriages between Germans and Mischlinge of the second degree (almost pure Germans), and Jews and Mischlinge of the first degree (almost pure Jews). Finally approved were marriages between two Mischlinge of the first degree. Thus did law isolate persons of first-degree status. Except by official permission, such persons could marry only among themselves, or other Jews—in which case their status changed immediately to Jewish.

Prohibited except by special decree were marriages between Mischlinge of the first degree and Germans, and marriage between first- and second-degree Mischlinge. Three categories of marriage were absolutely prohibited: two Mischlinge of the second degree, second-degree Mischlinge and Jew, and—of course, the worst of all—German and Jew.

The laws of blood and honor also proscribed *Rassenschande*, or race defilement via illicit sexual relations. Extramarital sex or sex within illegal marriages was forbidden. But at Hitler's insistence, only men—be they Jewish or German—could be sent to prison for violations. Here the Nazis combined racism with sexism.[42] It was Hitler's belief that women were weak and possessed little willpower, and thus could not really be held accountable for sexual deviance. But if a woman lied during court proceedings, she could be found guilty of perjury and sent to prison.[43]

The Nazis took Rassenschande seriously. In 1942, during a crucial period of World War II, no fewer than sixty-one Jews were

---

41. It seems odd today, but in 1935, Jews still had some civil rights—an important point for the argument to be developed later in this chapter.

42. For a discussion of sexism in Nazi Germany, see Claudia Koonz, *Mothers in the Fatherland: Women, Family and Nazi Politics* (New York: St. Martin's Press, 1987).

43. At Heydrich's orders, however, a lawful conviction of a German would result in immediate deportation of his Jewish partner to a concentration camp.

convicted of race defilement, compared to fifty-six for currency violations and fifty-seven for passport fraud. Most interestingly, ignorance was no defense against Rassenschande. As Hilberg notes, "Any German man wishing to have extramarital intercourse with *any* woman had the legal duty of inspecting her papers to make sure that she was not Jewish under the law."[44] Romance suffered grievously under the Nazis: the exotic, the whimsical, the erotic—these fare poorly in the face of "due process."

All this seems amazing at the close of the twentieth century. At the least, it is hard to follow. Before we evaluate its significance, there is one more complication—and complex it is!—to consider. The Nuremberg laws proscribed and regulated future marriages, but what was to be done about existing marriages, and particularly the offspring of those unions? As time passed, and Jews came under ever greater discriminations, such questions became matters of life and death.

In 1938 there were still thirty-thousand mixed marriages in Germany. On 28 December of that year, Hermann Göring issued a directive that divided those couples into two categories: privileged, meaning those exempt from "concentration," and not privileged. All mixed couples who reared their children as Christians were privileged; those who reared their offspring as Jews were not. For childless couples, privilege was granted when the husband was German and the wife Jewish; the opposite—Jewish husband, German wife—was not privileged. For this last case, Göring had hoped that his decree would force a German woman to divorce her Jewish husband.

Decree after decree, detail after detail: All of this occurred before the systematic mass murder even began. The significance of the laws of blood and honor is not in its logic and certainly not in its stupefying detail. In retrospect, its significance is that it sheds light on the darkness that was to follow.

Hitler gave the bureaucracy a job: to clean the country of Jews. They proceeded as bureaucrats proceed: they formulated

---

44. Hilberg, *The Destruction of the European Jews*, vol. 1, p. 162.

precise definitions; they registered those who fit the definition; they opened files for each registrant; they segregated Jews; they concentrated them; they killed them. In the words of Zygmunt Bauman: "Bureaucracy made the Holocaust, and it made it in its own image."[45]

For Christopher Browning, "the mere existence of a corps of Jewish experts created a certain bureaucratic momentum behind Nazi Jewish policy."[46] That momentum led more or less directly, we know now, to Auschwitz. Jean Amery also emphasized the importance of the laws of blood and honor: "I do not believe that I am inadmissibly projecting Auschwitz and the Final Solution back to 1935 . . . when I read the laws, I did indeed already hear the death threat—better the death sentence."[47] Raul Hilberg agrees: "When in the early days of 1933 the first civil servant wrote the first definition of 'non-Aryan' into a civil service ordinance, the fate of European Jewry was sealed."[48]

In trying to understand the genesis of the Holocaust, I have emphasized habit, routine, and tradition. Yet how could habit, how could routine, how could tradition create Auschwitz? Auschwitz was unprecedented. Bureaucrats had directed killings, to be sure; but no one, nor any organization, had ever collected vast numbers of people in one place, sorted them out, gassed them, and converted them to ash. No one had ever designed a factory that killed up to twenty-thousand people per day.

No: a Key to our understanding is that Auschwitz was a creative product of the imagination. And so we have a missing link. For bureaucrats who follow habit and tradition and routine would seem to make poor inventors. Nonetheless Raul Hilberg shows us that these bureaucrats did, in fact, become inventors. His strength, and a great one it is, is telling us in detail what happened; he shows that the Holocaust is not some abstract force of history, but real people perpetrating unimaginable deeds. About

45. Bauman, p. 105.
46. Christopher Browning, *The Path to Genocide: Essays on Launching the Final Solution* (Cambridge: Cambridge University Press, 1992), p. 37.
47. Amery, p. 26.
48. Hilberg, *The Destruction of the European Jews*, vol. 1, p. 288.

why this process happened, Hilberg has little to say. To address the "why" question, we need to understand two concepts: chaos and functionalism.

functionalism

Even before Germany attacked the Soviet Union, Franz Neumann, a German political philosopher, had written a most remarkable book, entitled *Behemoth*.[49] Neumann posed two questions: Has Germany a political theory? and Is Germany a state?

Neumann argued that Nazi ideology—as one normally thinks of the term—was not a set of interconnected ideas. Perhaps, he said, the function of Nazi ideology was to hide, rather than reveal: "the so-called non-rational concepts of blood, community, folk, are devices for hiding the real constellation of power and for manipulating the masses."[50]

Neumann concluded that Nazi ideology was a sham.[51] The answer to Neumann's first question was no. Ideologies that the Nazis used (or discarded) were merely techniques of domination, not taken seriously for their content by the very German leaders who purported them.

---

49. Neumann had been arrested in 1933, but was able to leave Germany. The book, over five hundred pages, was completed in 1942 at Columbia University, where Neumann was affiliated with the Institute for Social Research. I cite the 1963 version (New York: Octagon Books) which contains an appendix of one hundred pages.

The title of the book is taken first from Hobbes, whose analysis of Leviathan—a coercive state founded on individual rights—is well known. Less known is his study of government during the seventeenth century English civil war, which depicts a nonstate, anarchy and chaos: the Behemoth. In a preface, Neumann explained that Hobbes had borrowed both titles, *Leviathan* and *Behemoth*, from Jewish mythology, where the former was the ruler of the desert, the latter of the sea. Both were monsters of Chaos.

50. Neumann, p. 464.

51 In *Hitler's Weltanschauung* (Middletown, CT: Wesleyan University Press, 1972), Eberhard Jäckel maintains that Nazi ideology was a coherent set of ideas, consistent within its own premises: "Volk," will, superiority of men, virtue of war, and—most importantly—the cunning and depravity of Jews. Many historians accept Jäckel's analysis. My point is not to deny the authenticity of this position, but rather to argue that alongside the interconnectedness, chaos existed as antithesis.

Perhaps we err in focusing exclusively on ideas in and of themselves. Nazis were exceptionally anti-intellectual, and gave little credence to any system of ideas. Nazis were, concluded one analyst, men "who held thought itself in contempt and regarded ideas as mere weapons in the political fight for power."[52] Power was expressed not through words, but deeds, typically violent ones. In fascist regimes, that power was directed by, dictated by and for, a strong party as the focal point for all action.

Is Germany a state? There were, Neumann purported, four centers of power in Nazi Germany: the monopolistic economy, the one-party system, the army, and the bureaucracy.[53] There were also "thousands of technical rules." Yet there was no legislature—that had been abolished by Hitler—and no "realm of law." "We are confronted with a form of society," he concluded, "in which the ruling groups control the rest of the population directly, without the mediation of that rational though coercive apparatus known as the state."[54] Thus, in the modern sense of the term, Neumann concluded, Nazi Germany was not a state.[55]

Writing his book in the 1930s, Neumann knew little of the Holocaust. Yet his thesis merits our attention. There was bureaucracy, to be sure; but there was also chaos. And the Holocaust could not have happened in the absence of either partner of this

---

52. Fritz Stern, *The Politics of Cultural Despair: A Study in the Rise of the German Ideology* (Berkeley: University of California Press, 1961), p. 194. For Hungarian philosopher György Lukács, Nazi ideology was a demagogic synthesis of the philosophy of German imperialism, the application of American advertising techniques to German politics and propaganda (cited in Jäckel, p. 17).

53. This categorization was to be a great influence on Raul Hilberg, who studied under Neumann. Note that Hitler's role is de-emphasized in this scheme.

54. Neumann, p. 470.

55. Robert Koehl, "Feudal Aspects of National Socialism," *American Political Science Review*, 54 (1960): 926, maintains that Nazism is best conceptualized as feudalism. As a form of government, feudalism is characterized by a series of power relationships. For abstract law and the state the Nazis attempted to substitute personal loyalty to Hitler. Beneath the leader, as one would find in a feudal society, "the Nazi scene was filled with ever-changing groups and clusters of protagonists [whose] relationship to each other was only semi-hierarchical."

pair. To put it another way, the Holocaust arose out of the dialectics of bureaucratic rationality and stateless chaos. The implications of this insight are profound.

Historians have developed two ways—termed *functionalism* and *intentionalism*—of thinking about the origins and dynamics of the Holocaust.[56] I briefly present the latter, and then develop the former. For I should say ahead of time that as a sociologist I find functionalism more sensible. It portrays the Holocaust dialectically, just as I have said above: as bureaucratic rationality within a culture of chaos.

Intentionalism was born at the Nuremberg war crimes trials, when American prosecutors presented Nazi crimes as a carefully orchestrated conspiracy. This view is, first and foremost, Hitler-centric. Hitler is at the center of everything to do with the Holocaust, and there is a direct line between his earliest anti-Semitic diatribes and the death camps that were built years later. According to Lucy Dawidowicz, the first and foremost scholar of intentionalism, Hitler's plan was presented as a blueprint in *Mein Kampf*. "Once Hitler adopted an ideological position," she wrote, "he adhered to it with limpetlike fixity."[57]

The functionalist position, on the other hand, proposes two correctives about Hitler: (1) He is a "brooding and sometimes distant leader, who intervened only spasmodically, sending orders crashing through the system like bolts of lightening."[58] He is primary, no doubt; but he is not the only innovative actor; others, even in middle-level positions, play important roles. (2) He is flexible; he behaves more like a skilled politician, rather than an

---

56. This debate has been reviewed often and by many. I found most useful Saul Friedlander, "From Anti-Semitism to Extermination," pp. 11–18 in Furet; Marrus, pp. 40–46; and Hans Mommsen, Foreword to Karl Schleunes, *The Twisted Road to Auschwitz* (Urbana: University of Illinois Press, 1990).

57. Lucy Dawidowicz, *The War Against the Jews, 1933–1945* (New York: Holt, Rinehart & Winston, 1975), p. 111. Dawidowicz, perhaps the first American scholar to study the Holocaust, is a strong critic of functionalism, and would not use—and would not approve of—the term *intentionalist* to describe her work. As a student, Dawidowicz lived in Eastern Europe during the rise of Nazism. Her memoir of that experience, *From That Place and Time* (New York: Norton, 1989), is fascinating reading.

58. Marrus, p. 40.

obsessed politician who implements a master plan—the elimi-
nation of all Jews—regardless of the political and military costs.

Functionalists see the period from 1933, when Hitler came
to power, to 1941, when he began the mass killing of Jews, as a
time of evolving policy. Though there was terrible discrimination
against Jews, few were killed. Even as late as 1940, Nazi bureaucrats developed plans—memos were sent back and forth—for a
massive, forced emigration of Jews to the distant island of
Madagascar.

For functionalists there is no necessary relation between a
specific ideology and a specific action. Most certainly, Nazi leaders hated Jews. But did they from the beginning have a specific
plan to kill them all? For functionalists, the Nazis stumble-
bumbled into the Holocaust—bit by bit, piece by piece. They invented Auschwitz not in one fell swoop, but day by day, solving
problems by trial and error as they arose. Ultimately, of course,
they did invent Auschwitz, but they did it for office politics, to
advance their bureaucratic careers.

Consistent with Neumann's work, functionalists de-emphasize the role of the state in the Holocaust; they focus on its substitute, the Nazi Party. According to German historian Hans
Mommsen, National Socialism "presented a completely new type
of party, fundamentally different from the Communist and the
traditional democratic parliamentary parties." It was a structure
"which allowed an unprecedented short-term mobilization of all
available political energies to achieve particular political ends,
especially in foreign and military areas."[59]

Beneath Hitler, however, lines of Party authority were
vague and fluid; there were constant struggles for power and
position among rivals. Decisions were made not to advance
some rational goal of the state, but to gain or consolidate political power. Thus between Hitler and the traditional German
bureaucracy, in this gray area of chaos, came the "cumulative
radicalization"—to use Mommsen's insightful phrase—that led
to the Holocaust. The road to Auschwitz, according to historian

---

59. Hans Mommsen, "National Socialism: Continuity and Change." In
Laqueur, pp. 181, 183.

Karl Schleunes, was not a straight one. From the first anti-Semitic statements of Hitler to the Auschwitz death factory, the road was "twisted."

Let us explore these ideas of cumulative radicalization and twisted road. We begin by asking the question: How does a rational bureaucrat turn into a mass murderer? To address this question, we need to discover "what patterns of social structure and what patterns of personal immersion in a social situation serve to implement the program of an extremist movement."[60]

We begin by thinking about the bureaucracy. The glue that holds the organization together is compliance.[61] "I just followed orders," was the bureaucrat's defense at the Nuremberg war trials. Sociologist Fred Katz suggests that this view of the bureaucrat is one-sided, for along with each form of compliance is a form of autonomy, or discretionary activity. Routinization, he writes, "includes not only definite controls, but definite sectors of autonomy." Within their well-defined tasks, and this is an important point, these bureaucrats had some freedom to innovate, to invent solutions. "Their inventiveness in the course of their work, their flexibility when they wanted to be flexible, all demonstrated autonomy." Eichmann, for example, "displayed a great deal of ingenuity and adaptability in devising ways of getting trainloads of victims to their final destinations."[62]

Intentionalists have emphasized the importance of the Nuremberg laws. At the rally that honored their passage, Hitler said: "You have now agreed to a law whose full significance will only be recognized hundreds of years from now."[63] These laws seemed to represent careful planning and rational (though, by

---

60. Fred E. Katz, "Implementation of the Holocaust: The Behavior of Nazi Officials," *Comparative Studies of Society and History* 24 (1982): 512. See also Katz's *Ordinary People and Extraordinary Evil* (Albany: State University of New York Press, 1993).

61. Amitai Etzioni, *A Comparative Analysis of Complex Organizations* (New York: Free Press, 1961). Sociologists have identified three possible types of compliance: alienative—we follow though we do not believe we ought to; calculative—we follow because it is in our best interest; and normative—we follow because everyone else follows.

62. Katz, "Implemention of the Holocaust," pp. 515, 522.

63. Quoted in Yahil, p. 72.

our standards, twisted) behavior. They seemed to presage the Holocaust that was to follow.

Yet I want to develop a different interpretation, this one based on insights from chaos and functionalism. In presenting the details of the blood and honor laws, I probably gave the impression that they were carefully written over a long period of time. Today we think of our own Congress: hearings, testimony, drafting, writing, compromise, rewriting, and so forth. In fact, the laws were drafted and finalized, helter-skelter, in less than two days.[64]

And what of the bureaucrat who drafted these laws? Bernhard Lösener, the "racial expert" from the interior ministry, had been a Nazi Party member since 1930. Yet Lösener does not fit our image of a Nazi bureaucrat. For he seems, in retrospect, to be neither banal nor evil. By the time he drafted the blood and honor laws, Lösener had become disillusioned with the Party for two reasons: its interference in the affairs of the German Lutheran Church, and its persecution of Jews, particularly those of mixed lineage. Most historians now believe that he wrote the blood and honor laws to protect as many as possible: full Jews were beyond the pale, but part Jews could be, and to a degree were, protected.[65]

So we see that the intentionalist view of the Nuremberg laws is wanting. They were hardly the product of careful and deliberate planning; and they were, at least in the eyes of their composer, not driven by virulent anti-Semitism. It was a twisted, not a straight, road that led to the infamy of Auschwitz.

Leni Yahil, an Israeli scholar, has developed a fascinating interpretation of the laws of blood and honor. In her view, the Nuremberg laws were developed to resolve a problem that vexed the Nazis, one that had caused considerable friction between the Party and the various bureaucracies. The problem was not what to do about the Jews; the problem (remarkable in retrospect) was

---

64. For instructive details, see Schleunes, p. 122ff.
65. Lösener's apologia seems legitimate: he did work to protect Mischlinge, and learning of Jewish massacres in 1941, he transferred from his job. In 1944 he was arrested, purportedly for a minor role in the plot against Hitler. And most incredibly, after the war he was employed by the American Jewish Joint Distribution Committee.

what to do about the anti-Semites! "Anti-Jewish action," she writes, "was one expression of the tensions prevailing among the various centers of power in the Reich."[66]

By 1934, only a year after Hitler took power, government anti-Semitism had become problematic; the international boycott of German goods was hurting the economy. Considerable tension arose between the Nazi SA[67] and civil police: the former were destroying Jewish-owned shops; the latter tried to stop such "wanton destruction." The Bavarian minister of the interior denounced "criminal" elements in "anti-Semitic trespassing." Economic minister Schacht warned that unless "illegal actions against Jews came to a halt, he would not be able to acquire the raw materials for armaments or the foreign policy." Frick, the minister of the interior, made a more interesting distinction: "In the law-abiding state of Germany, only by means of the law is it possible to remove Jews from their positions."[68] In other words, anti-Semitism is okay, but only if it is expressed rationally as due process of law.

Law means policy; policy means implementation; and implementation means bureaucracy. For the Nazi state to function, anti-Semitism had to be carefully systematized. Each of the ministries—interior, foreign, treasury, and so on—wanted a piece of the action.

To control "Jewish affairs," each mid-level official had to outdo his[69] rival. "The departments involved hastily busied themselves with supporting legislation, even if only to retain their share of responsibility." Careers were built, or lost! Power was expanded, or lost! The bureaucratic winners were those

---

66. Yahil, p. 68.

67. Also known as the stormtroopers, the SA was founded in the early 1920s. Led by Earnst Rohm, the SA was characterized by illegal military activity and virulent anti-Semitism. Rohm's power, as well as his open homosexuality, became a problem within the Nazi Party. On 30 June 1934, SS officers assassinated Rohm and other SA officials in what was called "the night of the long knives." Thereafter the authority of the SA diminished greatly.

68. Yahil, pp. 69, 71.

69. I use the sexist "his" here purposefully, for almost all Nazi officials were men. For instructive exceptions to this Nazi misogyny, see Koonz, *Mothers in the Father Land*.

who (and here again is that important concept) invented the most comprehensive policy. The result of all this action was the "systematic mass murder of the Jews, which no one had previously imagined possible."[70] Such are the powers of bureaucratic invention!

forgetting

Reading about the Nuremberg laws of blood and honor, it is easy to be smug. That was Nazi Germany, and it was a long time ago, we say to ourselves. We interpret the previous sections as though their contents were not only terrible, but unique. Yet Nazi definitions are less unusual than we would like to think. Here I consider two examples: the definition of races—both popular and legal—in the United States, and the incarceration of American Japanese in concentration camps during World War II.

the "one-drop rule"

How do we define the races in our contemporary United States? By popular usage, the product of a mixed white-black marriage is deemed "half-black" or even "quarter-black,"[71] rather than the corresponding and rarely used terms "half-white" or "quarter-white." We also have a long history of prohibiting marriages between the races; the word describing that phenomenon—

---

70. Mommsen, "National Socialism," pp. 199–200.

71. We have specific terms, some outdated, to describe various racial mixtures. A "mulatto," according to the United States census from 1850 to 1920, was any person in whom the mixture of black and white is visible. In more technical usage, a "mulatto" was a person who was half white and half black. A "quadroon" was one-quarter black. An "octoroon" was one-eighth black. In Louisiana, there were distinctions made for persons who were as little as one-sixty-fourth black, and for mixtures between mulattoes and blacks. A three-quarters black was called a "griffe" or a "sambo." And a seven-eighth black was a "sacatra" or "mango." Complications arose as mixed black-whites mated with each other, or with Indians. This latter combination was called a "mustees," a term derived from the Latin American word *mestizo*. For a review of these terms, see Joel Williamson, *New People: Miscegenation and Mulattoes in the United States* (New York: Free Press, 1980), p. xii.

miscegenation—has always been a negative label, both in law and culture.

In both common usage and law, race in the United States has been defined in terms of the "one-drop" rule: A single drop of black blood makes a person black. Courts have used the term "traceable amount rule." In *Plessy v. Ferguson* (U.S. 163 537), the 1896 ruling that established the separate-but-equal interpretation of the law, the U. S. Supreme Court endorsed the one-drop rule.

The one-drop rule also become encoded into state law. And it was administered and enforced! In 1948, a Mississippi man was given a five-year prison sentence for violating the antimiscegenation law; he claimed not to be black, but the state proved that his great-grandmother was a slave girl and his conviction was upheld. Thirteen years after the passage of the Nuremberg laws, and three years after the end of the war, the State of Mississippi not only still prevented interracial marriage, but used the more rigorous criterion of one-eighth than even the Nazis, who stopped at one-quarter, dared.

Five other states also had a one-eighth criterion, and until 1970, the State of Louisiana defined a negro as anyone with a "trace of black ancestry." In that year a legal suit was brought on behalf of a child whose ancestry was allegedly only one part of 256 black. In the mid-1980s the Louisiana courts were still haggling over the racial status of a woman who was purportedly "three-thirty-second" black;[72] in the mid-1990s, various agencies of the federal government were examining, with considerable controversy, the implications of such racial definitions for the census of 2000.[73]

The one-drop rule is distinct in two ways: It applies only to blacks; no other minority group (e.g., Native Americans) is so regulated. And it is distinctly American, for it is found in no other

72. For the fascinating (and instructive) details of this case, see Calvin Trillin, "American Chronicles: Black or White," *New Yorker*, 14 April 1986, pp. 62–78. At one point, the defendant suggested visiting the President of the United States. "She would ask him if he thought she looked colored."

73. See Lawrence Wright, "One Drop of Blood," *New Yorker*, 25 July 1994, pp. 46–55, for the ridiculous and profound arguments over this issue.

country in the world. Yet in America its use has been not only persistent, but widespread, crossing various political and ideological lines. It has been used, writes one scholar, by "judges, affirmative action officers, and black protesters as well as by Ku Klux Klansmen."[74]

american concentration camps

The phrase grates badly in our ears. Concentration camps were Nazi inventions, not ours. Yet the United States government did build and administer concentration camps for the Japanese American population during World War II. To be sure, they were not slave labor camps; nor were they death camps. Nonetheless, this is a shameful story in twentieth-century American history.

Shortly after Pearl Harbor, the United States government forced some 112,000 Japanese—American citizens as well as legal aliens—to move to so-called "relocation centers," concentration camps surrounded by barbed wire. The Japanese were never more than 2.1 percent of the population of California, and 0.1 percent of the entire United States population. Nonetheless, there was a long history of prejudice and discrimination against them. In 1905, for example, an anti-Japanese campaign led by the *San Francisco Chronicle* produced the following front-page headlines: "Japanese a Menace to American Women" and "The Yellow Peril: How Japanese Crowd Out the White Race."[75] A 1920 California state law, parts of which were later declared unconstitutional, prohibited the transfer of land to Japanese nationals, and barred noncitizen Japanese from serving as guardians for their own minor children.

Even during the war, the United States made important distinctions between the Japanese and the German enemy: our

---

74. For an invaluable summary of the one-drop rule, see F. James Davis, *Who Is Black?* (University Park: Pennsylvania State University Press, 1991). My quote is taken from p. 5. This material is also reviewed in Gunnar Myrdal's classic book, *An American Dilemma* (New York: Harper & Brothers, 1944), p. 113ff.

75. Quoted in Roger Daniels and Harry Kitano, *American Racism* (Englewood Cliffs, NJ: Prentice-Hall, 1970), p. 47.

anti-German attitudes arose out of politics; our anti-Japanese out of racism. For the former we attributed guilt to specific individuals: there were always "good Germans." Not so for the Japanese. "The evil deeds of Hitler's Germany were the deeds of bad men; the evil deeds of Tojo and Hirohito's Japan were the deeds of a bad race."[76]

Franklin Roosevelt's executive order of 11 February 1942 was the legal authority for the evacuation. The U. S. Army, which had generated most of the pressure for the order, also implemented it. Asked about distinctions between aliens and citizens, General John L. De Witt insisted that "A Jap is a Jap."[77] Under the army's interpretation, a person of Japanese heritage was considered to be anyone who had as little as "one-sixteenth Japanese blood," as well as "Japanese who were married to Caucasians, Chinese, Filipinos, Negroes, Hawaiians, and Eskimos."[78] Under such rules, all Japanese living in the three West Coast states[79]—regardless of their nationality—were deported to ten camps located in the interior.

And what of the bureaucrat in charge of this operation? The first director of the so-called War Relocation Authority was Milton Eisenhower. His career did not suffer: he was later to become president of Johns Hopkins University, and a highly visible figure as brother of the president of the United States. Other prominent politicians refused to criticize, or even supported, the operation. California governor Culbert Olson, a

---

76. Daniels and Kitano, p. 34.

77. Quoted in Daniels and Kitano, p. 60.

78. Audrie Girdner and Anne Loftis, *The Great Betrayal: The Evacuation of the Japanese-Americans During World War II* (London: Macmillan, 1969, p. 125). Okinawans were also included in the order, though they were not of Japanese ethnicity and generally viewed the Japanese as imperialists. Such distinctions meant little to white Americans, and so Okinawans spent the war behind barbed wire.

79. Interestingly, Japanese living in Hawaii, where they constituted fully one-third of the population, were not deported anywhere. As Daniels and Kitano explain, the reasons were more practical than ideological: such incarceration would have caused severe labor shortages and over-taxed shipping on what was rapidly becoming the forward operational base for the Pacific war (p. 62).

Democrat, and his Republican attorney general, Earl Warren, generally supported the operation.[80]

the social construction of race

Today we think of *Jew* as a religious or ethnic category. In pre-war Germany, Jews were counted as *Israelites*. Nazis defined *Jew* as a racial category. In this practice the Germans were no different than other Europeans, or—to an extent—Americans. *Jew* was used then as today we might use the term *black*. What was unique was the German effort to carefully define the racial parameters of Judaism.

Whenever race is discussed, fears of race mixing are never far away. For it is not so much the boundary, but the border crossing, that has dominated racist thinking. What Germans feared the most was race mixing. They conceptualized race mixing in terms of what anthropologists call the "hypo-decent rule."[81] According to this rule, persons of mixed racial heritage are categorized as a member of the group with the lesser social power and prestige. Thus a negative label is given to the progeny of an inter-racial union.

The American definition of *mixed Japanese* was remarkably similar to the German definition of *mixed Jew*; only the American definition was more stringent: one-sixteenth, as opposed to the one-eighth of the German definition of *Jew*, was required. During the war years, an American citizen with one great-grandparent who was Japanese was legally defined as Japanese. While it is true that the concept was not operationalized with any

---

80. In 1942 Warren, who later as chief justice of the U. S. Supreme Court became known as a champion of individual rights, wrote: "It will interest you to know that some of our airplane factories in this state are entirely surrounded by Japanese." It was also true, though Warren did not mention it, that the Japanese had been in most of these areas long before there were any aircraft factories. Quoted in Roger Daniels, *Concentration Camps USA: Japanese Americans and World War II* (New York: Holt, Rinehart and Winston, 1972), p. 76. In three separate opinions, the Supreme Court of the United States refused to strike down the legality of the evacuations.

81. For a discussion, see Melvin Harris, *Patterns of Race in the Americas* (New York: Norton, 1964), p. 56.

zeal, it is also true that American citizens suffered grievously as a result of these definitions.

Americans also used the hypo-decent rule to define *negro* or *colored*. Even the complex vocabulary of mixed white and black reminds us of the German effort to carefully define Jewish lineage. Most significantly, the one-drop rule is still widely applied in popular culture to define African-Americans.

There is a lesson to be learned here, one that goes far beyond the Holocaust. From these three examples, we should do no less than reconsider in its entirety our notion of "race." Most people think of "race" as a fixed biological category. Yet these examples show that race categories are cultural inventions.[82] Who is Jewish? or black? or Japanese? The answers to these questions are deeply rooted in politics and culture. Nor are the answers harmless. Prejudicial definitions of African American heritage have led—and still lead—to grievous suffering in our own country.

krema

Let us summarize this chapter with a remarkable story of one man within the culture of Nazi bureaucracy.

In 1946 the Russian army arrested a senior engineer from the German firm Topf & Sohne, which had designed and produced the crematoria at Auschwitz and other concentration camps.[83] According to the interrogation of Kurt Prufer, the operation of the Krema (his pet name for the ovens) was problematic: "the strain on the furnaces was colossal," because the ovens could not cope with the number of corpses that needed incineration. "So [in 1942] I decided to build a crematorium with a higher capacity." Prufer's design, which used the fat from burn-

---

82. Larry Reynolds, "A Retrospective on 'Race': The Career of a Concept," *Sociological Focus* 25 (1992): 1–15.

83. All quotes are from Gerald Fleming, "Engineers of Death," *New York Times*, 18 July 1993, p. E-19. The information herein came from Russian archives, which became available to American scholars in 1993.

ing corpses as fuel for the furnace, was innovative: "The Krema was to be built on a conveyor belt principle. That is to say, the corpses must be brought to the incineration furnaces without interruption. When the corpses are pushed into the furnaces, they fall onto a grate, then slide into the furnace and are incinerated. The corpses serve at the same time as fuel for the heating of the furnaces."

Why would Prufer construct such a grisly machine? Repeating an explanation often used after the war, he claimed: "I was a German engineer and a key member of Topf and I saw it as my duty to apply my specialist knowledge . . . in order to help Germany win the war."

Prufer had one regret: that he could not obtain a patent for his invention; the whole enterprise was a state secret. Nonetheless, Topf & Sohne eventually got its patent. On 3 January 1953, eight years after the fall of the Nazis, the Federal Republic of Germany issued the patent (No. 861,731) for "Process and Apparatus for the Incineration of Carcasses, Cadavers and Parts Thereof."

Imagine Prufer within the gray zone. He was surely an ordinary—dare I say banal—man. A Weberian vision sheds light, for Prufer was first and foremost acting as an expert, and a creative one at that, within a bureaucratic structure. He had a technical problem, in this case, how to maximize corpses into ash, which he solved with brilliant instrumental rationality.

That Prufer's definition of the problem—and that his solution—was intricately connected to Nazi culture is certainly true. That Prufer's problem and solution were also disconnected to any moral concern is perfectly consistent with ideology and practice in any modern society.

American culture mass-produces Kurt Prufers. I do not say that we build Kremas, or that we commit genocide against Jews (or African Americans, a more likely target for contemporary United States). What I am suggesting is that modern life—with its emphasis on process rather than substance—produces a context out of which horrific things might happen.

The same modern world that produced the automobile also produced the thermonuclear bomb. It had—it has—become acceptable to debate the costs *and benefits* of weapons of mass destruction. Question: Do we drop this or that type of bomb? Answer: Calculate the military, financial, political benefits and risks, and from that calculus make a decision (disregard losses— even civilian ones—from the enemy country as irrelevant).

It is to the most troubling characteristic of Nazism—its peculiar modern nature—that we now turn our attention.

4 modernity

There is a certain similarity between the measures which need to be taken when we draw a broad biological analogy between bodies and malignant tumors, on the one hand, and a nation and individuals within it who have become asocial because of their defective constitution, on the other hand.
—Konrad Lorenz, 1940, winner of the Nobel Prize for Biology, 1973

We can no longer afford to take that which was good in the past and simply call it our heritage, to discard the bad and simply think of it as a dead load which by itself time will bury in oblivion.
—Hannah Arendt, 1950

Without modern civilization and its central achievements, there would be no Holocaust.
—Zygmunt Bauman, 1989

I grew up in Los Angeles (always abbreviated L.A.), or more accurately, in San Fernando Valley. The Valley: Since then it has become a place of some fame or notoriety—is there a difference? It became, one might say, "totally awesome." But during my childhood it was perhaps less noteworthy: a rural area in transition, from chicken ranches (I lived on one), orange and grapefruit groves, to tract housing.

In the Valley we were the vanguard of modernism.

Ten thousand miles away from L.A., the Nazis (an acronym for National Socialist German Workers Party), most infamously the SS (these two letters had become a word unto itself), had obliterated the Jewish world. But it might as well have been a different planet, for all I knew. The old world was a place we Jews—the lucky ones anyway—had left, and with good reason too. We traded, I was told, poverty for progress; superstition for science; in short: we traded history for the future.

In the wake of Auschwitz, Jews were not talking. "Where were you born?" I asked my mother. "I don't remember," she replied. To the same question a year or so later, she answered: "Near Leningrad." (It was two decades later that an old aunt told me that she was from Dnepropetrovsk, some thousand miles to the south, in what is now Ukraine.) To others, she said that she was born on the Lower East Side of New York; actually she had lived in Harlem when it was a Jewish neighborhood.

There was no past, at least not one worth noting. This was not just ideology, it was the physical presence of Los Angeles. For, save a few trees, there was nothing of any age nearby. The oldest buildings were a decade or two at the most. Even the people were new, having arrived in the Valley but a few years back. Grandparents were few and far between. Mine still had foreign accents, but they had Americanized their names. Q: What is the ethnicity of "Markle?" A: It is an abbreviation of "Markowitz," a Serbian name, though these Jews—my father's side—had lived somewhere east of Budapest. The stories of their past, of their journeys to the new land—these were told with silence.

So my childhood, it seemed to me, was not part of any particular history, or even story. I had completely forgotten the Russian songs that I sang (or so I am told) as a toddler. Yiddish was spoken all around me, but never to me. I, not helped by an ineptitude in languages, never learned the tongue. In my world, no one dwelled on the past. It was, in a peculiar California way, an existential—today we would say postmodern—world that we lived in. So for me, when I think about the modern world today, and the meaning of the very idea of modernity, it signifies a place isolated from history and tradition, or perhaps even one opposed to tradition and history.

Where did my family come from? Did any of my relatives perish in the camps? I am ignorant. I speak (and think in) the language of a northwestern island of Europe because of some fluke of history. My past does not exist in any meaningful way before my own memory. As poet Richard Michelson laments:

> I am a Jew a generation after the Holocaust.
> Poorer, my grandfather says, without a past,
> than he, who has no future.

Looking backward, it amazes me that during the time of this boring and banal and safe childhood, the civilization of European Jewry (which had by some volcanic accident spewed me like so much lava onto the shores of the Pacific Ocean) was being murderously destroyed, life by precious life.

In this chapter I argue that Nazi society was quintessentially modern. As such it had more in common with our own culture and society than we would like to admit. I begin with Hannah Arendt's conception of Nazi society as totalitarian. I then consider the hallmark of any modern society: its practice of science, particularly medicine. I conclude by pondering the meaning of what it means to be enlightened: what modernity had to do with the Holocaust, and what that means for our future and our safety.

total domination

Hannah Arendt's 1951 book, *The Origins of Totalitarianism*, was not solely about the Holocaust, but it supplied a broad context to interpret that infamy. Moreover, in that book Arendt constructed an explanation—the most thought-provoking ever written, I think—of the central place of Auschwitz[1] within Nazism.

She began working on the book in 1944.[2] As she proceeded to write, and to learn more about Auschwitz, civilization as she understood it appeared "lifeless, bloodless, meaningless and unreal."[3] Arendt's approach is different, more abstract and at the same time more historical, from approaches we have examined so far. Her task was nothing less than trying to reconcile a so-called progressive Western civilization with a supposedly atavistic Nazi genocide.

---

1. Here I use Auschwitz not in the concrete sense, as a specific place, but as shorthand for all concentration camps.

2. Arendt had difficulty deciding on a title for the book. Her working title was *The Three Pillars of Hell*. It was later published in England with the title *The Burden of Our Times*, a title that she did not like. For details of her travail in writing *Origins*, see Elisabeth Young-Bruehl, *Hannah Arendt: For Love of the World* , p. 199ff.

3. Hannah Arendt, *The Origins of Totalitarianism*. I use the 1973 edition (New York: Harcourt, Brace and Jovanovich), p. viii, with three new prefaces written in 1966–67.

For Arendt, Nazism was decidedly not atavistic, nor should it be understood as a singularly German phenomenon. Rather, Arendt viewed Nazism as an example of a uniquely modern phenomenon she termed *totalitarianism*.[4] The implications of totalitarianism were enormous: "Suffering, of which there has always been too much on earth, is not the issue, nor is the number of victims. Human nature as such is at stake."[5]

Arendt asked: What is the relationship between the structure of totalitarianism and the content of its ideology? The answer, an echo of Neumann: virtually nothing. For the totalitarian movement, ideology[6] is action; and action is terrorism. Total terror[7] always trumps ideology. The content of propaganda is important only in that it leads to terror.[8]

---

4. According to Arendt, totalitarianism resulted from the crystallization of anti-Semitism, imperialism, and racism. Conditions to produce this form of governance arose toward the end of the nineteenth century and were triggered by World War I: a weakened modern state and the rise of imperialism; the demise of the class system and its values; and the atomization and individualization of modern mass society.

The concept is not new. The first reference to the term, according to the Oxford English Dictionary, was in 1928. Unfortunately, the concept was cheapened in contemporary political discourse when Jeanne Kirkpatrick, U.S. ambassador to the United Nations during the Reagan presidency, claimed that all communist governments—and only communist governments!—were totalitarian.

5. Quoted in Margaret Canovan, *Hannah Arendt: A Reinterpretation of Her Political Thought*, p. 23.

6. In previous chapters of this book, I have used "ideology" as an interconnected set of social and political ideas, derived from (and reflecting) economic or class positions. Arendt uses the term in its existentialist sense, as a way of accounting for action.

7. During the rise of Nazism, the terror was "bloody": "Terrorism had become a kind of philosophy," Arendt wrote, "to express frustration, resentment, and blind hatred, a kind of political expressionism which used bombs to express oneself." Eventually the administration of the camps became more bureaucratized, characterized by the "absolutely cold and systematic destruction of human bodies," which Arendt terms "total terror" (*The Origins of Totalitarianism*, p. 332). This policy change was not noted by memoirists, who reported a considerable amount of random violence at the camps, even toward the end of the war. See my article, Markle et al., "From Auschwitz to Americana."

8. Where the rule of terror is perfected, propaganda disappears entirely. As Himmler said of the concentration camps: "Education consists of discipline, never of any kind of instruction on an ideological basis" (quoted in Arendt, *The Origins of Totalitarianism*, p. 344).

Claims of a "Jewish conspiracy," which Nazis repeated ad nauseam, allowed, permitted, then demanded a terrorism against the Jews: "The assumption of a Jewish world conspiracy was transformed by totalitarian propaganda from an objective, arguable matter into the chief element of the Nazi reality; the point was that the Nazis *acted* as though the world were dominated by the Jews and needed a counterconspiracy to defend itself."[9]

Today we read Nazi propaganda with some amazement. It is cruel, to be sure; but it is also amazingly crude, hardly the output from a nation, to use Jean Amery's phrase, of "poets and thinkers." But within the context of a totalitarian society, such propaganda took on a frightening reality: "Racism for them was no longer a debatable theory of dubious scientific value, but was being realized every day in the functioning hierarchy of a political organization in whose framework it would have been very 'unrealistic' to question it."[10]

Do you want a job?—How many of your grandparents are Aryan? Do you want a promotion?—Is your physiognomy Aryan? Do you want to live?—Are you Jewish? In such a climate, one soon learns not to question the logic of race, the content of ideology.

Now I come to the crux, for my purpose, of Arendt's argument: that the ultimate expression of terror, and therefore the ultimate expression of totalitarianism, was the concentration camp. For most analysts, the camps are inexplicable: with a war raging, the Nazis continued to operate these costly and—from a military perspective—nonfunctional places. Thinking of the camps as superfluous or accidental, according to Arendt, entirely misses the point. As unlikely as it may sound, "these camps are the true central institution of totalitarian organizational power." "The uselessness of the camps, their cynically admitted anti-utility, is only apparent. In reality they are more essential to the preservation of the regime's power than any of its other institutions."[11]

---

9. Arendt, *The Origins of Totalitarianism*, p. 362.
10. Arendt, *The Origins of Totalitarianism*, p. 362.
11. Arendt, *The Origins of Totalitarianism*, pp. 437, 456.

Concentration camps serve as laboratories to act out "the fundamental belief" of totalitarianism: total domination. "Total domination, which strives to organize the infinite plurality and differentiation of human beings as if all humanity were just one individual, is possible only if each and every person can be reduced to a never-changing identity of reactions, so that each of these bundles of reactions can be exchanged at random for any other."[12]

Under scientifically controlled conditions, the Nazis were able to eliminate "spontaneity itself as an expression of human behavior" and transform the human personality "into a mere thing." Totalitarianism strives, she wrote, "not for despotic rule over men, but toward a system in which men are superfluous."[13] This principle was most fully realized in the gas chambers, which, if only because of their enormous capacity, could not be intended for individual cases but only for people in general.

Arendt's *Origins* contains one more key insight for my analysis. For the entire system to work, we must understand one crucial fact: The victims must be innocent! Let us examine the logic (I use this term purposely) of this remarkable claim. For the guilty, punishment should follow the crime; punishment of the guilty may be cruel, even heinous, but it will not seem arbitrary. But arbitrariness is the basis for domination. For punishment to be entirely arbitrary, the victim must be innocent in every respect. A survivor imagines the following conversation: A Jew asks: "For what purpose, may I ask, do the gas chambers exist?" The German answers: "For what purpose were you born?"[14]

For Arendt, the real lesson of the Holocaust is this: Auschwitz proves that "everything is possible."[15] The victims

---

12. Arendt, *The Origins of Totalitarianism*, p. 438. Here the influence of Heidegger's (and Sartre's) existential thought is evident: totalitarian leaders, denying their own freedom and destroying that of others, are "inauthentic," and therefore lose their humanity.

13. Arendt, *The Origins of Totalitarianism*, pp. 438, 457.

14. David Rousset, quoted in Arendt, *The Origins of Totalitarianism*, p. 449. His memoirs were translated from French as *A World Apart* (London: Secker and Warburg, 1951).

15. Arendt, *The Origins of Totalitarianism*, p. 437. In celebration of the fiftieth anniversary of D-Day in 1994, U. S. president Bill Clinton stood at the Brandenburg Gate in Berlin and proclaimed the triumph of freedom. The lesson for us to learn, he orated, was that "everything is possible."

cannot believe the truth of what is about to happen; their innocence prevents comprehension: "If . . . victims are aware of being innocent—that is, that there is no rational basis for their
status as victims—there follows an almost inevitable and falla-
cious conclusion. They can only assume that their oppression
proceeds from a mistaken judgment or a momentary lapse of
rationality by their oppressor."[16] Rash action, especially illegal
or violent behavior, would affirm guilt; for normal times to
return, according to this logic, victims should do nothing
recklessly.

No rational person, and we hope that we are such, believes
that everything is possible. Can a nation of Europeans, inheri-
tors of Beethoven and Goethe, really—as part of a coherent
plan—burn babies? The answer, a resounding Yes! shows indeed
that there are no boundaries to protect us from the possibility of
everything.

What are we to make of Arendt's thesis? I should begin by
expressing admiration: she wrote *Origins* as the war was just ending, when little was known of the Nazi genocide.[17] Nonetheless,
there are several limitations to Arendt's understanding of the
Holocaust.

First: I have presented only half of Arendt's argument.
Arendt's method in *Origins* was more complex, but also more
problematic, than I have so far revealed. For she analyzed not
only Nazi Germany, but gave equal attention throughout to the
Stalinist Soviet Union. Thus the concept of totalitarianism, upon
which the book rests, applies equally to the two cases.

Here Arendt fails. That innocent people, millions of them,
were killed by Stalin is a tragedy of incalculable magnitude. Yet,
for my intellectual purposes, that slaughter is different from—

---

16. Kren and Rappoport, p. 74. The authors continue: "The fact that one
is innocent, in the sense of not being guilty of the oppressor's accusations,
clearly works against adoption of effective action because of fear that such
action may contaminate or discredit one's primary claim to innocence"
(p. 75).

17. When the 1973 edition was published, Arendt declined to revise her
text. "What I had learned [in the intervening years] was interesting enough,
but it hardly required substantial changes in either the analysis or the argument of my original presentation" (p. xxiv).

and non-comparable to—the Nazi genocide. Unlike Nazis, the Soviets did not execute children! This is really another way of asserting that the Soviets murdered on the basis of (perceived) political opposition, rather than ethnic identity. The Soviets conceptualized their victims as guilty.[18]

Throughout her book, Arendt compares and contrasts Hitler and Stalin. Though they were the two most infamous mass murderers of the twentieth century, they were unalike: Stalin was an ethnic minority, a Georgian; it is inconceivable that a racemonger such as Hitler could have minority status. Stalin had other characteristics hardly imaginable in Hitler: he was a divinity student, a party functionary who followed orders, an uninspiring speaker—not charismatic at all.[19]

Second: For Arendt there is a leader, and then there are masses of followers.[20] "The chief characteristic of mass man is not brutality and backwardness," she wrote, "but his isolation and lack of normal social relationships." But it is perhaps naive to view German citizenry as so uprooted, so detached, so atomized. It is known, for example, that common citizens used SS terror to their advantage. How does one get even—settle an old argument perhaps—with neighbors? Denounce them to the SS. In some instances, citizens dressed as SS to scare—or even extort! their

---

18. Arendt analogizes the Soviet camps to purgatory, the Nazi camps to hell.

19. See Allan Bullock, *Hitler and Stalin: Parallel Lives* (New York: Random House, 1992). Bullock's goal is to compare the two leaders, but a close reading of the text reveals more differences than similarities between the two.

20. In the United States, postwar sociologists developed the idea of "mass society." They viewed individuals who joined social movements—not just Nazism but a wide variety of American protest movements—as irrational. Their behavior, it was claimed, was a nonfunctional response to an anomic mass society. Today, most scholars of social movements have a different, more rationalist, view of why people join social movements. According to the "entrepreneurial model" of resource mobilization theory, membership—even mass membership—is not terribly important in the success or failure of a social movement. What seems determinative is a well-trained professional staff (called "issue entrepreneurs") who create and define new issues as problematic. For an explication of this view, see my and Frances McCrea's, *Minutes to Midnight: Nuclear Weapons Protest in America* (Newbury Park, CA: Sage Publications, 1989).

neighbors.[21] In short, Arendt's analysis ignores the dense social organization of Nazi society and the creative behavior of its citizenry.

For Arendt, the real problem—and the root cause of totalitarianism—is the "curse" of the industrial revolution: "Loneliness, the common ground for terror, the essence of totalitarian government . . . is closely connected with uprootedness and superfluousness which have been the curse of modern masses since the beginning of the industrial revolution."[22] I will return to this critique of the industrial revolution shortly, but for now let me point out that this is a rather one-sided view of the past century of Western history.

Third: In totalitarian systems, the identity of the enemy is irrelevant. Victims might include anyone, any group. Yet anti-Semitism, for all its problems as a sole explanation of the Holocaust, seemed historically and culturally central to the very idea and practice of Nazism. Even more, the murder of the Jews was perpetrated—officially, at least—as a secret.[23] It is hard to imagine, as Arendt's explanation would demand, that secrecy could be the basis of totalitarianism.

Finally: Arendt almost completely ignored the role of another ideological system, one that came not from Adolf Hitler or other Nazis. To appreciate this ideology, we must examine the thought

---

21. Robert Gellately, *The Gestapo and German Society: Enforcing Racial Policy, 1939–1945*. (New York: Oxford Clarendon, 1991). Like any other society, wartime Germany contained people of all sorts, brave as well as weak, humane as well as anti-Semitic. For an insightful portrayal, see Ursula Hegi's novel, *Stones From the River* (New York: Poseidon Press, 1994).

22. Arendt, *The Origins of Totalitarianism*, p. 475. As one becomes lonely, one also loses solitude. "Self and world, capacity for thought and experience, are lost at the same time" (p. 477). In 1950, David Reissman wrote *The Lonely Crowd* (New Haven: Yale University Press, 1950), a book that depicted Americans as living in crowds, but nonetheless always lonely.

23. While the Holocaust may have been a secret de jure, it was not a secret de facto. Large segments of German society, from state bureaucrats to townspeople, had considerable knowledge of what was happening to the Jews. Nor was the Holocaust a secret in the United States. As David Wyman has shown in *Paper Walls: America and the Refugee Crisis, 1938–1941* (Amherst: University of Massachusetts Press, 1968) and *Abandonment of the Jews: America and the Holocaust, 1941–1945* (New York: Pantheon, 1984), American officials in the Roosevelt administration knew what was happening at Auschwitz and other concentration camps. In the United States, readers of daily newspapers were also apprised of the Holocaust as it was happening. For an analysis of contemporaneous newspaper coverage of the Holocaust, see my article, Markle et al., "From Auschwitz to Americana."

of some of the most renowned scientists and physicians—Americans as well as Germans—of the early twentieth century.

gardening

Metaphors are more than phrases. They help us think in new ways and see novel relationships. Metaphors might even help us invent new ideologies.

In the early twentieth century it was common to think of society as a garden.[24] Some people were flowers; some were weeds. Biologists were the gardeners. Their function was to scientifically determine status: Which was a weed? which a flower? The biologist weeded the garden, preventing the weed from growing at the flower's expense, making sure that the flower—perhaps more delicate, but certainly more beautiful—would have the space to grow.

In 1930, R. W. Darre, the future Nazi minister of agriculture, asserted: "He who leaves the plants in a garden to themselves will soon find to his surprise that the garden is overgrown by weeds." What is needed, Darre asserted, is a gardener who "ruthlessly eliminates the weeds which would deprive the better plants of nutrition, air, light and sun." What is true for gardens must also be true for society: "a people can only reach spiritual and moral equilibrium if a well-conceived breeding plan stands at the very *centre* of its culture."[25]

Note that Darre's statement, motivated by a biological ideology, was not inherently anti-Semitic.[26] Nor was it dependent in any direct way on the thoughts of Adolf Hitler or other Nazis. It was, however, dependent on a medical establishment that shared (at least parts of) the Nazi ideology. For among Hitler's select, it was the physicians who were to be the chief gardeners of Nazism.

Physicians were among the earliest and strongest supporters of Hitler. As early as 1929, forty-four physicians formed the

---

24. The argument that follows borrows heavily from Zygmunt Bauman, *Modernity and Ambivalence* (Ithaca: Cornell University Press, 1991), p. 26ff.

25. Quoted in Bauman, *Modernity and Ambivalence*, p. 27.

26. Indeed, several noteworthy Jewish biologists of that time advanced the gardening metaphor.

National Socialist Physicians' League to coordinate Nazi medical policy and to "purify the German medical community of the influence of Jewish Bolshevism."[27] By 1933, the league boasted a membership of almost three thousand physicians. In the election that preceded Hitler's appointment as chancellor, nine physicians were elected as Nazi members of parliament; 6 percent of Germany's physicians were members of the Nazi party compared with 3 percent of all teachers and less than 1 percent of judges.

In a 1933 address to the National Socialist Physicians' League, Hitler claimed that he could do without lawyers, engineers, and builders, but not without physicians: "You, you, National Socialist doctors, I cannot do without for a single day, not a single hour. If not for you, if you fail me, then all is lost. For what good are our struggles, if the health of our people is in danger." In another speech, Hitler called his Nazi revolution "the final step in the overcoming of historicism and the recognition of purely biological values." The Bavarian cabinet minister declared in 1934 that National Socialism is nothing more than "applied biology."[28]

Applied biology began not with Jews, as we might guess, but with Germans. On 14 July 1933 the Nazis passed the Law for the Prevention of Genetically Diseased Offspring, known as the sterilization law. This law gave Aryan physicians, upon approval from a "genetic health court," the authority to sterilize individuals suffering from a variety of "genetic" diseases. These afflictions included, among others, feeblemindedness and schizophrenia, genetic deafness or blindness, and severe alcoholism. The motive for sterilization was, in the minds of the perpetrators, sound genetics; they wished to improve the nation's gene pool. Between 1933 and 1937, physicians sterilized four hundred thousand Germans.

---

27. Robert Proctor, *Racial Hygiene: Medicine Under the Nazis* (Cambridge: Harvard University Press, 1988), p. 65. The Nazis routinely conflated Jews and Bolsheviks. There is, of course, a long history of Jewish activism in left politics. In Germany, Karl Marx had a rabbinical genealogy; and the leader of the left immediately after World War I was Rosa Luxemburg, a Jew who was assassinated by right-wing German nationalists. Jews were also prominent in 1917 in the new Soviet leadership. In addition to Leon Trotsky, six of twenty-one members of the Central Committee were Jewish. Nonetheless, the great majority of Jews were not leftists, nor were the majority of leftists Jewish. In the Stalinist purges of the 1930s, Jews were murdered all out of proportion to their numbers.

28. Quoted in Proctor, p. 64.

In the so-called "euthanasia" program, instituted in 1939, German physicians murdered German citizens. Scientists argued that it was not cost-effective to care for various defectives, people whose "lives were not worth living." Based on a rather elaborate approval procedure, physicians eventually murdered approximately seventy thousand adults and five thousand children. The method of killing and disposal of bodies seems, in retrospect, to presage future infamy. Some children received mortal injections of morphine or various poisons; others were gassed with carbon monoxide, purchased in pressurized cylinders from chemical factories. Bodies were cremated immediately to avoid an epidemic, parents were told in a standardized letter.[29]

"At the heart of the Nazi enterprise," Robert Jay Lifton has written, "was the medicalization of killing—the imagery of killing in the name of healing. In fact, Nazi doctors were able to obliterate "the boundary between killing and healing."[30]

Before the Nazis were a glimmer in Adolf Hitler's mind, professional science had set the stage for a final solution: "When the Nazis took over, the pre-existing scientific discourse allowed the doctors to become the priests of the cult of German blood as well as its medical keepers and the exterminators of its potential polluters." This symbiosis—between Nazi power and biological doctrine—proved to be monstrous: "The Nazi extermination programme was a logical extension of sociobiological ideas and eugenics doctrines . . . which flourished widely in Germany well before the era of the Third Reich."[31] German perpetrators murdered in the name of science. They began by murdering Germans; they concluded by slaughtering Jews.

---

29. Werner Catel, responsible for the program to murder children, was appointed after the war as professor of pediatrics and director of the Children's Clinic at the University of Kiel in Northern Germany. In 1979 he co-edited a textbook to be used by nurses assigned to children's hospitals.

30. Robert Jay Lifton, *The Nazi Doctors* (New York: Basic Books, 1986), p. 14. Asked how he could reconcile killing with his Hippocratic Oath, a Nazi doctor responded to Lifton: "Of course I am a doctor and I want to preserve life. And out of respect for human life, I would remove a gangrenous appendix from a diseased body. The Jew is the gangrenous appendix in the body of mankind" (p. 16).

31. Stephen Chorover, *From Genesis to Genocide* (Cambridge: MIT Press, 1979), p. 109.

Let us now examine what is meant by "Nazi science" or "Nazi medicine."[32] First I should note: the phrase sticks in my throat. It would seem to be an oxymoron. I used to think that science and medicine were the quintessence of democracy; even more, I thought that they could not survive outside democratic culture.[33] But this is not true. Effective science, and by that I mean everything from laboratory problem solving to technical application to profound theorizing, happened—and happened often—in Nazi Germany.[34]

Most historians have attempted to account for the horrible excesses of Nazi science in one of two ways: as perverted by politicians, or as perverted by scientists. I think that each of these accounts is at best narrow, at worst deeply flawed. Both lead us away from a proper understanding of Nazi medicine—as an important expression of Nazi social structure and culture.

In the first view, Nazi science is not really science, but rather a science bent out of shape, a mirror of an ugly society. In this account, Hitler and his henchmen expelled Jewish scientists and corrupted liberal values, in so doing, they destroyed legitimate science.[35] This verson of history notwithstanding, the Nazis did

---

32. This section is based on Proctor.

33. Robert K. Merton, one of the best known of all postwar sociologists, posited that certain institutional norms—universalism, organized skepticism, communality, and disinterestedness—were necessary for the conduct of good science. These norms, he concluded, were to be found in democracies; lacking these norms, as in a totalitarian society, the scientific effort would be greatly diminished.

34. And as well in the Soviet Union. American politicians (though not American scientists) continually underestimated the ability of Soviet scientists to produce an atomic, and then a thermonuclear, bomb. When such weapons were produced, Americans typically—and incorrectly—credited not scientists, but spies. According to this historiography it was stolen information, not discovered technique, that so quickly allowed the Soviet Union to produce such weaponry.

35. This was the view during the war years. According to J. D. Bernal, Nazism enthroned irrationality over reason, and in so doing "reduced scientific criticism to impotence." He concluded that "The destruction of science in Germany . . . may be one of the major tragedies in the development of civilization" (*Social Function of Science* [New York: MacMillan, 1939, pp. 211–12]. Joseph Needham added: "German science has been largely destroyed" (*An Attack on International Science*, Cambridge: [Cambridge University Press, 1941]).

not destroy German science[36] and medicine. In particular, the disciplines of human genetics, anthropology, and psychology—all components of what Nazis called "applied biology"—flourished. One hundred fifty medical journals published continuously and more than thirty new medical journals were founded during the Nazi period.

In some ways, Nazi medicine was actually progressive by today's standards. Nazi physicians and public health officials emphasized the relation between environment and disease: they funded research on the adverse effects of X rays and heavy metals, and conducted the first studies indicating the dangers of asbestos; they promoted whole grain foods and were suspicious of additives; they militated against excessive alcohol and tobacco consumption. In 1938, they labeled cigarettes "Germany's deadliest consumer poison." And in 1939, the city of Dresden enacted a law that prohibited smoking in all public places.[37]

In the second view, science was perverted not by politicians, but by ambitious, dishonest, or fraudulent scientists. Nazi physicians betrayed their Hippocratic Oath and committed terrible crimes. Anthropologists, who lacked prestige and power in the

----

It is true that the Nazis imprisoned many noted scientists, mostly Jewish, and forced others to leave. German physics was particularly hard hit. Albert Einstein and Erwin Schrödinger emigrated. One of the ironies of the war is that relativistic physics, termed "Jewish physics" by the Nazis, formed the theoretical basis for building the atomic bomb.

Five future Nobel Laureates in biology were forced to leave; leading figures in medicine, such as Sigmund Freud, also fled for their lives. Between 1933 and 1938 some ten thousand Jewish physicians lost their jobs: some fled; many were murdered in concentration camps.

36. German physicists designed new rockets—which were to wreak havoc over England—and created the first electron microscopes; chemists first synthesized polyvinyl chloride, fabricated paper from oil, and harnessed geothermal energy.

37. Proctor, p. 239; and Proctor, "Nazi Doctors, Racial Medicine, and Human Experimentation," in George Annas and Michael Grodin, The Nazi Doctors and the Nuremberg Code: Human Rights in Human Experimentation (New York: Oxford University Press, 1992), p. 28. During this time, German scientists published the research on the deleterious effects of cigarettes. See my (with Ronald J. Troyer) Cigarettes: The Battle Over Smoking (New Brunswick, NJ: Rutgers University Press, 1983).

pre-Nazi era, sold their professional souls for political gain. "Finally they were respected as the experts that were to straighten out the problems of workers, soldiers, and murderers alike."[38] No doubt there is some truth in this account. Scientists—then and now—seek prestige and power. So do many in other professions. The weakness of this analysis is twofold: it confines inappropriate ambitions to Nazi scientists, and it treats the scientist as an isolated individual, rather than as a member of a profession and a citizen of a society.

Thinking of Nazi medicine as an anomaly or a perversion leads us, in my judgment, away from understanding. A better approach, it seems to me, comes from the work of Thomas Kuhn, a contemporary philosopher of science.[39] According to this account, Nazi scientists and physicians designed experiments and conducted protocols that were consistent with their worldview and the prevailing "knowledge" of their time. That we judge this racist is not the point; rather, Nazi physicians used the logic and techniques of science to pursue problems that they saw as scientifically relevant.

From a Kuhnian perspective, Nazi medicine became "normal science." It was unremarkable, not unusual at all in its day-to-day activities. Nazi scientists designed experiments, collected data, analyzed data, and published their results in scholarly journals; their success or failure in these activities influenced the relative advancement of their careers. Their behavior, in other words, was similar to that of scientists throughout the ages and in other cultures.

---

38. Benno Muller-Hill, *Murderous Science* (New York: Oxford University Press, 1989), p. 13.

39. Thomas Kuhn, *The Structure of Scientific Revolutions* (Chicago: University of Chicago Press, 1972). For Kuhn, day-to-day laboratory science, which he termed *normal science*, involves routinized behavior aimed at solving a series of shared problems. These problems are defined as important, as worth solving, because they are part of what Kuhn called a *paradigm*. Kuhn's central insight is that all scientific activity is derived from a paradigm, which is inevitably a reflection of culture and social structure. Thus science is seen not as intellectually independent from, but rather as a crucial part of, the surrounding world. For a review of the relation of science and society, see my (and Sheila Jasanoff, James Petersen, and Trevor Pinch) *The Handbook of Science and Technology Studies* (Newbury Park, CA: Sage Publications, 1995).

In his book, *Racial Hygiene*, Robert Proctor follows this Kuhnian perspective. He sees Nazi medicine neither as an anomaly nor a perversion. He does not examine individual physicians or their specific experiments; nor does he grant much attention to Hitler's Nazis. Rather, Proctor's analysis traces the pre-Nazi development of theories of racial hygiene and the successive symbiosis between Nazi political culture and medicine.[40]

Proctor shows how, in a certain sociohistorical context, the interaction between science and power led (and therefore still could lead) to unprecedented crimes. Nazis—physicians and politicians—believed that knowledge and control of human genetics was the "key to human destiny." They argued that Germany was "teetering on the brink of racial collapse" and that racial hygiene was needed to save Germany from "racial suicide." "Nazis took the major problems of the day—problems of race, gender, crime and poverty, and transformed them into medical or biological problems."[41] Thus physicians justified unpleasant tasks (e.g., murdering a mentally defective person) as necessary for the organic health of the larger society in the same way that contemporary physicians would justify the discomfort (and some risk) of immunizing a child for the benefit of society.

Proctor's conclusions are frightening: Scientists and physicians were not merely instruments of Nazi mass murder; they were creatively involved in the theorizing, in the planning, in the initiation, in the administration, and in the execution of the Holocaust! Far from being coerced into supporting the inhumane racial policies and programs of Nazi politicians, he argues, Germany's scientists and physicians helped formulate both their language and their legislation. Racial science became, in the Third Reich, normal science. Physicians became the gardeners of their culture, exterminating all undesirable weeds.

---

40. I found Mario Biagioli's discussion, "Science, Modernity and the 'Final Solution,' " in Saul Friedlander, *Probing the Limits of Representation: Nazism and the Final Solution* (Cambridge: Harvard University Press, 1992), p. 185ff., helpful in presenting Proctor's ideas.

41. Proctor, *Racial Hygiene* p. 286. Nazis were experts at what sociologists term the *medicalization* of a wide variety of conditions. Racial hygiene, properly applied, would eliminate human disease—"not just schizophrenia or flat feet, but also criminality, alcoholism and homosexuality."

medical experiments

Between 1939 and 1945, Nazi scientists conducted at least seventy formal medical experiments in concentration camps; at least seven thousand persons were forced to be the subjects for these experiments. Each experiment followed standard scientific method and attempted, to the extent possible, to control all extraneous variables. Each followed a carefully designed and elaborate protocol which designated how subjects were chosen, how materials were collected, and the relationship of data to the larger purpose of the experiment.

All protocols were subject to elaborate approval processes: typically they were planned at major universities and research centers in Germany and Austria, whose laboratories analyzed blood and tissue samples collected from prisoners; the army medical corps and the medical services of the SS coordinated the experiments, usually conducted by the two hundred German physicians who were stationed at concentration camps.[42]

There were two broad categories of experiments: those primarily concerned with medical practice, and those concerned with racist ideology.[43]

medical treatment

Within this first category there were two types of experiments: those related to survival and rescue, and those involving treatment. All

---

42. See Lifton. Some Jewish physicians were forced, and some volunteered, to help in these experiments. For accounts by two such physicians, see Miklos Nyiszli, *Auschwitz: A Doctor's Eyewitness Account* (New York: Frederick Fell Inc., 1960), and Elie Aron Cohen, *The Abyss: A Confession* (New York: Norton, 1973).

43. Specific data from this section come from Nava Cohen's article on "Medical Experiments" in the *Encyclopedia of the Holocaust* (p. 956ff.). Cohen makes the following ethical distinction: Experiments on medical practice have "objectives compatible with medicine, but whose means were unethical"; on the other hand, the very purpose of racial experiments "violated medical ethics" and were "irreconcilable with the accepted norms of medical research."

I am not comfortable with this means-end distinction which seems to confer some legitimacy on any experiments whose objectives are compatible with traditional medicine. This same means-end distinction has spawned a strange debate among medical ethicists: whether or not to use the data from Nazi experiments. I cannot imagine that the victims, having been treated as un-humans, should today be treated as data. This would be their ultimate dishonor.

survival and rescue experiments were conducted at Dachau. They were designed to test the human potential for survival under harsh conditions, with the ultimate goal of saving German lives.

The purpose of high-altitude experiments was to help design equipment that might save air crews subject to high-altitude disasters. They were conducted by a physician from the German Experimental Institute for Aviation in Berlin and by an air force physician. Victims were put into pressure chambers. It was known that personnel could not survive for long at altitudes greater than 3.7 miles without oxygen and special equipment. At simulated eight-mile altitudes, experimental victims had spasms and lost consciousness; at nine miles, they had severe breathing problems. Nonetheless, experiments continued until altitude simulated thirteen miles, the maximum altitude at which Axis aircraft operated. Data collection was augmented by film of the victim's trauma. Of approximately two hundred subjects, seventy to eighty lost their lives as a result of the experiments.[44]

Freezing experiments, designed by two professors from Kiel University, attempted to establish the most effective method of treating persons who had been exposed to prolonged cold, either in freezing seas or on land. Victims of the first type of experiment were put into a tank of ice water and kept there for seventy to ninety minutes, or as long as it took for them to lose consciousness. Physicians then attempted to revive them. Of three hundred subjects, eighty to ninety lost their lives. In experiments involving dry cold, sixty victims were put naked into the snow-covered courtyard and kept there for nine to fifteen hours. These experiments were terminated prematurely (at least from the experimenter's perspective) because the screams of the prisoners disturbed Dachau's civilian population.

Other experiments were designed to improve medical treatment, particularly related to battle injuries and immunization against disease.[45] At Ravensbruck physicians conducted two experi-

---

44. After the war, the U.S. Army expressed interest in this research. In fact, the army hired Siegfried Ruff, one of the principal investigators of the high altitude experiment. Others who participated in the research were recruited into the American program, Operation Paperclip, designed to exploit German scientific talent. Justifying American actions, one official claimed that there was no need to continue "beating a dead Nazi horse" (quoted in Linda Hunt, "U.S. Coverup of Nazi Scientists," *Bulletin of the Atomic Scientists*, April 1985, p. 20).

ments on the treatment of war wounds, both on Polish female prisoners. They injected prisoners with gangrene bacilli and then treated them with sulfanilamide, a new drug at the time. The original experimental protocol caused no deaths, so physicians injected increasing concentrations of bacilli. Eventually, seventy-five died. In a second set of experiments, physicians broke or smashed bones of healthy prisoners, who were then given various treatments.[46] Eleven of twenty-four victims died, the remainder were maimed for life.

Here are some other examples of experiments related to the treatment of war wounds: At Dachau and Ravensbruck, physicians injected pus into soft tissue to cause severe gangrene.[47] Of sixty victims, all non-Jewish religious prisoners, nineteen lost their lives. At Auschwitz and Buchenwald, physicians inflicted on victims second- and third-degree burns; at Dachau, four victims were shot point-blank and then treated with an experimental anticoagulant. All died.

Several experiments had as their goal the more effective treatment of disease. In one experiment conducted by civilian physicians at Dachau, twelve hundred prisoners—most of them Roman Catholic priests—were given malaria. Thirty died from the disease; another three hundred to four hundred died from treatment overdoses. Similar experiments, all with disastrous effects, were designed to test treatments for typhus and yellow fever.

racial experiments

There were two categories of racial experiments: those designed to promote racist ideology, and those designed to facilitate the destruction of the Jews. At Auschwitz, Josef Mengele studied twins and dwarfs. Few details of the dwarf experiments survive; in studying twins, Mengele's goal was to establish a genetic cause for twinning. He hoped that the future application of this principle might

---

45. Numerous experiments on treatment of chemical warfare injuries were also conducted.

46. In a particularly grisly variation of this protocol, limbs of mentally ill patients were amputated for possible transplantation to soldiers. Victims were then put to death.

47. Karl Gebhardt, eventually sentenced to death for his work in the Ravensbruck experiments, was a former president of the German Red Cross.

eventually double the birthrate of the Aryan population. He conducted various clinical tests: blood, X-ray, and bone measurement. He injected twins with various substances, often in the eyes, apparently in an attempt to change eye color. He then killed them with chloroform injections to the heart. He also studied the course of various diseases, especially tuberculosis, on Gypsies: one twin pair received a disease inoculum, the other was the control. In total, Mengele's experiments involved some fifteen hundred twins; about two hundred survived.[48]

Nazi physicians conducted a wide range of serological and anatomical experiments. For example, 115 Jews in good health were killed in gas chambers at Sachsenhausen; their corpses were then sent to the University of Strassburg where a research team attempted to prove that the skeletal structure of communists and Jews was inferior.

At Auschwitz physicians sterilized men, women, and children with large doses of X rays, which caused severe burns. They sent the castrated testicles to the Breslau Institute for histopathological examination. Almost all victims were then sent to gas chambers. Several experiments were designed to find the most efficient way to sterilize large numbers of people. At Auschwitz and Ravensbruck, Dr. Carl Clauberg developed a procedure where he, and ten assistants, could sterilize one thousand women per day: they injected caustic chemicals into the uterus, which also severely damaged the ovaries. In a second part of the protocol, they removed women's ovaries and sent them to Berlin to confirm damage to ovarian tissue.

the american connection[49]

It was the United States, not Germany, that first actually practiced eugenics. Defined as the science of improving the biologi-

---

48. For a recollection of these experiments by one of the twin victims, see Eva Mozes Kor, "The Mengele Twins and Human Experiments: A Personal Account." In Annas and Grodin, pp. 53–60. Ms. Kor is president and founder of Children of Auschwitz Nazi Deadly Lab Experiments (CANDLES).

49. There was also a British connection. Eugenics was founded, and the term coined, by Frances Galton and "adopted by the whole of the infant British Sociology." In 1929, Karl Pearson, whose statistical techniques are widely and routinely used by contemporary sociologists, claimed that "the survival of the unfit is a marked characteristic of modern town life" (quoted in Bauman, *Modernity and Ambivalence*, p. 33). In recent years some eugenical ideas have reappeared in the work of a new discipline termed *social biology*.

cal quality of the human race, eugenics promotes selective breeding and the concomitant deletion of harmful genes from the human gene pool. Eugenicists hoped to identify people with "good" genes and encourage them to have large numbers of progeny; those with "bad" genes would be discouraged—or prevented—from breeding.[50]

Decades before the Nazis took power, eugenic thought had been translated into legislation. In 1907 the State of Indiana passed the first laws that permitted the forced sterilization of the mentally ill and criminally insane; by the late 1920s, twenty-eight American states had such laws. In 1922, Calvin Coolidge argued: "The laws of biology have demonstrated that Nordic peoples deteriorate when mixing with other races."[51] Eleven years before Hitler took power, a U.S. president, not some rabble-rouser, was purporting what today we would deem the worst sort of vulgar racism.

By 1930 some fifteen thousand individuals, all incarcerated in prisons or mental institutions, were sterilized, most against their will. By the beginning of the war, more than thirty-nine thousand individuals, almost half of them in California, had been sterilized on eugenic grounds.[52]

Many American scientists supported Nazi racist policies and even applauded Hitler. Clarence G. Campbell, president of the American Eugenetic Research Association, offered this toast, "To that great leader, Adolf Hitler," at the 1935 International Population Congress in Berlin. And in a 1942 issue of the prestigious *Journal of Heredity*, American geneticist T. Ellinger praised the Nazis' "large scale breeding project, with the purpose of eliminating from the nation the hereditary attributes of the Semitic race." In the same year that gas chambers were installed at Auschwitz, Ellinger proclaimed that it is more "merciful to kill the unfortunate outright."[53]

---

50. For further information, see Daniel Kevles, *In the Name of Eugenics: Genetics and the Use of Human Heredity* (New York: Knopf, 1985), and Elazar Barkan, *Retreat of Scientific Racism: Changing Concepts of Race in Britain and the United States Between the World Wars* (Cambridge: Cambridge University Press, 1992).

51. Quoted in Bauman, *Modernity and Ambivalence*, p. 36.

52. Philip Reilly, *The Surgical Solution: A History of Involuntary Sterilization in the United States* (Baltimore: Johns Hopkins University Press, 1991).

53. Stefan Kuhl, *The Nazi Connection: Eugenics, American Racism and German National Socialism* (New York: Oxford University Press, 1994), pp. 27, 60.

Eugenics reached its peak between the two world wars before it was discredited by Nazi practices. But it did not disappear. In 1972, the United States Public Health Service made an astonishing admission: it had begun in 1932—and had continued for four decades—a clinical experiment that monitored, but did not treat, black men who had advanced syphilis. "The study had nothing to do with treatment; no new drugs were tested; neither was any effort made to establish the efficacy of old forms of treatment. It was a non-therapeutic experiment, aimed at compiling data on the effects of the spontaneous evolution of syphilis on black males."[54] The so-called Tuskegee Study of Untreated Syphilis, used as subjects 399 black men who suffered from advanced syphilis. Two hundred and one black males free of the disease served as controls.

Physicians who regularly examined the men, some the entire four decades, offered no treatment; they did not tell the men that they had syphilis.[55] According to experimental design, they monitored the progression of the disease. Investigators prevented the men, the so-called subjects, from seeking treatment at other government facilities; so intent were they to prevent treatment that investigators even procured draft deferments from World War II for these men. Upon the death of each subject, investigators conducted an autopsy as part of the experimental design.

Even in 1972 public health officials, though highly critical of the study that their institution had sponsored, offered certain defenses on behalf of the research. They claimed that the treatment available in the 1930s, mostly heavy metals such as arsenic and bismuth, caused more harm than good. Nonetheless such treatment was standard medical practice at that time; moreover, as penicillin became available in the mid 1940s, it too was withheld from the experimental subjects.

---

54. James H. Jones, *Bad Blood: The Tuskegee Syphilis Experiment* (New York: Free Press, 1981), p. 2. This is the best and most complete reference for this issue.

55. Most thought they were being treated for "rheumatism or bad stomachs": some were told that they had "bad blood" (Jones, p. 5). Data collection involved the analysis of spinal fluid, obtained from the men through painful lumbar punctures which often induced severe headaches.

The Tuskegee study was still collecting data on the few surviving subjects when a reporter broke the story in the *Washington Star* on 25 July 1972. Citizens and scientists alike professed shock and outrage. Congress conducted hearings.

Nonetheless: The research was no secret, certainly not within the medical community. Between 1936 and 1973 (after public disclosure), thirteen articles about the Tuskegee research were published in medical journals. From the first article, "Untreated Syphilis in the Male Negro: A Comparative Study of Treated and Untreated Cases," to the last, "Aortic Regurgitation in the Tuskegee Study of Untreated Syphilis,"[56] the design and intent of the study were known to any casual reader of medical journals.

Nor was the study a secret among public health officials. In addition to the U.S. Public Health Service in Washington, the study was cosponsored by the Macon (Alabama) County Health Department, the Veterans Administration Hospital in Tuskegee, the Tuskegee Institute,[57] and—later on—the prestigious Centers for Disease Control in Atlanta.

It seems obvious to us that the study, in which white physicians knowingly allowed harm to come to their black subjects, was profoundly racist. Did the investigators hate blacks? Probably not. Their motives were more complex, probably influenced as much by belief in science as by belief in race differences.[58]

---

56. *Venereal Disease Information* 17(1936): 260–65; *Journal of Chronic Diseases* 26(1973): 187–94. Other articles were published in prestigious journals such as the *Milbank Memorial Fund Quarterly* and the *Archives of Internal Medicine*.

57. A black institution founded by Booker T. Washington.

58. Jones emphasizes the prevailing racism among public health officials and physicians which permitted, even encouraged, such studies. Nonetheless he presents a sympathetic portrait of the principal investigators of the Tuskegee study, claiming that they were truly interested in alleviating syphilis among blacks. According to prevailing medical thought, syphilis was believed to affect blacks very differently from whites. Were this proved false (as it was!), these public health officials thought that it would be easier to fund syphilis eradication programs for blacks. They were "racial liberals by the standards of the 1930s. Within the medical profession they were truly progressive" (p. 172).

Critics have not focused on the sexist nature of this research. The study never even addressed, and therefore could not choose to ignore, syphilis among women. The research design entirely excluded females. Moreover, in not treating men, investigators gave no consideration of the risk to the disease for the subjects' female sexual partners.

In 1972, John Heller, who served as project director from 1943 to 1948, made two claims: "there is nothing in the experiment that was unethical or unscientific."[59] The ethical claim is difficult to buy. In addition to allowing harm, investigators showed a profound disrespect for their patients as human beings by not informing them—worse, by lying to them—about their condition.[60] The scientific claim is a curious one. Proponents such as Heller mistakenly—and very dangerously—justify any scientific activity as long as it is well designed. To put it bluntly: This argument, so rooted in our scientific culture, sounds very much like Nazi logic.[61]

enlightenment?

Tuskegee and Auschwitz are not identical, but they are obviously related to one another. Both Tuskegee and Auschwitz, it seems to me, can only be understood as products of our modern, rational, scientific world.

---

59. Quoted in Jones, p. 8.

60. Contemporary regulations designed to protect human subjects revolve around these criteria: that the experimenter "do no harm," or at least that any potential harm (as in experimental treatment) is outweighed by potential expected good; and that the experimenters "respect" their subjects, usually through an "informed consent" which explains the goals of the experiment, and its risks, to the subject. These rules, which do not always work so well, were derived from the Nuremberg trials of Nazi physicians. Partly as a result of the Tuskegee revelations, they were formalized in the National Research Act of 1974, which mandates approval of all federally funded proposed research with human subjects.

61. The American prosecutor at Nuremberg claimed that the concentration camp experiments were "insufficient and unscientific," "a ghastly failure, as well as a hideous crime." According to Robert Lifton, *The Nazi Doctors*, Nazi doctors corrupted their Hippocratic Oath. In so doing, they subverted the science of healing into a practice of killing. For Lifton, Nazi medicine was not just corrupted; it was inverted. Thus Lifton goes to great lengths to show that Mengele's work was unscientific. Only by this method can Lifton delegitimize Mengele *as a scientist*.

As Robert Proctor, *Racial Hygiene*, laments: "one is almost left with the impression that if such experiments had been 'good science,' this would somehow make a difference in our attitudes toward them."

Opponents attacked the legitimacy of the Tuskegee study by claiming that it was "bad" science. This tactic was especially prominent in a 1993 PBS television documentary, *Bad Blood*. For a discussion of good science versus bad science in the Tuskegee experiment, see Arthur Caplan, "When Evil Intrudes," *Hastings Center Report* 22 (1992): 29–32.

The scientific enlightenment, which arose in Europe in the eighteenth century, was predicated on two related notions: (1) that human beings could control, even dominate, nature; no mere victims of fate, humans could and would control their destiny, and (2) this control, expressed through instrumental reason and logic, and embodied in the method of science, could be used in a wise and judicious way to improve the condition of human-kind. Henceforth, human beings would act in rational ways— they could weigh costs against benefits, means against ends—to improve their own, and their fellow citizens', lot in life.

Part of this belief was that science could and should be used to solve social problems. This way of looking at the world, this ideology, is termed *scientism*, and it has characterized most West-ern societies for the past two hundred years.[62] A variant of scientism is biologism, the belief that social problems can be solved through applied biology. When biologism is combined with racism, the result can be explosive.[63]

The Nazi experience discredited biologism, at least in its vul-gar eugenical form. For some thinkers, Auschwitz casts doubt on scientism as well. For the gardening metaphor is entirely consis-tent with, and in many ways grew out of, scientism. It is the sci-entist who prunes the trees, uproots the weeds, and especially authorizes (or diagnoses) some plants as weeds, others as flowers.

After Auschwitz, could one still think of history as the un-folding of a scroll, where fate and ignorance are replaced, slowly

---

62. "Scientism is present where people draw on widely shared images and notions about the scientific community and its beliefs and practices in or-der to add weight to arguments which they are advancing, or to practices which they are promoting, or to values and policies whose adoption they are advo-cating." Politicians and scientists are "predisposed to make use of the avail-able cultural resources to rationalize and justify beliefs and attitudes" which are a "function of the social and political system of which they are a part." Ian Cameron and David Edge, *Scientific Images and Their Social Uses* (London: Butterworth, 1979), pp. 3, 5.

63. According to John Lukacs, biological determinism provides an ideo-logical base for reactionary worldviews. "The experience of science and medi-cine under the Nazis is by no means the first, and by no means the last, time intellectuals have hoisted a banner proclaiming that biology is destiny" (quoted in Proctor, *Racial Hygiene*, p. 297).

but progressively, with reason and enlightenment? Perhaps reason and mass murder are not the antithesis of one another. Perhaps modernity and scientism are intrinsically related to Auschwitz. Hannah Arendt, whose ghost haunts this book, wrote: "Progress and Doom are two sides of the same medal."[64]

This notion, that enlightenment may lead to disaster as well as to Beethoven's Ninth Symphony, was by no means original.[65] In the 1940s, Theodor Adorno and his colleagues[66] undertook a difficult intellectual task: to understand the malaise of modern civilization. For them, the Holocaust arose as a (but not the only) logical outcome of what they termed the *dialectic of enlightenment.* Surely one cannot deny the progressive elements of our modern scientific world. Yet there is another side, another part of the whole. "No universal history leads from savagery to humanitarianism, but there is one leading from the slingshot to the megaton bomb."[67]

Through so-called instrumental reasoning, human beings not only dominate nature, but they destroy what is unique in themselves. In a technical society, human beings become just another product; the qualitative diminishes as the quantitative overwhelms. "Progress thus turned out to spawn its antithesis, a barbarism all the more brutal because of its use of modern techniques of control."[68]

---

64. Arendt, *The Origins of Totalitarianism*, p. vii.

65. In 1880, for example, Friedrich Nietzsche wrote: "A century of barbarism is beginning, and the sciences will be its handmaiden." Martin Heidegger, with whom Arendt studied, was similarly pessimistic about the value of the Enlightenment.

66. Prior to the Nazi takeover, Adorno and his colleagues—including Max Horkheimer, Erich Fromm, Herbert Marcuse, and Walter Benjamin—were at the University of Frankfurt. With the exception of Benjamin, who committed suicide prior to his capture by the Nazis, these scholars fled to the United States. My presentation will flow more easily by focusing on Adorno's two books: *Dialectic of Enlightenment* (New York: Herder and Herder, 1972), written in 1944 with Horkheimer, and *Negative Dialectics* (New York: Seabury Press, 1987), written in 1966. For the analysis of Adorno's thought, I have learned much from Martin Jay, *Adorno* (Cambridge: Harvard University Press, 1984), and Gilian Rose, *The Melancholy Science: An Introduction to the Thought of Theodor W. Adorno* (New York: Columbia University Press, 1978).

67. Adorno, *Negative Dialectics*, p. 320.

68. Jay, p. 38.

After the war, Adorno and several colleagues struggled to understand the implications of Auschwitz for our modern world. Like Arendt, they believed that the Holocaust was an explicitly modern phenomenon. In *The Authoritarian Personality*,[69] written in 1950, they sought to uncover the causes of prejudice in any and all modern societies. Using the techniques of modern social science, they attempted to identify individuals with a "pre-fascist" authoritarian personality. Such individuals, they hypothesized, would be "at the same time enlightened and superstitious, proud to be an individualist and in constant fear of not being like all the others, jealous of his independence and inclined to submit blindly to power and authority."[70]

Adorno concluded that individual prejudice resulted from parent-child relationships.[71] For him, prejudiced persons tended to be ones whose socialization emphasized dominance, intolerance, conformity, and sexual repression. Such individuals would be incapable of appreciating novel experiences and would lack critical self-reflection.

On the face of it, this would seem to be what I termed in chapter 2 a *pathology* explanation. It is, in fact, partly psychological. But Adorno and his colleagues were fundamentally dialecticians: individuals were simultaneously a product of psychology, culture, and history. "The prejudiced person," they wrote, "must largely be considered the outcome of civilization," characterized by increased division of labor, monopolistic institutions, and the success of competition.[72] Whether or not the authoritarian

---

69. Theodor Adorno, Else Frenkel-Brunswik, Daniel Levinson, and R. Nevitt Sanford, *The Authoritarian Personality* (New York: Harper, 1950). The study was designed and conducted in New York, where the authors had fled from the Nazis. Soon after the end of the war, Adorno and Horkheimer moved back to Germany.

Susan Buck-Morss's book, *The Origin of Negative Dialectics* (New York: Free Press, 1977), p. 181ff., helped me understand *The Authoritarian Personality*.

70. Adorno et al., p. ix.

71. Here Erich Fromm's (and Freud's) influence is evident. Fromm maintained that each society has its own libidinal structure, derived from a combination of basic human drives and social factors. When the social structure of a society changed, so did the social function of its libidinal structure. When the rate of change between the two varied, Fromm argued, an explosive situation could result.

72. Adorno et al., p. 389.

personality becomes fascist in behavior would depend "on the most powerful economic interests . . . about which the great majority of people would have little to say."[73]

What are we to make of Adorno's thesis? As with Arendt,[74] Adorno developed many of these ideas in the 1940s, when rather little was known about the Holocaust. Moreover, Adorno, like Arendt, had an agenda writ large: not just the Holocaust, but all contemporary modern life. One sign of intellectual influence, and this more for Adorno than Arendt: a half century later, their ideas and insights are still vigorously debated.

For my purposes, the principal problems with Adorno's work are similar to the limitations of Arendt's study. Adorno's analysis exists either at an abstract "macro" level or a psychological "micro" level. In between modernity on the one hand, and authoritarian personalities on the other, there is no middle. We read of anti-Semitism, to be sure. But Adorno gives scant attention to institutional anti-Semitism.[75] He pays little heed to organized religion or educational curriculum. These institutions, on which sociologists focus so much of their attention, are underdeveloped in Adorno's analysis.

Another problem, I think, is that modernity is almost always presented as a regressive force. Adorno and his colleagues claimed to be dialecticians, but—perhaps understandably —they became quite pessimistic after Auschwitz. Like Arendt, some Frankfurt theorists tended to be quite hostile toward anything in politics or culture, and particularly in science and technology, which was new. After Auschwitz they retreated into an analysis of aesthetics, and saw change not as leading to progress, but rather to chaos.

One final criticism: The data collected and analyzed in *The Authoritarian Personality* never confirmed Adorno's hy-

---

73. Adorno et al., p. 158.

74. Though their analyses had much in common (and they must have known each other), Arendt and Adorno, two intellectual giants of the midcentury, did not cite one another. In a letter to Karl Jaspers, Arendt referred to Adorno as a "repulsive" human being!

75. Adorno's conception of anti-Semitism is close to Hitler's "emotional" anti-Semitism.

pothesis. Modern society probably produces authoritarian personalities, a concern to all those who worry about future holocausts.
But Adorno and his colleagues failed to predict in any consistent
way the correlates and antecedents of such a personality.[76]

a dialogue

So far in this book, my attempt to understand the Holocaust has
been in the form of a dialogue: mostly with scholars and survivors, but also with artists and writers. Aside from Primo Levi, I
have been most influenced by three scholars: Hannah Arendt,
Richard Rubenstein, and Zygmunt Bauman. Arendt's insights
cannot be overestimated. In the 1940s, before the Holocaust was
even named, her writings were framing future dialogue.

Rubenstein (a theologian) and Bauman (a sociologist) belong to
a second generation of scholars. Following Arendt, each has sought—
as have I—to see individual behavior not as isolated or idiosyncratic,
but rather as nested within social structure; in turn, each has seen contemporaneous bureaucracy as historically located. In the final analysis, each sees the Holocaust as a (not the) result of modernity.

Rubenstein and Bauman begin with the ideas of Max Weber. "I was struck," Rubenstein wrote, "by the degree to which
Weber's model of bureaucracy as a coldly rational impersonal
instrument for domination could be taken as a blueprint" for the
Nazis.[77] Thus bureaucratic behavior—with its focus so narrowly
on task, on technique, on cost efficiency—seems to permit, seems

---

76. In fact, one retrospective analysis of the authoritarian personality was
subtitled: "An Inquiry Into the Failure of Social Science Research to Produce
Demonstrable Knowledge." See David McKinney, *The Authoritarian Personality
Studies* (The Hague: Mouton, 1973).

77. Richard Rubenstein, "Anticipation of the Holocaust in the Political Sociology of Max Weber." In Lyman Letgers (ed.), *Western Society After the Holocaust*
(Boulder: Westview Press, 1983), p. 166. Rubenstein did not suggest in any way
that Weber was a forerunner of Nazism, only that "Weber's reflections on the organization, methods, and personnel of bureaucracy have a chilling aura of proph-
ecy about them." His thesis was controversial, to say the least. Here is the reply of
Guenther Ross "Response to Rubenstein," a renowned scholar of Max Weber: "My
disagreement with Professor Rubenstein is total. There is just about no sentence in
his presentation that I can accept on empirical or analytical grounds" (p. 187).

to allow, seems to—dare we say it—"anticipate" administered mass death.

For Bauman as well, the "potential" for a Holocaust exists in the "instrumental rationality" of bureaucratic culture. Viewing humans as—to use Descartes's phrase—masters and possessors of nature: "Bureaucratic culture prompts us to view society as an object of administration, as a collection of many 'problems' to be solved, as nature to be 'controlled,' 'mastered' and 'improved' or 'remade.'" If Jews are defined as a legitimate problem, if a garden needs weeding, then there is surely a "rational" way to proceed. "Our knowledge of bureaucratic rationality is at its most dazzling," Bauman wrote, "once we realize the extent to which the very idea of the [Final Solution] was an outcome of the bureaucratic culture."[78]

Here murder, even mass murder—especially mass murder!—becomes not some irrational, atavistic outburst, but rather the quintessence of our modern world, another rational business decision. The most shattering lesson that we learn from the Holocaust, Bauman declares, is that "the choice of physical extermination as the right means . . . was the product of routine bureaucratic procedures: means-end calculus, budget balancing, universal rule application."[79]

The Holocaust is writ large: not only a product of our (note the pronoun) civilization, but a sign of its "progress." In *The Cunning of History*, Rubenstein concludes: "The Holocaust bears witness to *the advance of civilization*, I repeat, to the advance of

---

78. Bauman, *Modernity and the Holocaust*, p. 15.
79. Bauman, *Modernity and the Holocaust*, p. 17. The Jewish Councils, which the Nazis put in charge of the ghettos, also used means-end rationality to try to save as many Jews as possible. But in the final analysis, according to Bauman, they assisted the Nazis: "The Nazis saw to it that rationality meant co-operation, that everything the Jews did to serve their own interest brought the Nazi objectives somewhat nearer to full success . . . The Jews could therefore play into the hands of their oppressors, facilitate their task, bring closer their own perdition, while guided in their action by the rationally interpreted purpose of survival" (p. 137). Here Bauman differed from Arendt, who accused the Judenrat not so much of rational behavior, but of immoral behavior (see Alan Milchman and Alan Rosenberg's review of Bauman's book in *Holocaust and Genocide Studies* 5 [1990]: 337–342.).

civilization, to the point at which large scale massacre is no longer a crime."[80]

It is not that modernity automatically results in a Holocaust, but that it is a potential inherent in modernity. The Holocaust, Bauman maintained, was "an outcome of a unique encounter between factors by themselves quite ordinary and common" in our modern culture. The Holocaust was "born and executed in our modern rational society, at the high stage of civilization and at the peak of human cultural achievement, and for that reason it is a problem of that society, civilization and culture."[81] Strong words indeed! For Rubenstein and Bauman use the Holocaust to call into question, to deconstruct, our cherished notions of civilization and its progress. Though their scholarly vision is somewhat different from my own,[82] I find their visions strong and challenging.

Let me return to a Bauman metaphor which I cited in chapter 1. The Holocaust, he wrote, can be viewed as "a window, rather than a picture on the wall. Looking through that window,

---

80. Rubenstein, *The Cunning of History,* p. 90.

81. Bauman, *Modernity and the Holocaust,* p. x.

82. For Rubenstein, bureaucracy and secularism, both products of modernity and progenitors of the Holocaust, are themselves products of a biblical tradition. He focuses on Luther's intolerance and hatred, a natural product of his "dichotomous division of mankind into the elect and the reprobate" (*The Cunning of History,* p. 93). Rubenstein's dialogue, then, is theological, specifically Judaic.

In the last chapter of his *Modernity and the Holocaust,* Bauman announces the beginning of a project: "The construction of a theory of morality capable of accommodating in full the new knowledge generated by the Holocaust" (p. 169). I am uncomfortable with his consequent discussion of evil, which he sees as a personal attribute, not as a cultural outcome. Moreover, in attempting to see the world in terms of personal good and evil, Bauman denies the gray zone—the center of my own understanding. Finally, I am suspicious of the attempt, a secularized theodicy, to have as an outcome of the Holocaust a more moral society.

As a scholar interested in dialogue, I have an additional complaint about both authors. Each is reluctant to acknowledge his intellectual debts. Citations to Weber are common; there are a few acknowledgments to Arendt, though I find them perfunctory; but each author ignores Adorno, Horkheimer, and other Frankfurt scholars to whom he is obviously indebted. Building on their foundations, joining an ongoing dialogue, would have made both books much stronger.

one can catch a glimpse of many things otherwise invisible." In the concluding chapter, I want to look through that window. What I hope to glimpse is the stealthy and furtive shadow of a future memory.

5   after

Ich bin ein Berliner.
—John F. Kennedy, 1962

*I would rather be a Jew than a German. They live with a past that is
more difficult for them.*
—Lucy Dawidowicz, 1985

*What remains is a central, deadening sense of despair over the human
species. . . . If one keeps at the Holocaust long enough, then sooner or
later the ultimate personal truth begins to reveal itself: one knows,
finally, that one might either do it, or be done to.*
—George Kren and Leon Rappaport

Memories of a survivor: Toward the conclusion of his epic film,
Shoah, Claude Lanzmann asks Itsak Zuckerman, one of the
few survivors of the Warsaw uprising, to summarize his experience. Zuckerman does not play media games. He pauses too long
and then reaches back across four decades of memory; he averts
his eyes and with some difficulty almost mumbles: "I began
drinking after the war. It was very difficult." Then he adds: "If
you could lick my heart, it would poison you."

Memories of a tourist: Jerusalem, 1980. I am at Yad Vashem,
the museum of the Holocaust in Jerusalem. I walk from one exhibit to the next, each lit by harsh spotlights, blackness in between. I don't know what to think; I don't know what to feel. I
am overwhelmed.

Today I reach back over only one decade of memory; I remember little. I have saved one peculiar memory, not of an exhibit of Nazi memorabilia, but of two other tourists, a Hasidic
man and his son. The man, my age, with long pais, and dressed in
the obligatory black suit and hat, looking appropriately somber

amidst the surrounding Holocaust relics. Perhaps he is thinking of childhood stories, of family (even parents) who perished. The boy, about ten and dressed identically, is misbehaving—playing with the odd lighting, dancing in and out of the shadows. He is bored: this is not his story.

I also remember, but it is a shadowy and dim memory, a memorial constructed from tiny lights. Years later Raul Hilberg tells me: "You and I know that the Yad Vashem memorials are 70 percent kitsch." Then, he says, and this I remember clearly: "The children's memorial with all those lights—what's the difference between that and the walkway between Terminal B and Terminal C at United Airlines in Chicago?"

Now, when I fly out of O'Hare Airport, I have a problem. I am unable to exercise control over an improbable image; that passageway reminds me (ridiculously, I know) of the Holocaust. Holocaust has become (again, this is Hilberg's term) "holokitsch."

in memoriam

Warsaw: November 1990.

It is a red-letter day for Poland. Tomorrow will mark the first free election in the history of Poland. The candidates are charismatic Lech Wałęsa, winner of the Nobel Prize for peace, star of the American media, and Tadeusz Mazowiecki, quiet and scholarly, currently the prime minister. Wałęsa has just hinted (rather heavily) that the Catholic Mazowiecki has Jewish ancestry. "I can prove that my forefathers were all Poles," Wałęsa says. "I am clean. I am a Pole."

Five decades ago there were 3.5 million Jews in this country, 3.2 million of whom were murdered by the Nazis with more than a little cooperation from the Polish people. Today only about fifty thousand still live here. Wałęsa's charge is disgraceful. Mazowiecki cannot decide whether to ignore the charge or give it publicity and credibility through denial.

Here at an academic conference, I am one of thirty professors on a bus tour of the city. Tours are always strange and disorienting: one speeds by, or perhaps stops for a few moments at, various noteworthy places in history. Some cognitive leap, or perhaps simple osmosis, is supposed to occur in this bus ride through time and over hallowed ground. I expect and wait to feel some given emotion: perhaps disgust, perhaps awe.

It's raining and thus hard to see through the fog and wet streaks on the bus windows. We drive past the Palace of Culture, a huge structure built by the Russians, which all Poles seem to dislike—obviously a proxy for hating Russians. Joke: Where is the best view of Warsaw? From the Palace, because then you don't see the Palace! Since the fall of the communist government this joke is told in public. We do not stop to see the view.

We drive by the only synagogue left (there were thirty) from prewar Warsaw. The Nazis did not destroy this one, the finest of all; rather they turned it into a barn for their horses. Now it is restored, a synagogue once again. There is no time to stop at this place of torahs, prayer shawls, and horse manure. I rub the window with my sleeve; the waters part for a brief moment, but I cannot feel the place. Like the Hasidic boy at Yad Vashem, I cannot grasp this story.

We drive faster now. I try to grasp the significance of various palaces, including the one where the Warsaw Pact was signed. A symbol of the cold war, this particular palace is in eclipse.

Then we come to the Murano quarter, the site of the Warsaw ghetto. Three hundred thousand human beings did not survive here, starved on an official ration of 180 calories per day and sent to gas at Treblinka. Most wanted to join the transports just to escape. Ludwig Fischer, the SS governor of the Warsaw district, said: "The Jews will die from hunger and destitution, and a cemetery is all that will remain of the Jewish question." I try to feel the tragedy of the place, but the ghetto has long been obliterated. In its place are ugly apartment blocks. "Artificial" is the term Primo Levi used to describe this site. I feel empty. There is no hallowed ground here.

Out of the bus, I walk to the memorial that commemorates the ghetto. It stands in a plain square-block park: yellow grass, no trees. It is made from black granite originally (and ironically) purchased by the Nazis to memorialize Hitler. The sculpture depicts brave fighters on top, starving people on bottom. I think of Raul Hilberg, for whom memorials ought not be too modern or too "socialist." "It's just Stalinist realism," he said to me a few months earlier, "interchangeable with similar statues in Moscow and Leningrad." Even more, Hilberg said that this particular memorial is "interchangeable with certain kinds of fascist artifacts."

Hilberg's negative words had shaped my memory even before my eyes have seen the monument. Who am I to dispute one of the best known of all Holocaust scholars? I think about his lines; I stare at the statue. I weep.

As I wipe away the tears, we get into the bus and drive past the home of Lazarus Zamenhoff. In 1887, he developed Esperanto (the word means "hopeful") as an international language. Zamenhof, a Jew, hoped that a common language might help avoid war. We do not stop here either, but rather turn south along the Vistula. I watch the water flow.

At home, I read about Holocaust memorials and monuments, the Warsaw memorial in particular. I am trying to reshape and refine my own memory. What is, and what should be, the message of a particular memorial? Ultimate suffering and tragedy, or survival and hope? Passive victims on their way to slaughter, or brave predecessors of Zion?

For some, I read, commemoration should be uplifting: Memorials to the Holocaust "should not just recall the barbarism of the Nazi regime," one critic wrote. In addition, "they should stir a revolt of the conscience, a rebellion of the mind, which is inseparably bound to the essence of true democracy."[1] So stated, the politics of memorials are explicit: They should mourn the tragedy, but they should also teach. But what is it that should be taught?

For James Young, a perceptive critic of Holocaust memorials, these monuments not only "reflect particular kinds of political and cultural knowledge," but they also . . . "determine the understanding future generations will have of this time." Yet "once created, memorials take on lives of their own, stubbornly resistant to the state's original intentions."[2] So the Warsaw ghetto

1. Adolf Rieth, *Monuments to the Victims of Tyranny* (New York: Praeger, 1968).

2. James E. Young, "Israel's memorial landscapes: Sho'ah, Heroism, and National Redemption," in Peter Hayes (ed.), *Lessons and Legacies: The Meaning of the Holocaust in a Changing World*, (Evanston: Northwestern University Press, 1991), pp. 173, 281.

memorial might contain cultural archetypes: "The lumbering mytho-proletarian figures of the Stalinist era."[3] But to the embarrassment of the state, the memorial has become a gathering site for all sorts of political protest. Even Palestinians assert their freedom from Israel in this place.

Armed with this knowledge, this understanding, my reconstructed memory, I do not wish back my tears.

collective memory

On the surface, this chapter concerns the way we think about the Holocaust today. At a deeper level, it is about time and memory and history.

Consider by analogy the French Revolution. Every generation of historians writes about that event not only as a past occurrence, but because of its ongoing relevance for contemporary culture. They use the French Revolution to ask: What is meant by freedom? What price does one pay for it? How might its quest devolve into violence and chaos? Some historians see the French Revolution as a glimmer of hope, to be realized at a later date; others see in it the mob's ugly violence.[4]

I wish to meditate about our "collective memory"[5] of the Holocaust. As the twentieth century draws to a close, what is the Holocaust to mean for us: A signal to the end of progress? A disastrous misstep in the upward progressive climb of human kind? A myth, even, as some outrageously maintain? What is our

---

3. Young, *The Texture of Memory: Holocaust Memorials and Meaning* (New Haven, Yale University Press, 1993), p. 157. Chapter 6 of this book tells the fascinating story of Nathan Rapaport's Warsaw sculpture.

4. My own discipline, sociology, was born in France as a conservative reaction to the mob violence from that revolution.

5. Here I use Maurice Halbwachs' concept, which begins with an individual's memory and follows the process by which that memory becomes (or fails to become) authoritative history. Thus does memory incorporate a political and economic component to go along with the psychological one that we all understand. Halbwachs' book, *On Collective Memory* was published in 1941. Three years later, while he was living in Paris, the Gestapo arrested and deported him to the Buchenwald concentration camp, where he died in 1945. His book was reissued by the University of Chicago Press in 1992.

responsibility to history? Who deserves honor? Who does not? What do we teach and what do we forget? Finally: What do we learn about ourselves?

To begin, I need to explore the connection between history, memory, and the future. In other words, I need to think about the meaning of time.

Time, we understand from common sense, is linear: past, present, and future. Causation, supposedly, is one-way: the present is dependent on the past, the future upon the present. But for sociologists, the world of our existence is more complicated. For we understand that the past not only molds the present, but at the same time, the present sculpts the past.

This proposition—that the present forms the past—holds true for both memory and history. As we grow older and progress through our life cycle, our view of our own past changes. After Auschwitz, survivors typically describe idyllic childhoods: gone are petty family disputes, troubles at school (save those from anti-Semitism), and banal existences—swept away by train, gas, and flame.

A character in Cynthia Ozick's novella, *The Shawl*, says of the Holocaust: "Before is a dream. After is a joke. Only during stays. And to call it a life is a lie."[6] The Holocaust must remain unframed and unsettled, unforgotten—and always, welcome or not, central. A survivor remembered attending his first funeral in America: "I couldn't understand all the fuss," he told me: "the weeping, the wailing, the procession, the fine words . . . after Auschwitz," he said, "what was the big deal?" The Holocaust, in vivid color, was reality, is reality, will always be reality. Life after the Holocaust, by contrast, is pale.

Survivors may think of the Holocaust through their gut. Contemporary Americans, a generation and a continent removed, think about the Holocaust through language. For the words we use, our available vocabulary, are nothing less than the building blocks of our thought.

Today we think of a phenomenon called "the Holocaust." Until relatively recently, however, the Nazi mass murder of the

---

6. Cynthia Ozick, *The Shawl* (New York: Knopf, 1989), p. 58.

Jews had no commonly accepted name. According to the *Encyclopedia of the Holocaust*, the term comes from an ancient Greek word *holokauston*, a sacrifice consumed by fire. In the Book of Samuel, *holocaust* means a burnt offering to God. Gradually it came to mean large-scale human destruction.[7]

Not until the 1950s did the term *Holocaust* become synonymous with the Nazi genocide of the Jews. The U.S. Library of Congress did not create the subject heading "Holocaust—Jewish, 1939–1945" until 1968. Now the word *Holocaust*, (always capitalized, presumably for grammatical respect) refers to a specific, bounded historical event.

The point is this: Until a phenomenon has a commonly agreed upon name, it lacks a certain cognitive reality. The way in which we define a subject and identify it determines, at least in part, the way that we think of it, its meaning for us. With a name, we gain an identity, a certain clarity; but as a boundary, the name also excludes as foreign that which is on the other side.

historiography

The past is in constant flux.[8]

Let me illustrate with an American example that is relevant, I hope, to the Holocaust. I live in Michigan. Prior to the 1830s, the people who inhabited this area—perhaps lived on the spot now described as my property—were the Potawatomi, one of the Algonquin forest tribes. In 1830, according to my encyclopedia, they "ceded" their lands to the U.S. government and moved west.

Perhaps.

---

7. Many scholars, dissatisfied with biblical genealogy of the term, *Holocaust*, sought an alternative. The Hebrew word for holocaust, *Sho'ah*, was first used in 1940 to refer to the destruction of European Jews. Some scholars, Americans included, now choose that term to describe the Nazi genocide. I considered using Sho'ah for this book, but decided instead to employ the more commonly used English word. I also wanted to avoid a term that had such a singular historical referent.

8. For a sociological treatment of this subject, and one with relevance to the Holocaust, see my own and Frances McCrea's "Forgetting and Remembering: Bitburg and the Social Construction of History," *Perspectives on Social Problems* 2 (1991): 143–59.

Students in Michigan schools learn little of the Potawatomi. They are not part of "our" (white, European) history. But let us for a moment imagine a history of the Potawatomi written by a Potawatomi historian. Most likely this is what we would read: that there was a great cataclysm, a great mass murder, visited upon the Potawatomi by the white race; that this genocide is the central and defining tragedy of Potawatomi history; that to have forgotten it is, in itself, a great crime and a great insult.

I say this not to equate[9] the fate of the Native Americans to the fate of the Jews, but rather to illustrate from the outside—from an example unfortunately unknown to most white Americans—the tremendous importance of historiography. We know not the Potawatomi dead, nor their stories. To admit their tragedy is to condemn ourselves.

I hope that the relevance of this example is obvious: In attempting to learn about the Holocaust, we first must learn about Holocaust historians. For historians, to put it bluntly, create history for us. And here is a corollary lesson: to comprehend the Holocaust, we must understand that history is a mirror; as we paint and primp the past, we change nothing less than the images of ourselves.

I want to consider two attempts, both in recent years, to reinterpret the Holocaust, to put that event into a different historical perspective. First I discuss the Bitburg incident; then I assess the "historians' debate." Each will tell as much about storytellers as it does about the story.

bitburg[10]

On 5 May 1985, the attention of the world was focused suddenly—and strangely—on Bitburg, a small town in what was

---

9. The two examples are not homologous, but certainly analogous. "In the same decade when the United States was putting into practice a constitution which many consider the first true political product of the Enlightenment," Vincent Pecora has written, "it was also systematically eradicating a supposedly inferior native population in its search for Lebensraum and calmly pursuing race slavery" ("Habermas, Enlightenment and Antisemitism," in Friedlander, *Probing the Limits of Representation*, p. 163.

10. The published literature on Bitburg is staggering. By 1986, one year after the incident, G. H. Hartman had edited *Bitburg in Moral and Political Perspectives* (Bloomington: University of Indiana Press). In 1987 I. Levkov edited an encyclopedic volume, *Bitburg and Beyond: Encounters in American, German and Jewish History* (New York: Shapolsky). The two volumes together exceeded one thousand pages.

then West Germany. For on that day Ronald Reagan, president of the United States, paid a memorial visit to a military cemetery. Among the thousands dead were the graves of some fifty Waffen SS. The controversy over Reagan's visit represented nothing less than "the imperatives of historical memory, national responsibility, forgiveness and justice, politics and morality."[11]

Reagan was really making four historical claims about the war and the Holocaust:

1. that Germans were victims;
2. that unnecessary guilt has been imposed on them;
3. that Germany is (and has almost always been) an ally; and
4. that our real enemy has always been the Russians.

First: Germans were victims of Nazism. German soldiers "were victims," he said, "just as surely as the victims in the concentration camps." Reagan's moral calculus seems rough at best: surely young men drafted as soldiers cannot be blamed too much for state policy.[12] Yet it is absurd to conflate the guilty German soldiers, career officers, and SS, with the victims of the camps. We are capable of finer and more sensible distinctions.[13]

Second: "They have guilt feelings that have been imposed on them," the president said, "and I just think it's unnecessary." Even more: "The German people have few alive that remember even the war and certainly none that were adults and participating in any way." Ronald Reagan was an adult, in his thirties, at · the close of the war. One would presume that his German counterparts would have memories of those times.[14]

---

11. Alvin Rosenfeld, "Another Revisionism: Popular Culture and the Changing Images of the Holocaust." In Hartman, p. 91.

12. Let alone civilians, though their apathy—and perhaps their votes for Adolf Hitler—do not make them blame-free. All quotes in this section are cited in Markle and McCrea, "Forgetting and Remembering."

13. As Elie Wiesel said: "I do not believe in collective guilt or collective responsibility. Only the killers are guilty. Their sons and daughters are not." He urged Reagan to "find another way" to commemorate German suffering. "Your place is with the victims," he maintained. For an incisive discussion of collective guilt, see Amery, p. 72ff.

14. The pre-Bitburg maneuvering appears almost Orwellian. For it was Yom Hashoa, the Day of Holocaust Remembrance, on which Reagan made the speech comparing dead German soldiers with victims of the Holocaust. On the

Germany as our historic ally—the third Bitburg claim—was not invented by Reagan. Seventeen years after the greatest carnage in history, John F. Kennedy identified Germany as the land of freedom, to be emulated and exemplified by citizens of the world. In retrospect, Kennedy's speech was a truly amazing effort to reinterpret history. Reagan developed Kennedy's vision by asserting "the friendship between the American and German peoples—a great blessing that has grown rich and strong over three centuries of shared national experience."

Kennedy's real enemy—Reagan's final claim—was of course the Soviet Union.[15] Bitburg and its SS graves were, for Reagan, a metaphor for anticommunism, not the Holocaust. Reagan characterized World War II as "the war against one man's totalitarian dictatorship." If the war and Holocaust could be remembered as Hitler's (*and only Hitler's*) fault, then Reagan could remember German soldiers differently: "not as Nazi aggressors but as brave anticommunists" misled by a "crazed and evil leader."[16] As an editorial in a West German newspaper summarized: "You cannot have both good Germans in the alliance and bad Germans as a standard of depravity. That would not only split West Germany, but would deprive the alliance of the tacit understanding . . . that the past is past."[17]

Reagan's visit to Bitburg was more than a political trip. By visiting that particular cemetery, Reagan (whether he knew it or not!) was attempting to rewrite Holocaust history.

---

president's reluctance to visit a concentration camp, an administration official explained: "The President was not hot to go to a camp. You know, he is a cheerful politician. He does not like to grovel in a grisly scene like Dachau." As Arthur Schlesinger noted: "He fought the war on the film lots of Hollywood . . . and apparently got many of his ideas of what happened from subsequent study of *Reader's Digest*."

15. That the Soviet Union has always been our real enemy has long been purported by textbooks of American history. In high school texts in particular "the morbid fear of communism becomes an overriding passion—to the point where in some books the whole of American history appears as a mere prologue to the struggle with the 'reds' " (Frances Fitzgerald, *America Revised: History Schoolbooks in the Twentieth Century* [Boston: Little Brown, 1979], p. 56).

16. Stephen Brockman, "Bitburg Deconstruction," *Philosophical Forum* 17 (1986): 168.

17. Quoted in W. R. Dormer, "Paying Homage to History," *Time*, 13 May 1985, pp. 16–19.

the historians' debate

Bitburg was the tip of an iceberg. For more than a decade several highly regarded conservative West German historians have been writing revisionist histories of the Holocaust.[18] Unlike some recent writings,[19] the works of these historians in no way deny the existence of the Holocaust, nor do they diminish its tragedy. Rather they make various historical claims, attempting to "normalize" the Holocaust, to free Germans from their historical ballast. Let me present a few of these claims in capsulated form:

1. World War II is best conceptualized as a continuation of World War I; the two wars together should be thought of as the "European Civil War."
2. The Nazi genocide was not the first, nor the last. Even in the twentieth century the Turks slaughtered 1.5 million Armenians, and millions were killed by the Bolsheviks. Neither of those nations carry the collective guilt of the Germans.
3. Auschwitz was a replication of the Bolshevist gulag. In fact, the gulag was the causal prerequisite of Auschwitz.[20]

This last claim has been purported most forcefully by Ernst Nolte. The Nazis, he argued, did not invent radical genocide. Rather they learned about "Asiatic Barbarism" (Nolte's term) from the Soviet gulags: "Did the National Socialists . . . carry out

----

18. The "debate" was initiated by the Frankfurt School sociologist Jürgen Habermas, who attacked the writings of several of his conservative opponents, especially Andreas Hillgruber and Ernst Nolte. My understanding of this argument has been enhanced by two books: Richard Evans, *In Hitler's Shadow: West German Historians and the Attempt to Escape From the Nazi Past* (New York: Pantheon, 1990), and Charles Maier, *The Unmasterable Past: History, Holocaust and German National Identity* (Cambridge: Harvard University Press, 1988); and by Norbert Kampe's article, "Normalizing the Holocaust? The Recent Historians' Debate in the Federal Republic of Germany," *Holocaust and Genocide Studies* 2 (1987): 61–80.

19. I am not inclined to confer legitimacy on these works by citing them.

20. Other claims made by the revisionist historians include: that because of international Jewish opposition to Nazism, Hitler was justified in deporting Jews; that the death camps were understandable, given the collapsing eastern front; and that resistance to Hitler was not brave, but foolish; and so on.

an 'Asiatic' deed only because they regarded themselves and their kind as the potential or real victims?" Even more: Bolshevik terror was a necessary precondition for the Nazi Holocaust: "Was not the Gulag Archipelago prior in history to Auschwitz? Was not 'class murder' by the Bolsheviks the logical and real precondition of 'race murder' of the Nazis? Was not the Gulag more original than Auschwitz? Auschwitz," he concludes, "was above all a reaction born out of the anxiety of the annihilating occurrences of the Russian Revolution." It was a "copy"—still more horrifying than the original, but a copy all the same.[21]

today

How ought we evaluate these historiographic debates? American history has created a glorious past for us; German historians, by contrast, grew up with a past which was evil incarnate. As Lucy Dawidowicz pointed out in the quote leading this chapter, theirs is a difficult past to live with. I would expect German academics to try to exorcise their own demons—to "historicize" and "contextualize" the Holocaust. For history is too important to be left to the past. "The Historians' controversy," one critic has correctly summarized, "was thus not just about history but about culture, not primarily about facts but about values, and not just about the past but also about the future of Germany."[22]

I believe that the effort to blame the Bolsheviks for the Holocaust—and this claim is at the center of the conservatives' efforts—is misplaced and dishonest. Even worse: it repeats Hitler's own justifications. In constructing our own histories, we need to confront our past, not to construct alibis.

Nolte and his colleagues minimize the Holocaust. It becomes a sideshow to the clash of European empires; it becomes one of many genocides. It would be a terrible mistake to forget any of these tragedies. The stories of genocide—be the victims Armenians, Native Americans, or Khmer—need to be told.

---

21. Quoted in Richard King, "Reforming German History," *Virginia Quarterly Review*, Spring 1990, p. 357.
22. King, p. 358.

For me, however, the Holocaust is unique because it occurred at the center of European civilization, and it occurred with an unprecedented modern ferocity. So far in this book, I have focused on Auschwitz as an example of Nazi infamy, and justifiably so; there is no precedent for the 1.5 million murdered at that site.

I have not yet discussed concentration camps which—unlike Auschwitz—served exclusively as extermination camps. These places had a single purpose: the mass murder of all Jews, regardless of age or sex or ability to work. No selections, no slave labor: everyone transported to a death camp was murdered. The mortality statistics are truly mind-boggling: at Treblinka, Sobibór, Chełmno, and Bełżec, the Nazis murdered 870,000, 250,000, 320,000 and 600,000, respectively. Here are the number of survivors from those camps: seventy from Treblinka, fifty at Sobibór, three at Chełmno (two of whom are dramatically interviewed in the film, *Shoah*), and at Bełżec, *one* human being did not perish amidst the onslaught.

What is there to say.

It is difficult to know what to think in light (perhaps darkness is a better metaphor) of these numbers. Perhaps it is less difficult to know what *not* to think: Auschwitz (and certainly Triblinka, Sobibór, Chełmno and Bełżec) were no copies.

Primo Levi minced neither words, nor judgments, accusing Ernst Nolte and his colleagues of "banalizing the Nazi slaughter."[24] Levi's argument is twofold. First: While the Auschwitz obviously came after the Soviet Gulag, it was not in any way Asiatic. Rather the Holocaust was "perfectly European." German chemical plants produced the Zyklon B used to gas countless innocents; other German manufacturers used the hair from massacred women, while German banks invested the gold extracted from the teeth of the murdered.

Second: The Gulag was in no way a precedent for the death camps. "The first was a massacre among peers" which "did not divide humanity between supermen and submen." The second,

---

23. Primo Levi, "The Dispute Among German Historians. Pp. 163–166 in *Mirror Maker: Stories and Essays* (New York: Schocken Books, 1989), p. 163. Other Levi quotes in this and the next paragraph come from this short essay.

by contrast, was founded on an ideology saturated with a world split in two." Particularly significant for Levi were the symbols of the second: from the tattoos used to mark the victims, to the "selections" for death, to the rat poison used to kill them. Nothing about the Gulag was even close to Treblinka and Chełmno, which did not supply labor and were not concentration camps, but were "black holes meant for men, women, and children guilty only of being Jewish, where one got off the train only in order to enter the gas chambers, from which no one ever came out alive." And let us remember: the Nazis, not the Soviets, specifically targeted babies and children for execution. Levi concludes his four-page essay with the admonition: Germany "cannot and must not whitewash her past."

I find Levi's arguments compelling.

Bitburg purports a different lesson. "The Bitburg ceremony replicated a fatal past, both in terms of its presentation and its abuse of historical memory."[24] In Ronald Reagan's history, the Holocaust was an abhorrent freak, a tragic accident, a blip in the long and steady line of historical progress; the Holocaust, in this same telling, obscured a more important struggle between good and evil, one expressed for four decades in the name of the cold war.

But the Bitburg incident escaped Reagan's sound-bite politics and demonstrated the reasons why leaders, be they presidents or dictators, have always feared memory and history. Official stories—history told by the powerful—is inherently conservative. Such history maintains but one permissible story. But told from the margins of culture and society, history has many voices, none exclusively privileged. This marginal history is, and must be, a continuing story "for overcoming of the present as well as the past."[25]

Thus, like the conservative German historians, Reagan's Bitburg also minimizes the Holocaust. In Bitburg's history, we are safe within the warmth of our hearths. We need not, and indeed

---

24. Eric Rentschler, "The Use and Abuse of Memory: New German Film and the Discourse of Bitburg." *New German Critique* 36 (1985), p. 85.

25. Brockman, p. 160.

should not, ask disturbing questions, let alone ponder their answers.

Even if we dismiss Bitburg revisionism, It is nonetheless hard to grasp the historical significance of the Holocaust. It was not a political revolution; no social class rose to power because of the Holocaust. Nor were economic systems changed much; no financial collapse occurred. New religions did not arise, nor did the Holocaust have any impact on science. Finally, the Holocaust itself led to no changes in national boundaries.

Even the analogy to the black plague, which also left in its wake uncountable millions of dead bodies, is unsatisfactory. The plague, unlike the Holocaust, was a natural and unselective phenomenon. The Holocaust, by contrast, selectively stripped Jews from their communities, which were otherwise unchanged and able to conduct business as usual.[26]

Nonetheless, I think of the Holocaust as a pivotal event in Western civilization. If the French Revolution some two hundred years ago showed that human liberation is within our grasp (though not our hold), the Holocaust shows that our necks can just as easily be broken.

For Jürgen Habermas, the Holocaust was an "irreversible rupture" in human history. At Auschwitz: "something happened, that up to now nobody considered as even possible. There one touched on something which represents the deep layer of solidarity among all that wears a human face." What we know now, that we did not know before, is that everything is possible. Auschwitz, Habermas concluded, "has changed the basis for the continuity of the conditions of life within history."[27]

If the Holocaust is unprecedented, then it is difficult to consider it within the confines of ordinary discourse.

Read the words of memoirist Sara Nomberg-Przytyk: "We were not so much mesmerized by the flames as by the sea of human blood. Burning flesh gives off a sweet, choking odor that makes you feel faint." She concluded: "It is difficult for me to

---

26. Kren and Rappoport, p. 129.
27. Quoted in Andreas Huyssen, "Monument and Memory in a Postmodern Age. *The Yale Journal of Criticism* 6 (1993), p. 260.

say how we were able to live through those times, conscious of human life oozing out of existence everywhere. How is it that we did not all go crazy? How is it that we were able to vegetate, keeping our composure in this unbearable world? The time arrived when a screem tore itself involuntarily out of one's throat."[28] Writers seek metaphors such as hell or otherworldliness to grasp at the essence of the Holocaust; others seek complex analogies. For Kren and Rappoport, the Holocaust is the "moral equivalent of the Copernican revolution." After the Holocaust, they write, we can no longer assert that our morals form the center of our universe. "The historical development of [Western civilization's] moral instrumentalities—law and religion—was a failure ending in Auschwitz."[29]

For me, the ovens and flames do no less than deconstruct our view of civilization and progress. The Holocaust steals our innocence; the Holocaust challenges our smug acceptance of the good world. To study the Holocaust is to know that tomorrow is not safe—not only for us, but for the world which has created us. "Our world is not literally an Auschwitz," conclude Kren and Rappoport," but the Nazi Holocaust did happen; and now the only visions of the world that can be taken seriously are those that come through the irrevocably ash-darkened prisms of post-Holocaust sense and sensibility."[30]

anamnesis

Felix Nussbaum's painting *The Damned*, graces—or perhaps I should say haunts—the cover of this book. Nussbaum finished it in 1943, about seven months before the Nazis murdered him at Auschwitz. The composition of the work is complex. The background shows the remains of a civilization: tattered banners, representing pestilence flags, flap over empty streets; crows, another symbol of death, fly overhead. In the midground, skeletons are pallbearers for caskets soon to be filled; a high wall—a prison?—shows a graffiti of death images.

---

28. Nomberg-Przytyk, p. 81.
29. Kren and Rappoport, pp. 131–32.
30. Kren and Rappoport, p. 143.

In the foreground, looking towards us and away from the past, are the dammed. The figure in the center is a self-portrait, quite typical of Nussbaum paintings; by his side is his wife, Felka Platek, a Polish Jewish artist. There are ten other people; some are Felix and Felka at various ages, in various poses. The total, twelve, might represent the lost tribes of Israel, or perhaps Christ and the apostles, this latter symbol especially evident in Nussbaum's sketch for *The Damned*. All the faces show fear, horror, despondency or blank resignation. The colors, expressionist brilliant in earlier works, are browns, grays, and black for this apocalypse.

Until a few years ago, the life and work of Felix Nussbaum had been forgotten. Now we know a little. He was born in Osnabrück, Germany, to a middle-class Jewish family. At age eighteen, he began to study art, first in Hamburg, later in Berlin, at the Academy of Fine Arts. In 1932, he was awarded a prestigious fellowship to study at the Prussian Academy's Villa Massimo in Rome. But the following year, the Nazis, now in power, withdrew the fellowship. Thus began Nussbaum's odyssey: exile in Belgium, arrest with the Nazi invasion of that country, escape from an internment camp in France, return to Belgium, where friends hid him and his wife. Throughout this time of trial, until his capture, Felix Nussbaum painted his travail.

He was forty years old when he was murdered—in August 1944, at Auschwitz—just one month before the Russians liberated the camp.

For the next thirty years, he was unknown to the outside world. His work, like that of so many other artists, would have remained invisible were it not for the efforts of two men: Wendelin Zimmer, an art critic, and Peter Junk, a librarian—both non-Jews, both residents of Osnabrück.

"Although I had been writing art reviews for the *Neue Osnabrücker Zeitung* for five years," wrote Zimmer, "I had never come across the name of Felix Nussbaum."[31] The year was 1970. Relatives of Nussbaum had brought several of his works to Osnabrück. They were in "extraordinarily bad condition,"

---

31. Emily D. Bilski, *Art and Exile: Felix Nussbaum, 1904–1944* (New York: The Jewish Museum, 1985), p. 8.

damaged from dampness and lack of stretchers. The paintings showed "abraded layers of pigment, cracked and flaked paint and perforations in the canvases."

Zimmer helped organize a small Nussbaum exhibit, at which time the mayor of Osnabrück spoke of "restitution for the injustices committed in the name of an inhuman ideology against our fellow Jewish countrymen in Osnabrück and throughout Germany." Still, almost nothing was known of Nussbaum's life. The local newspaper published an editorial appeal, "Who Remembers Felix Nussbaum?" asking for information. "We had at last come to the realization," wrote Zimmer, "that the rediscovery of this artist involved more than just displaying his art. We had been accorded the unique opportunity to examine not only his work but also to reconstruct one of the six million lives our nation had so wantonly destroyed."[32]

Thus were the efforts of Zimmer and Junk twofold: to recover and exhibit Nussbaum's work, and to reconstruct and publicize his life as a symbol of the fate of Osnabrück's exterminated Jews. Toward that end, they founded a museum, in Osnabrück, devoted to his work. In 1985, they organized an exhibit of Nussbaum's work at the Jewish Museum in New York. "It was a labor of penance and mourning," Junk wrote, and as such could not be relegated to art historians, critics, and museum curators."[33]

Here is a slender connection: I saw three Nussbaum pieces in East Berlin in 1993, part of an exhibit of so-called decadent art. The paintings were at the Gropius Haus, an old mansion that was part of the headquarters (an extraordinary historical irony!) for the Nazi SS. Though I was sluggish and cranky from too much touring, the paintings stopped me cold. Nussbaum pierced my fatigue.

But this is Nussbaum's story—as well as Junk's and Zimmer's story—not mine. What I hope to accomplish is what Theodor Adorno called "anamnestic solidarity." This means that I use memory not just as recollection. As Zimmer and Junk understand, remembrance has both ethical and political power. My vision—our vision—of a just society must be grounded in our memories of victims.

---

32. Bilski, p. 9.
33. Bilski, p. 12.

A friend of Nussbaum's, living with him in Brussels, remembers the arrest of the artist. In the middle of the night, the SS stormed into the Nussbaum bedroom: "I can still hear the shrill cries of despair coming from the couple who had been awakened from a sound sleep." Junk continues: "Felix and Felka's piercing cries still echo today, imposing an obligation that led us to trace the course of Nussbaum's life."[34]

an ending?

I began chapter 2 with a discussion of Adolf Eichmann. His story ended with his execution, at the hands of the Israelis, in 1962. But was his execution an appropriate ending for his miserable life? Gershom Scholem, the great Jewish theologian, thought not.

Scholem had opposed the death penalty for Eichmann, but not for the obvious reasons. His opposition was not moral, as mine would have been. He did not—as I would—question the right of the Israelis to murder Eichmann for his crimes against humanity; he declared, in fact, that Eichmann "deserved the death penalty."[35]

Eichmann's death, for Scholem, was an "inappropriate ending" which "falsified the historical significance of the trial." The Jerusalem proceedings, he maintained, created an illusion by asserting a conclusion. "Such an illusion is most dangerous because it may engender the feeling that something has been done to atone for the unatonable." But the hanging of one "human or inhuman creature," for Scholem, concluded nothing.

Quite the contrary. One fears, he argued, that "instead of opening up a reckoning and leaving it open for the next generation, we have foreclosed it." It is to our interest, he maintained, "that the great historical and moral question, the question probing the depths which this trial has forced us all to face—How could this happen?—that this question should retain all its weight, all its stark nakedness, all its horror." It would have been better, he concluded, "if we did not have the hangman stand

---

34. Bilski, p. 16.
35. This and the following quotes are from Gersholm Scholem, pp. 299–300.

between us and our great question, between us and the soul-searching account we have to settle with the world."

So Eichmann's death was a false conclusion. Perhaps all conclusions are. How does one end without concluding? I end this book, as I began it, with my own experience.

Miami: August 1993.

This is my first visit to Miami, but I have not looked forward to the trip. Here for a meeting of the American Sociological Association, I stay at the Fountainbleu Hotel. With its six restaurants, seven bars, tropical swimming pool, and ostentatious architecture—too much of everything—the hotel embodies my prejudices of the city.

I have always thought of Miami as nouvelle Jewish: too much heat, too much water, too much beach, too many tourists, and—most of all—far too much money. I cannot connect with this living Jewish culture; I cannot grasp its story with the same intensity that I feel for dead European Jewish culture.

We decide to visit the memorial to the Holocaust a few miles to the south. I am determined not to like it, not to be affected, as I am moved by European commemorative sites. We park near the memorial at the edge of Miami's "art deco" area; its pink and blue buildings display a fifty-year-old, though newly renovated, charm. At first, the area seems an unlikely place for a Holocaust memorial. Not really, though, for art deco architecture was in part a German import, influenced by the Jugendstil and Bauhaus styles developed earlier in the century. So I am surrounded by German culture, albeit a derivative, after all.

The August sun beats upon us as we walk to the monument; I am sticky and cranky. The monument comes into my view; I crane my neck uncomfortably to see a giant arm with countless human flotsam and jetsam hanging desperately from it. Forty-two feet high, the bronze hand points or reaches, I cannot tell which. Most of the human figures cling desperately to the wrist, just below the tattoo. A handful of figures are scattered, helter-skelter, on the ground beneath. One shows two haggard, starving figures approaching one another. Close up, we see that they are male and female, lovers, one presumes, on the edge of death. I think of Karl Wolfskehl, who fled the Nazis and wrote shortly before his death in New Zealand:

If you knew what I knew,
Your laughter would sound low,
Low as the stifled moans
Over tombstones.

Tears drop from my eyes, frying on my cheeks.

The memorial, designed and sculpted by Kenneth Treister, was commissioned in 1985 and dedicated by Elie Wiesel in 1990. A pamphlet tells visitors that in addition to commemorating the victims, the memorial should "inform with factual representation." I understand the worth of informing, though writing this book has shown me the difficulty of depicting the Holocaust. For when I began the book, I knew (or thought I knew) what I wanted to say. Now I'm not so sure. And though it seems trite to say it this way, the act of writing has, for me, raised more questions than it has answered.

The pamphlet also says that the memorial should "serve as solace to survivors." I am suspicious of giving solace. I fear that the attempt will somehow lead to an assertion of purpose for mass death, an assertion that these deaths were not in vain. This do-good impulse to attribute some higher purpose for the Holocaust must be resisted. There is no justification, there should never be a justification—religious or otherwise—for the Holocaust. The dead were victims, not martyrs. For me, all theodicy is disingenuous. I think of Jacob Glatstein's poem: "The God of my disbelief is magnificent," he wrote:

The Torah we received at Sinai,
And in Lublin we gave it back.
Corpses do not praise God.

Under the heavy sun, I think about my maternal roots from Dnepropetrovsk. Of the considerable family left behind, I know nothing. I have learned some details of this story from Raul Hilberg's books. According to a 1926 census, there were 83,900 Jews in Dnepropetrovsk, about one-third of the total population of the city. After the German invasion of the Soviet Union in 1941, the mobile killing squads murdered several hundred thousand Ukrainian Jews. In Dnepropetrovsk, where fifteen thousand Jews were slaughtered in one action, a local army official complained that he did not receive prior notification; the massacre, he protested, had ruined his plans for a ghetto. By March 1942 there were, according to Nazi estimates, only 702 Jews remaining in the city.

My father was born in Pennsylvania. His father's family was from a village whose name I do not know, near Munkács (then located in the Hungarian empire), today called Mukačevo in western Ukraine. Only a few members from that family survived the Holocaust. As a child, I was frightened by their gaunt faces; I was more frightened by their tattoos. They never told, and I never asked to hear, their stories.

French historian Marc Bloch, who was shot by the Gestapo in 1944, said that the task of the historian was to create a dialogue between the living and the dead. Perhaps that is also my hope. But I have lost the connection.

Questions haunt me.

Are we all Nazis? The answer, though to a different question, is this: As reflexive individuals, we must begin to see (in the fine words of Roger Gottlieb) "the little slave holder in ourselves, the tiny reflection of the Nazi in our own souls." Is there a common thread that connects Beethoven's symphonies to Auschwitz? What should I feel when I listen to Wagner? Should I even listen? The Israelis have decided not, banning his music. In Berlin I did listen, and in a place haunted by Hitler's ghost. I believe that we must confront, not flee, the memory of history.

What does the Holocaust tell us about our own civilization and its discontents? Should I follow Cynthia Ozick, that fierce and brilliant critic, and boycott Bayer aspirin or BASF tapes? I choose not. I turn my face away from the Germanness of the perpetrators, the Jewishness of the victims, the uniqueness of the Nazi genocide—not to ignore a specific history, but to assert its universality.

Perhaps the import is not in the questions themselves, but in the attempt to create some dialogue. It is my hope that the very asking of these questions is itself a first act toward insurrection. "On and on the furnaces of destruction burn; nothing can make them go out," Ozick has written, "as long as there are you and I to remember who lit them, and why."

From shtetl to Auschwitz to Miami, a trip across time and space and memory, a trip beginning in the European hearth, passing through the flames of death, and ending in the August heat. I struggle, and hope that I continue to struggle, to grasp what the Holocaust means for civilization, for American culture, for me.

another ending

Here is another ending: no monuments or memorials; no historical setting. This ending is about people whose names I know. The story is mine, but only vicariously.

1990: a small village in Upper Austria.

We trace the final steps of the life of Marko Banjac, my wife's father. We walk through the field where he was buried. Everything is so peaceful here, in these rolling hills, high mountains in the distance. Slowly and with care, my wife picks a large and beautiful bouquet of wildflowers and lays it at the approximate spot of his grave. I feel as though she has consecrated the ground. At the bridge where he was shot, she tucks a few flowers in some loose bricks head high. We cry softly.

Back in the car, we drive to the house of the mayor, who murdered Marko in 1945. The Americans sentenced him to a few years of prison, after which he was released. He is now an old man, we are told. We park the car in front of his house. It is a beautiful home, large, surrounded with flowers, obviously the dwelling of a comfortable family.

We sit for a moment, then talk. We remember Nicholas Gage's book, *Eleni*, where the author describes a lifelong and obsessive search for, and then absolutely anticlimactic meeting with, the Greek communist who killed his mother during World War II.

In this quiet area we are conspicuous in our parked rental car. What should we do? Our pasts, our traditional understandings of acceptable behavior, have not prepared us for this moment. Our nightmares do not apply. Should we knock on his door? Then what: introduce ourselves? make a scene? seek some sort of revenge?

We sit and stare for several moments, confused, uncertain.

We drive away.

references

Adam, Uwe Dietrich. "The Gas Chambers." Pp. 84–95 in *Unanswered Questions*, ed. François Furet (New York: Schocken Press, 1989).

Adorno, Theodor. *Negative Dialectics* (New York: Seabury Press, 1987).

Adorno, Theodor, Else Frenkel-Brunswik, Daniel Levinson, and R. Nevitt Sanford. *The Authoritarian Personality* (New York: Harper, 1950).

Allardyce, Gilbert. "What Fascism is Not: Thoughts on the Deflation of a Concept." *American Historical Review* 84 (1979): 367–388.

Allen, Woody. *Without Feathers* (New York: Random House, 1972).

Alter, Robert. *Necessary Angels: Tradition and Modernity in Kafka, Benjamin and Scholem* (Cambridge: Harvard University Press, 1991).

Amery, Jean. *At the Mind's Limits* (New York: Schocken Press, 1990).

Arendt, Hannah. *Eichmann in Jerusalem: A Report on the Banality of Evil* (New York: Viking Press, 1963).

———.*The Origins of Totalitarianism* (New York: Harcourt, Brace and Jovanovich, 1973).

Askenasy, Hans. *Are We All Nazis?* (Secaucus, NJ: Lyle Stuart, 1978).

Astor, Gerald. *The Last Nazi* (New York: Donald I. Fine, 1985).

Barkan, Elazar. *Retreat of Scientific Racism: Changing Concepts of Race in Britain and the United States Between the World Wars* (Cambridge: Cambridge University Press, 1992).

Barnouw, Dagme. "The Secularity of Evil: Hannah Arendt and the Eichmann Controversy." *Modern Judaism* 3 (1983): 75-94.

Bauer, Yehuda. *A History of the Holocaust* (New York: Franklin Watts, 1982).

Bauman, Zygmunt. *Modernity and the Holocaust* (Ithaca: Cornell University Press, 1990).

————. *Modernity and Ambivalence* (Ithaca: Cornell University Press, 1991).

Bellow, Saul. *Mr. Sammler's Planet* (New York: Viking Press, 1969).

Bendix, Reinhard. *Max Weber: An Intellectual Portrait* (Garden City, NY: Doubleday, 1960).

Bernal, J. D. *Social Function of Science* (New York: Macmillan, 1939).

Biagioli, Mario. "Science, Modernity and the Final Solution." Pp. 185-205 in *Probing the Limits of Representation: Nazism and the Final Solution,* ed. Saul Friedlander (Cambridge: Harvard University Press, 1992).

Bilski, Emily. *Art and Exile: Felix Nussbaum, 1904-1944* (New York: The Jewish Museum, 1985).

Braham, Randolf. "Antisemitism and the Treatment of the Holocaust in Post-Communist East Central Europe." *Holocaust and Genocide Studies* 8 (1994): 142-163.

Breitman, Richard. *The Architect of Genocide: Himmler and the Final Solution* (New York: Knopf, 1991).

Brockman, Stephen. "Bitburg Deconstruction." *Philosophical Forum* 17 (1986): 159-174.

Browning, Christopher. *Ordinary Men: Reserve Police Battalion 101 and the Final Solution in Poland* (New York: Harper Collins, 1992).

————. *The Path to Genocide: Essays on Launching the Final Solution* (Cambridge: Cambridge University Press, 1992).

Buck-Morss, Susan. *The Origin of Negative Dialectics* (New York: Free Press, 1977).

Bullock, Allan. *Hitler and Stalin: Parallel Lives* (New York: Random House, 1992).

Burkhardt, Jacob. *Force and Freedom: Reflections on History* (New York: Pantheon Books, 1943).

Cameron, Ian, and David Edge. *Scientific Images and Their Social Uses* (London: Butterworth, 1979).

Canovan, Margaret. *Hannah Arendt: A Reinterpretation of Her Political Thought* (Cambridge: Cambridge University Press, 1992).

Caplan, Arthur. "When Evil Intrudes." *Hastings Center Report* 22 (1992): 29-32.

Chorover, Stephen. *From Genesis to Genocide* (Cambridge: MIT Press, 1979).

Cohen, Elie. *The Abyss: A Confession* (New York: Norton, 1973).

Cohen, Nava. "Medical Experiments." Pp. 957-966 in *Encyclopedia of the Holocaust,* ed. Israel Gutman (New York: Macmillan, 1990).

Daniels, Roger. *Concentration Camps USA: Japanese Americans and World War II* (New York: Holt, Rinehart and Winston, 1972).

Daniels, Roger, and Harry Kitano. *American Racism* (Englewood Cliffs, NJ: Prentice Hall, 1970).

Davis, F. James. *Who is Black?* (University Park: Pennsylvania State University Press, 1991).

Dawidowicz, Lucy. *The War Against the Jews, 1933-1945* (New York: Holt, Rinehart & Winston, 1975).

———. *From That Place and Time* (New York: Norton, 1989).

Denneny, Michael. "The Privilege of Ourselves: Hannah Arendt on Judgment." Pp. 245-274 in *Hannah Arendt: The Recovery of the Public World,* ed. Melvin Hill (New York: St. Martins, 1979).

Des Pres, Terrence. *The Survivor: An Anatomy of Life in the Death Camps* (New York: Oxford University Press, 1976).

Dicks, Henry. *Licensed Mass Murder: A Socio-Psychological Study of Some SS Killers* (New York: Basic Books, 1972).

Dormer, W.R. "Paying Homage to History." *Time* 13 May 1985, pp. 16-19.

Elliot, Gil. *Twentieth Century Book of the Dead* (New York: Sribner, 1972).

Elms, Alan. *Social Psychology and Social Relevance* (Boston: Little Brown, 1972).

Evans, Richard. *In Hitler's Shadow: West German Historians and the Attempt to Escape From the Nazi Past* (New York: Pantheon, 1990).

Etzioni, Amitai. *A Comparative Analysis of Complex Organizations* (New York: Free Press, 1961).

Fein, Helen. *Genocide: A Sociological Perspective* (Newbury Park, CA: Sage Publications, 1993).

Fenelon, Fania. *Playing For Time* (New York: Atheneum, 1977).

Fest, Joachim. *Hitler* (New York: Harcourt, Brace & Jovanovich, 1974).

Fitzgerald, Frances. *America Revised: History Schoolbooks in the Twentieth Century* (Boston: Little Brown, 1979).

Fleming, Gerald. "Engineers of Death." *New York Times* 18 July 1993, p. E-19.

Flood, Charles. *Hitler: The Path to Power* (Boston: Houghton Mifflin, 1989).

Friedlander, Saul. "From Anti-Semitism to Extermination." Pp. 11-18 in *Unanswered Questions*, ed. François Furet (New York: Schocken, 1989).

——— (ed). *Probing the Limits of Representation: Nazism and the Final Solution* (Cambridge: Harvard University Press, 1992).

Friedrichs, Otto. *The End of the World: A History* (New York: Fromm International Publishing Co., 1986).

Fromm, Erich. *Escape From Freedom* (New York: Ferrar and Rinehart, 1941).

Furet, François (Ed.). *Unanswered Questions: Nazi Germany and the Genocide of the Jews* (New York: Schocken, 1989).

Gamson, William, Bruce Fireman and Steven Rytina. *Encounters With Unjust Authority* (Homewood, IL: Dorsey, 1982).

Gellately, Robert. *The Gestapo and German Society: Enforcing Racial Policy, 1933-1945* (New York: Oxford Clarendon, 1991).

Georg, Willy. *In the Warsaw Ghetto* (New York: Aperture Foundation, 1993).

Gerth, Hans, and C. Wright Mills (eds.). *From Max Weber: Essays in Sociology* (New York: Oxford University Press, 1946).

Gilbert, Martin. *The Holocaust: A History of the Jews of Europe During the Second World War* (New York: Henry Holt & Co., 1985).

Girdner, Audrie, and Anne Loftis. *The Great Betrayal: The Evacuation of the Japanese-Americans During World War II* (London: Macmillan, 1969).

Grunfeld, Frederic. *Prophets Without Honor: A Background to Freud, Kafka, Einstein and their World* (New York: Holt, Rinehart and Winston, 1979).

Gutman, Israel and Robert Rozett, "Estimated Jewish Loses in the Holocaust" *Encyclopedia of the Holocaust* (Appendix 6), ed. Israel Gutman (New York: Macmillan, 1990).

Gutman, Israel, and Michael Berenbaum (eds.). *Anatomy of the Auschwitz Death Camp*. Published with the United States Holocaust Memorial Museum (Bloomington: Indiana University Press, 1994).

Halbwachs, Maurice. *On Collective Memory.* (Chicago: University of Chicago Press, 1992).

Hallie, Philip. *Lest Innocent Blood Be Shed* (New York: Harper & Row, 1979).

Harris, Melvin. *Patterns of Race in the Americas* (New York: Norton, 1964).

Hartman, G.H. (ed). *Bitburg in Moral and Political Perspectives* (Bloomington: Indiana University Press, 1986).

Hegi, Ursula, *Stones From the River* (New York: Poseidon Press, 1994).

Hilberg, Raul. *The Destruction of European Jews* (New York: Holmes & Meier, 1985).

———. "German Railroads, Jewish Souls." *Society* (April, 1986): 60-64.

———. "The Bureaucracy of Annihilation." Pp. 119-133 in *Unanswered Questions*, ed. François Furet (New York: Schocken Books, 1989).

———. *Perpetrators, Victims, Bystanders: The Jewish Catastrophe 1933-1945* (New York: Harper Collins, 1992).

Horkheimer, Max and Theodor Adorno. *Dialectic of Enlightenment* (New York: Herder and Herder, 1972).

Hunt, Linda. "U.S. Coverup of Nazi Scientists." *Bulletin of the Atomic Scientists* 41 (April, 1985): 16-24.

Huyssen, Andreas. "Monument and Memory in a Postmodern Age." *The Yale Journal of Criticism* 6 (1993): 249-262.

Jäckel, Eberhard. *Hitler's Weltanschauung* (Middletown, CT: Wesleyan University Press, 1972).

Jasanoff, Sheila, Gerald Markle, James Petersen and Trevor Pinch. *The Handbook of Science and Technology Studies* (Newbury Park, CA: Sage Publications, 1995).

Jay, Martin. *Adorno* (Cambridge: Harvard University Press, 1984).

Jones, James. *Bad Blood: The Tuskegee Syphilis Experiment* (New York: Free Press, 1981).

Kádár, György. *Survivor of Death, Witness to Life* (Nashville: Vanderbilt University, 1988).

Kafka, Franz. *The Penal Colony* (New York: Schocken Books, 1961).

————. *The Trial* (New York: Schocken Books, 1968).

Kampe, Norbert. "Normalizing the Holocaust? The Recent Historians' Debate in the Federal Republic of Germany." *Holocaust and Genocide Studies* 2 (1987): 61-80.

Katz, Fred. "Implementation of the Holocaust: The Behavior of Nazi Officials." *Comparative Studies of Society and History* 24 (1982): 510-527.

————. *Ordinary People and Extraordinary Evil: A Report on the Beguilings of Evil* (Albany: State University of New York Press, 1993).

Kelman, Herbert and V. Lee Hamilton. *Crimes of Obedience: Toward a Social Psychology of Authority and Obedience* (New Haven: Yale University Press, 1989).

Kerr, Philip. *Berlin Noir* (London: Penguin Books, 1993).

Kevles, Daniel. *In the Name of Eugenics: Genetics and the Use of Human Heredity* (New York: Knopf, 1985).

Kierkegaard, Soren. *Fear and Trembling* (Princeton: Princeton University Press, 1983).

Kilham, W. and L. Mann. "Level of Destructive Obedience as a Function of Transmitter and Executant Roles in the Milgram Obedience Paradigm." *Journal of Personality and Social Psychology* 29 (1974): 696-702.

King, Richard. "Reforming German History." *Virginia Quarterly Review* 66 (Spring, 1990), 355-366.

Koehl, Robert. "Feudal Aspects of National Socialism." *American Political Science Review* 54 (1960): 921-933.

Koonz, Claudia. *Mothers in the Fatherland: Women, Family and Nazi Politics* (New York: St. Martins Press, 1987).

Kor, Eva Mozes. "The Mengele Twins and Human Experiments: A Personal Account." Pp. 53-60 in *The Nazi Doctors and the Nuremberg Code: Human Rights in Human Experimentation*, ed. George Annas and Michael Grodin (New York: Oxford University Press, 1992).

Kren, George, and Leon Rappoport. *The Holocaust and the Crisis in Human Behavior* (New York: Holmes & Meier, 1980).

Krinsky, Carol. *Synagogues of Europe: Architecture, History and Meaning* (Cambridge: MIT Press, 1985).

Kuhl, Stefan. *The Nazi Connection: Eugenics, American Racism and German National Socialism* (New York: Oxford University Press, 1994).

Kuhn, Thomas. *The Structure of Scientific Revolutions* (Chicago: University of Chicago Press, 1972).

Lachs, John. *Responsibility of the Individual in Modern Society* (Brighton: Harvester, 1981).

Lagerwey, Mary. *Gold-Encrusted Chaos: An Analysis of Auschwitz Memoirs* (Western Michigan University: Unpublished Ph.D. Dissertation, 1994).

Laks, Syzmon. *Music of Another World* (Evanston: Northwestern University Press, 1989).

Lang, Beryl. *Act and Idea in the Nazi Genocide* (Chicago: University of Chicago Press, 1990).

———. "Hannah Arendt and the Politics of Evil." Pp. 41-57 in *Hannah Arendt: Critical Essays*, eds. Lewis Hinchman and Sandra Hinchman (Albany: State University of New York Press, 1994).

Lanzmann, Claude. *Shoah: An Oral History of the Holocaust. The Complete Text of the Film* (New York: Pantheon, 1985).

Laqueur, Walter. *Fascism: A Reader's Guide* (Berkeley, CA: University of California Press, 1976).

Leitner, Isabella. *Fragments of Isabella* (New York: Crowell, 1978).

Lendavi, Paul. *Anti-Semitism Without Jews* (New York: Doubleday, 1971.

Levi, Primo. *Mirror Maker: Stories and Essays* (New York: Schocken Books, 1889).

————. *Other People's Trades* (New York: Summit Books, 1989)

————. *The Drowned and the Saved* (New York: Vintage International Press, 1989).

Levkov, I. *Bitburg and Beyond: Encounters in American and German Jewish History* (New York: Shapolsky, 1987).

Lifton, Robert J. *The Nazi Doctors* (New York: Basic Books, 1986).

Linden, R. Ruth. *Making Stories, Making Selves: Feminist Reflections on the Holocaust* (Columbus: Ohio State University Press, 1993).

Lukacs, John. *The End of the Twentieth Century and the End of Progress* (New York: Ticknor & Fields, 1993).

Maier, Charles. *The Unmasterable Past: History, Holocaust and German National Identity* (Cambridge: Harvard University Press, 1988).

Markle, Gerald, Mary Lagerwey, Todd Clason, Jill Green and Tricia Meade. "From Auschwitz to Americana: Texts of the Holocaust." *Sociological Focus* 25 (1992): 179-202.

Markle, Gerald, and Frances McCrea. "Forgetting and Remembering: Bitburg and the Social Construction of History." *Perspectives on Social Problems* 2 (1991): 143-159.

Marrus, Michael. *The Holocaust in History* (Hanover, NH: University Press of New England, 1987).

————. "The History of the Holocaust: A Survey of Recent Literature." *Journal of Modern History* 59 (1987): 114-160.

McCrea, Frances, and Gerald Markle. *Minutes to Midnight: Nuclear Weapons Protest in America* (Newbury Park, CA: Sage Publications, 1989).

McKinney, David. *The Authoritarian Personality Studies: An Inquiry Into the Failure of Social Science Research to Produce Demonstrable Knowledge* (The Hague: Mouton, 1973).

Melson, Robert. *Revolution and Genocide* (Chicago: University of Chicago Press, 1992).

Merton, Thomas. *Raids on the Unspeakable* (New York: New Directions, 1966).

Miale, Florence, and Michael Seltzer. *The Nuremberg Mind: The Psychology of the Nazi Leaders* (New York: Quadrangle, 1975).

Milchman, Alan, and Alan Rosenberg. Review of *Modernity and the Holocaust*, by Zygmunt Bauman. *Holocaust and Genocide Studies* 5 (1990): 337-342.

Milgram, J. Stanley. "Behavioral Study of Obedience." *Journal of Abnormal and Social Psychology* 67 (1963): 371-378.

———. *The Individual in a Social World* (Reading, MA: Addison-Wesley, 1971).

———. *Obedience to Authority* (New York: Harper & Row, 1974).

Miller, Arthur. *The Obedience Experiments* (New York: Praeger, 1986).

Momsen, Hans. "National Socialism: Continuity and Change." Pp. 178-210 in *Fascism: A Reader's Guide*, ed. Walter Laqueur (Berkeley: University of California Press, 1976).

———. Foreward to Karl Schleunes, *The Twisted Road to Auschwitz* (Urbana: University of Illinois Press, 1990).

Moore, Barrington. *Injustice: The Social Basis of Obedience and Revolt* (White Plains, NY: M. E. Sharpe, 1978).

Mosse, George. *The Crisis of German Ideology: Intellectual Origins of the Third Reich* (New York: Grosset and Dunlop, 1964).

Muller-Hill, Benno. *Murderous Science* (New York: Oxford University Press, 1989).

Myrdal, Gunnar. *An American Dilemma* (New York: Harper & Brothers, 1944).

Needham, Joseph. *An Attack on International Science* (Cambridge: Cambridge University Press, 1941).

Neumann, Franz. *Behemoth* (New York: Octagon Books, 1963).

Nomberg-Przytyk, Sara. *Auschwitz: True Tales From a Grotesque Land* (Chapel Hill: University of North Carolina Press, 1985).

Nyiszli, Miklos. *Auschwitz: A Doctor's Eyewitness Account* (New York: Frederick Fell Inc., 1960).

Oliner, Samuel and Pearl Oliner. *The Altruistic Personality: Rescuers of Jews in Nazi Germany* (New York: Free Press, 1968).

Ozick, Cynthia. *The Shawl* (New York: Knopf, 1989).

———. "On Christian Heroism." *Partisan Review* 49 (1992): 44-51.

Pane, Stanley G. "Fascism in Western Europe" Pp. 11-21 in *Fascism: A Reader's Guide*, ed. Walter Laqueur (Berkeley: University of California Press, 1976).

Pawel, Ernst. *The Nightmare of Reason: A Life of Franz Kafka* (New York: Farrar, Straus & Giroux, 1984).

Pecora, Vincent. "Habermas, Enlightenment and Antisemitism. Pp. 155-170 in *Probing the Limits of Representation: Nazism and the Final Solution*, ed. Saul Friedlander (Cambridge: Harvard University Press, 1992).

Pressac, Jean-Claude, and Robert-Jan Van Pelt. "The Machinery of Mass Murder at Auschwitz," Pp. 157-182 in Gutman, *Anatomy of the Auschwitz Death Camp*, eds. Israel Gutman, and Michael Berenbaum (Bloomington: Indiana University Press, 1994).

Proctor, Robert. *Racial Hygiene: Medicine Under the Nazis* (Cambridge: Harvard University Press, 1988).

———. "Nazi Doctors, Racial Medicine and Human Experimentation." Pp. 17-31 in *The Nazi Doctors and the Nuremberg Code: Human Rights in Human Experimentation*, ed. George Annas and Michael Grodin (New York: Oxford University Press, 1992).

Reilly, Philip. *The Surgical Solution: A History of Involuntary Sterilization in the United States* (Baltimore: Johns Hopkins University Press, 1991).

Reissman, David. *The Lonely Crowd: A Study in the Changing American Character* (New Haven: Yale University Press, 1950)..

Reith, Adolf. *Monuments to the Victims of Tyrany* (New York: Praeger, 1968).

Rentschler, Eric. "The Use and Abuse of Memory: New German Film and the Discourse of Bitburg." *New German Critique* 36 (1985): 67-90.

Reynolds, Larry. "A Perspective on 'Race': The Career of a Concept." *Sociological Focus* 25 (1992): 1-15.

Ritzer, George. *The McDonaldization of Society* (Newbury Park, CA: Pine Forge Press, 1993).

Robinson, Jacob. *And the Crooked Shall Be Made Straight* (New York: Macmillan, 1965).

Rose, Gilian. *The Melancholy Science: An Introduction to the Thought of Theodor W. Adorno* (New York: Columbia University Press, 1978).

Rosen, Norma. *Touching Evil* (New York: Harcourt, Brace & World, 1969).

Rosenfeld, Alvin. *Imagining Hitler* (Bloomington: Indiana University Press, 1985).

———. "Another Revisionism: Popular Culture and the Changing Images of the Holocaust." Pp. 90-102 in *Bitburg in Moral and Political Perspectives*, ed. G. H. Hartman (Bloomington: Indiana University Press, 1986).

Ross, Guenther. "Response to Rubenstein." Pp. 187-190 in *Western Society After the Holocaust*, ed. Lyman Letgers (Boulder: Westview Press, 1983).

Rousset, David. *A World Apart* (London: Secker and Warburg, 1951).

Rubenstein, Richard. *The Cunning of History: Mass Death and the American Future* (New York: Harper & Row, 1975).

———. "Anticipation of the Holocaust in the Political Sociology of Max Weber." Pp. 163-187 in *Western Society After the Holocaust*, ed. Lyman Letgers (Boulder: Westview Press, 1983).

———. *After Auschwitz* (Baltimore: Johns Hopkins University Press, 1990).

Ryback, Timothy. "Between Art and Atrocity," *Art News* 92 (December 1993): 116-121.

Sabini, John and Maury Silver. "Destroying the Innocent With a Clear Conscience: A Sociopsychology of the Holocaust." Pp. 329-358 in *Survivors, Victims and Perpetrators: Essays in the Nazi Holocaust*, ed. Joel Dimsdale (Washington, DC: Hemisphere Publishing, 1980).

Sartre, Jean-Paul. *Anti-Semite and Jew* (New York: Schocken Books, 1948).

Schleunes, Karl. *The Twisted Road to Auschwitz* (Urbana: University of Illinois Press, 1990).

Scholem, Gersholem. *On Jews and Judaism in Crisis* (New York: Schocken Books, 1976).

Segev, Tom. *Soldiers of Evil: The Commandants of the Nazi Concentration Camps* (New York: McGraw Hill, 1987).

Steiner, George. *Language and Silence* (New York: Atheneum, 1967).

Stern, Fritz. *The Politics of Cultural Despair: A Study in the Rise of German Ideology* (Berkeley: University of California Press, 1961).

Sutzkever, Abraham. *Selected Poetry and Prose* (Berkeley: University of California Press, 1991).

'Swiebocka, Teresa (ed). *Auschwitz: A History in Photographs*. Published for the Auschwitz-Birkenau State Museum (Bloomington: Indiana University Press, 1993).

Tec, Nechama. *When Light Pierced the Darkness: Christian Rescuers of Jews in Nazi-Occupied Poland* (New York: Oxford University Press, 1986).

Theroux, Paul. *The Great Railway Bazaar: By Train Through Asia* (New York: Houghton Mifflin, 1975).

Trillin, Calvin. "American Chronicles: Black or White." *New Yorker* (14 April 1986): 62-78.

Troyer, Ronald, and Gerald Markle. *Cigarettes: The Battle Over Smoking* (New Brunswick, NJ: Rutgers University Press, 1983).

Van Pelt, Robert-Jan. "A Site in Search of a Mission." Pp. 93-156 in *Anatomy of the Auschwitz Death Camp*, eds. Israel Gutman and Michael Berenbaum (Bloomington: Indiana University Press, 1994).

Volkov, Shulamit, "The Written Matter and the Spoken Word." Pp. 33-53 in *Unanswered Questions*, ed. François Furet (New York: Schocken Press, 1989).

Wiesel, Elie. *Night* (New York: Hill & Wang, 1960).

———. "Trivializing the Holocaust: Semi-Fact and Semi-Fiction." *New York Times* (16 April 1978), Section II:1–29..

Wiesenthal, Simon. *The Sunflower* (New York: Schocken Books, 1976).

Williamson, Joel. *New People: Miscegenation and Mulattoes in the United States* (New York: Free Press, 1980).

Wilner, Eleanor. *Sarah's Choice* (Chicago: University of Chicago Press, 1989).

Wolff, Kurt. *The Sociology of Georg Simmel* (New York: Free Press, 1950).

Wright, Lawrence. "One Drop of Blood." *New Yorker* 25 July 1994: pp. 46-55.

Wyman, David. *Paper Walls: America and the Refugee Crisis, 1938-1941* (Amherst: University of Massachusetts Press, 1968).

———. *Abandonment of the Jews: America and the Holocaust, 1941-1945* (New York: Pantheon, 1984).

Yahil, Leni. *The Holocaust: The Fate of European Jewry.* (New York: Oxford University Press, 1990).

Young, James. "Israel's Memorial Landscapes: Sho'ah, Heroism, and National Redemption." Pp. 279-304 in *Lessons and Legacies: The Meaning of the Holocaust in a Changing World*, ed. Peter Hayes (Evanston: Northwestern University Press, 1991).

———. *The Texture of Memory: Holocaust Memorials and Meaning* (New Haven: Yale University Press, 1993.

Young-Bruehl, Elisabeth. *Hannah Arendt: For Love of the World* (New Haven: Yale University Press, 1982).

Zimbardo, Philip. "Pathology of Imprisonment." *Society* 9 (1972): 4-8.

Zuccotti, Susan. *The Italians and the Holocaust: Persecution, Rescue and Survival* (New York: Basic Books, 1987).

Zweig, Stefan. *The World of Yesterday* (London: Cassell and Company, 1953).

author index

Adam, Uwe Dietrich, 16n. 38
Adorno, Theodor, 124nn. 66, 67,
    125nn. 69, 70, 72, 126, 148
Allardyce, Gilbert, 22n. 59
Allen, Woody, 57n. 57
Allport, Gordon, 45
Alter, Robert, 27n. 71
Amery, Jean, 1, 15n. 35, 28n. 73, 41,
    41n. 19, 103
Annas, George, 112n. 37, 118n. 48
Arendt, Hannah, 13, 35–40, 35n.5,
    36n. 7, 37nn. 8, 9, 38nn. 11, 12,
    39nn. 13, 14, 42, 55, 56, 60, 99,
    101–4, 101n. 3, 102nn. 7, 8, 103nn.
    9–11, 104nn. 12–15, 105n. 17, 107n.
    22, 124, 124n. 64
Askenasy, Hans, 55–57, 55n. 52, 56n.
    54
Astor, Gerald, 9n. 24

Barkan, Elazar, 119n. 50
Barnouw, Dagme, 39, 40, 40n. 15
Bauer, Yehuda, 34n. 2
Bauman, Zygmunt, 19, 19n. 49, 68–
    70, 68n. 6, 69n. 10, 70n. 12, 72, 83,
    83n. 45, 108nn. 24, 25, 118n. 49,
    119n. 51, 128, 128nn. 78, 79, 129,
    129nn. 81, 82
Bellow, Saul, 41, 41n. 21
Bendix, Reinhard, 71n. 16
Berenbaum, Michael, 15n. 36
Bernal, J. D., 111n. 35
Bettelheim, Bruno, 28n. 72
Biagioli, Mario, 114n. 40
Bilski, Emily D., 148nn. 32, 33, 149n.
    34

Braham, Randolph, 21n. 57
Breitman, Richard, 6n. 13
Brockman, Stephen, 140n. 16, 144n.
    25
Browning, Christopher, 42n. 22, 43nn.
    24–26, 44n. 27, 45, 45nn. 29, 30, 60,
    60n. 63, 83, 83n. 46
Buck-Morss, Susan, 125n. 69
Bullock, Allan, 106n. 19
Burckhardt, Jacob, 18n. 44

Cameron, Ian, 123n. 62
Canovan, Margaret, 13n. 31, 102n. 5
Caplan, Arthur, 122n. 61
Cassirer, Ernst, 19n. 48
Chorover, Stephen, 110n. 31
Ciardi, John, 1
Clason, Todd, 10n. 25, 102n. 7, 107n.
    23
Cohen, Elie Aron, 115n. 42
Cohen, Nava, 115n. 43

Daniels, Roger, 93n. 75, 94nn. 76, 77,
    79, 95n. 80
Darre, R. W., 108
Davis, James F., 93n. 74
Dawidowicz, Lucy, 86, 86n. 57, 131
Denneny, Michael, 40, 40nn. 16, 17
Des Pres, Terrence, 4n. 7
Dicks, Henry, 54–57, 54n. 50, 55n. 51
Dimsdale, Joel, 67n. 4
Dormer, W. R., 140n. 17

Edge, David, 123n. 62
Eichmann, Adolph, 31
Einstein, Albert, 36n. 6

Ellinger, T., 119
Elliot, Gil, 23n. 63
Elms, Alan C., 46n. 32, 49n. 39
Etzioni, Amitai, 88n. 61
Evans, Richard, 141n. 18

Fein, Helen, 26n. 69
Fenelon, Fania, 7, 7nn. 15, 16, 18, 8,
    8nn. 19, 20
Fest, Joachim, 17, 17n. 42, 18, 18n. 45
Fireman, Bruce, 60n. 65
Fitzgerald, Frances, 140n. 15
Fleming, Gerald, 96n. 83
Flood, Charles, 20n. 51
Frenkel-Brunswik, Else, 125nn. 69, 70,
    72, 126n. 73
Freud, Sigmund, 19n. 48
Friedlander, Saul, 86n. 56, 114n. 40,
    138n. 9
Friedrichs, Otto, 15n. 36
Fromm, Erich, 18n. 19
Furet, François, 16nn. 37, 38, 86n. 56

Gage, Nicholas, 153
Gamson, William, 60n. 65
Gellately, Robert, 107n. 21
Georg, Sergeant Willy, 13n. 32
Gerth, Hans H., 70n. 13, 72n. 18
Gilbert, Martin, 11n. 29, 20n. 50
Girdner, Audrie, 94n. 78
Glatstein, Jacob, 151
Goebbels, Josef, 33
Gottlieb, Roger, 152
Green, Jill, 10n. 25, 102n. 7, 107n. 23
Grodin, Michael, 112n. 37, 118n. 48
Grunfeld, Frederic, 19n. 48, 36n. 6,
    73n. 23
Gutman, Israel, 14n. 34, 15n. 36

Habermas, Jürgen, 145
Halbwachs, Maurice, 135n. 5
Hallie, Philip, 59n. 60
Hamilton, V. Lee, 53n. 47
Harris, Melvin, 95n. 81

Hartman, G. H., 138n. 10, 139n.
    11
Hayes, Peter, 134n. 2
Hegi, Ursula, 107n. 21
Heine, Heinrich, 77n. 37
Hilberg, Raul, 14n. 34, 16n. 37, 17n.
    39, 21n. 53, 63, 64, 64n. 1, 65n. 3, 68,
    74–76, 75nn. 28, 31, 32, 76nn. 33–35,
    78, 78n. 38, 82, 82n. 44, 83, 83n. 48
Himmler, Heinrich, 15n. 36, 63, 102n.
    8
Hinchman, Lewis, 39n. 14
Hinchman, Sandra, 39n. 14
Hitler, Adolph, 19, 20, 32, 84n. 51, 109
Horkheimer, 124n. 66
Hunt, Linda, 116n. 44
Huyssen, Andreas, 145n. 27

Jäckel, Eberhard, 84n. 51, 85n. 52
Jameson, Fredric, 12
Jasanoff, Shelia, 113n. 39
Jay, Martin, 124nn. 66, 68
Jones, James H., 120nn. 54, 55, 121n.
    58, 122n. 59
Junk, Peter, 148, 149

Kádár, György, 66
Kafka, Franz, 27, 27n. 71, 68, 73, 73n.
    22
Kampe, Norbert, 141n. 18
Kant, Immanuel, 40, 40n. 18
Katz, Fred, 88, 88nn. 60, 62
Kelman, Herbert, 53n. 47
Kennedy, John F., 131
Kerr, Philip, 58n. 58
Kevles, Daniel, 119n. 50
Kierkegaard, Soren, 57n. 57
Kilham, W., 69, 69n. 8
King, Richard, 142nn. 21, 22
Kitano, Harry, 93n. 75, 94nn. 76, 77,
    79
Koehl, Robert, 85n. 55
Koonz, Claudia, 81n. 42, 90n. 69
Kor, Eva Mozes, 118n. 48

Kremer, Dr. Johann, 11, 12
Kren, George, 69, 69n. 9, 105n. 16, 131, 145n. 26, 146, 146nn. 29, 30
Krinsky, Carol, 32
Kuhl, Stefan, 119n. 53
Kuhn, Thomas, 113n. 39

Lachs, John, 70n. 11
Lagerwey, Mary, 5n. 11, 10n. 25, 66, 102n. 7, 107n. 23
Laks, Syzmon, 7, 7nn. 15, 17, 8n. 21
Landau, Felix, 11
Lang, Berel, 27n. 70, 39n. 14
Lanzmann, Claude, 4n. 8, 63, 74n. 27, 75n. 29, 131
Laqueur, Walter, 22n. 60, 87n. 59
Leitner, Isabella, 10n. 25
Lendavi, Paul, 21n. 57
Letgers, Lyman, 127n. 77
Levinson, Daniel, 125nn. 69, 70, 72, 126n. 73
Levi, Primo, ix, 1, 5, 5n. 6, 6n. 14, 7n. 18, 10, 12, 12n. 30, 27n. 70, 65, 66, 133, 143, 143n. 23, 144
Levkov, I., 138n. 10
Lifton, Robert Jay, 110, 110n. 30, 115n. 42, 122n. 61
Linden, R. Ruth, 26n. 69
Loftis, Anne, 94n. 78
Lorenz, Konrad, 99
Lösener, Bernhard, 78
Lukács, György, 85n. 52
Lukacs, John, 17, 18, 18n. 43, 123n. 63

Maier, Charles, 141n. 18
Mann, L., 69, 69n. 8
Markle, Gerald, 10n. 25, 102n. 7, 106n. 20, 107n. 23, 112n. 37, 113n. 39, 137n. 8, 139n. 12
Marrus, Michael, 1n. 1, 22n. 58, 24n. 64, 75n. 30, 86nn. 56, 58
McCrea, Frances, 106n. 20, 137n. 8, 139n. 12

McKinney, David, 127n. 76
Meade, Tricia, 10n. 25, 102n. 7, 107n. 23
Melson, Robert, 24n. 65
Merton, Thomas, 38n. 10
Miale, Florence, 35, 36, 36n. 6, 54, 54n. 49, 56
Michelson, Richard, 100
Milchman, Alan, 128n. 79
Milgram, Stanley J., 31, 45n. 31, 47n. 34, 48–50, 48n. 36, 49n. 37, 50nn. 40, 41, 52, 52nn. 43–45, 53, 53n. 46, 59n. 62, 61, 61n. 67
Miller, Arthur, 56nn. 53, 55
Mills, C. Wright, 70n. 13, 72n. 18
Mommsen, Hans, 86n. 56, 87, 87n. 59, 91n. 70
Moore, Barrington, 60, 60n. 65, 61, 61n. 66
Mosse, George, 21n. 55
Muller-Hill, Benno, 113n. 38
Myrdal, Gunnar, 93n. 74

Needham, Joseph, 111n. 35
Neumann, Franz, 84, 84nn. 49, 50, 85, 85n. 54
Nietzsche, Friedrich, 124n. 65
Nolte, Ernst, 141, 142
Nomberg-Przytyk, Sara, 9n. 23, 10n. 25, 145, 146, 146n. 28
Nyiszli, Miklos, 115n. 42

Oliner, Pearl, 59n. 60
Oliner, Samuel, 59n. 60
Ozick, Cynthia, 41, 41n. 20, 136, 136n. 6, 152

Pane, Stanley G., 22n. 60
Pawel, Ernst, 72, 72n. 20, 73n. 24, 74, 74n. 26
Pecora, Vincent, 138n. 9
Petersen, James, 113n. 39
Pinch, Trevor, 113n. 39
Pressac, Jean-Claude, 15n. 36

Proctor, Robert, 109nn. 27, 28, 111n. 32, 112n. 37, 114, 114n. 41, 122n. 61, 123n. 63
Prufer, Kurt, 96, 97

Rappoport, Leon, 69, 69n. 9, 105n. 16, 131, 145n. 26, 146, 146nn. 29, 30
Reilly, Philip, 119n. 52
Reissman, David, 107n. 22
Rentschler, Eric, 144n. 24
Reynolds, Larry, 96n. 82
Rieth, Adolf, 134n. 1
Ritzer, George, 71n. 15
Robinson, Jacob, 35n. 5
Rose, Gilian, 124n. 66
Rosenberg, Alan, 128n. 79
Rosenfeld, Alvin, 17n. 41, 139n. 11
Rosen, Norma, 65
Ross, Guenther, 127n. 77
Rousset, David, 104n. 14
Rozett, Robert, 14n. 34
Rubenstein, Richard, 17n. 40, 23n. 63, 24n. 65, 70n. 13, 127–29, 127n. 77, 129nn. 80, 82
Ryback, Timothy, 5n. 9
Rytina, Steven, 60n. 65

Sabini, John, 67, 67n. 4, 68, 68nn. 5, 7
Sanford, R. Nevitt, 125nn. 69, 70, 72, 126n. 73
Sartre, Jean-Paul, 21n. 57, 42
Schiller, Friedrich, 8
Schlesinger, Arthur, 140n. 14
Schleunes, Karl, 86n. 56, 88, 89n. 64
Scholem, Gershom, 35n. 5, 149, 149n. 35, 150
Segev, Tom, 60n. 64
Seltzer, Michael, 35, 36, 36n. 6, 54, 54n. 49, 56
Silver, Maury, 67, 67n. 4, 68, 68nn. 5, 7
Simmel, Georg, 25, 25n. 68
Snow, C. P., 31
Steiner, George, 8, 8n. 22, 9

Stern, Fritz, 85n. 52
Sutzkever, Abraham, 13, 13n. 33
Swiebocka, Teresa, 15n. 36

Theroux, Paul, 65
Toynbee, Arnold, 23, 24
Trillin, Calvin, 92n. 72
Troyer, Ronald, 112n. 37
Tucholsky, Kurt, 73, 73n. 23, 74

Van Pelt, Robert-Jan, 15n. 36
Volkov, Shulamit, 21, 21n. 54, 22, 22n. 58

Wagner, Richard, 31
Warren, Earl, 95n. 80
Weber, Max, 68, 70n. 13, 71, 72
Wiesel, Elie, 28n. 72, 66, 139n. 13
Wiesenthal, Simon, 11n. 28
Williamson, Joel, 91n. 71
Wilner, Eleanor, 58n. 59
Wolff, Kurt, 25n. 68
Wolfskehl, Karl, 150, 151
Wright, Lawrence, 92n. 73
Wyman, David, 107n. 23

Yahil, Leni, 20n. 52, 88n. 63, 90nn. 66, 68
Young-Bruehl, Elisabeth, 13n. 31, 101n. 2
Young, James, 134, 134n. 2, 135n. 2

Zimbardo, Philip, 52n. 45
Zimmer, Wendelin, 147, 148
Zuccotti, Susan, 22n. 61
Zweig, Stefan, 24n. 66

subject index

Abraham, 57–59, 57n. 57
  and Genesis 22, 57
  and holocaust, 57, 57n. 56
  feminist version of, 58
Adorno, Theodor, 124, 124n. 66, 125n.
  69, 126, 126nn. 74, 75, 127, 129n. 82
alienation
  of modern life, 12
Allies, The, 3
altruism, 59nn. 60, 61
American Eugenetic Research
  Association, The, 119.
    See also medical experiments
American Jewish Joint Distribution
  Committee, The, 89n. 65
American Sociological Association,
  150
Amery, Jean, 83, 83n. 47
anamnestic solidarity, 148
anti-Semitism, 21n. 53, 24, 44, 54, 59,
  86, 88, 89, 90, 90n. 67, 102n. 4, 107n.
  21, 108, 136
  and Denmark, 22
  and France, 21
  and Germany, 21
  and Gypsies, 21
  and hatred of minorities, 22
  and Hitler, 19–21, 21n. 56
  and Italy, 22, 22n. 61
  and Jews, 21, 21n. 57
  and misogyny, 22
  and nationalism, 22
  and Poland, 21, 21n. 57
  and WWI, 20, 20n. 51, 21
  as a cultural code, 22, 22n. 60
  as central to Nazism, 107
  as ideology, 21

emotional, 20, 67, 126n. 75
institutional, 126
rational, 20, 21, 67, 90
archives
  Russian, The, 96n. 83
Arendt, Hannah, 13n. 31, 35n. 5, 52,
  54, 60n. 64, 61, 74n. 25, 76, 101–7,
  101n. 2, 102n. 4, 6, 105n. 17, 106n.
  18, 124n. 65, 125–27, 126n. 74, 128n.
  79, 129n. 82
  and analysis of the Stalinist
    Soviet Union, 105, 106.
  and her interpretation of
    Eichmann, 35–42.
    See also banality, Eichmann,
    normalcy and totalitarianism
Aryan, 6n. 13, 103
  and medical experiments, 118
  and the Reich Citizenship Law,
    79
  bureaucracies and schools, 76
  Christ as an, 31
  definition of, 77, 80, 80n. 40
  definition of non-, 83
  music, 7n. 18.
    See also Nuremberg laws of
    blood and honor
Auschwitz, 1, 5, 5n. 10, 9, 12, 15, 15n.
  36, 21, 27, 41, 66, 72n. 19, 83, 87, 88,
  96, 99, 101, 101n. 1, 104, 107n. 23,
  122, 126, 136, 141–43, 145, 146, 152
  and autism, 28n. 72
  and birth, 9, 9n. 24, 10n. 25. *See*
    also children
  and medical experiments,
    117–19, 118n. 48
  and scientism, 123, 124

Auschwitz *(continued)*
  and tourists, 1n. 1
  as world's largest cemetery, 16,
    16n. 38
  death toll of, 16n. 38
  implications of, 125
  killing center of, 4n. 6
  liberation of, 4n. 5, 16n. 38, 147
  maximum efficiency of, 16
  survivor of, 15n. 35.
  See also Oświceçim
Austria, 18n. 46
authoritarian personality, 126, 127
  and childrearing, 19, 19n. 47
  and Germans, 18, 19, 24
  and Nazism, 18, 19, 19n. 47
Authoritarian Personality, The, 125, 126

Bad Blood, 122n. 61
banality, 40n. 18, 41n. 20, 55, 97
  and childhood, 101
  and existence, 136
  of evil, 36–42, 61
  of Nazi slaughter, 143.
  See also Arendt, Eichmann and
    totalitarianism
Banjac, Marko, 28, 29, 153
Bauman, Zygmunt, 127, 129, 129n. 82
Bavarian Alps, 2
Beethoven, 8, 27, 105, 124, 152
Behemoth, 84, 84n. 49. *See also*
  Leviathan
Bełżec, 143
Benjamin, Walter, 124n. 66
Bergman, Ingmar, 3
Berlin
  and Brandenberg Gate, 104n. 15
  and Checkpoint Charlie, 32
  and Gropius Haus, 148
  and Humbolt University, 32
  and the Beth Café, 32
  and the German Experimental
    Institute for Aviation, 116. *See
    also* medical experiments

and the largest synagogue in the
    world, 32
  and the Oranien district, 32, 33
  Staatsoper, 31
  Wall, 32
biologists
  as gardeners, 108, 108n. 26.
  See also metaphor and physicians
Birkenau, 4n. 6, 15n. 36. *See also*
  Auschwitz and Brzezinka
Bitburg. *See* historiography
black plague, the
  as analogous to the Holocaust,
    145
Bloch, Marc, 152
Bolshevism, 109, 109n. 27, 141, 142
Book of Samuel, the, 137
Bosnia
  and ethnic massacre, 28
Braun, Eva, 2
Brzezinka, 15n. 36. *See also* Birkenau
Buchenwald, 117, 135n. 5
Buchmann, Lieutenant Hans, 44n. 28
bureaucracy, 87, 90
  and autonomy, 88
  and compliance, 88, 88n. 61
  and dehumanization, 70
  and hierarchy of authority, 71
  and history-making behavior, 67
  and instrumental rationality, 128
  and Max Weber, 71, 71n. 16
  and moral responsibility, 72
  and murder, 67. *See also* mass
    murder
  and obedience, 69.
  and the Nazi machine, 75, 78
  and trains, 63–66.
  as a mechanism of rationality, 71
  as an exercise of power, 72, 85.
  as cold, rational and impersonal,
    127
  as historically located, 127
  as inventive, 80, 81
  of destruction, 76

versus anarchy and chaos, 68.
See also chaos
bystanders, 17n. 39

Campbell, Clarence G., 119
Camp David, 2
C.A.N.D.L.E.S., 118n. 48
Catel, Werner, 110n. 29
Chamberlain, Neville, 3n. 4
chaos, 78, 84, 84n. 51, 85, 89, 126
    as a gray area, 87. *See also* gray
        zone
    monsters of, 84n. 49. *See also*
        Behemoth and Leviathan
    stateless, 86
Chełmno, 37, 143, 144
children
    and burning babies, 105
    at Auschwitz, 9, 9n. 24, 10, 10nn.
        25, 26
    mass murder of, 106, 110n. 29, 144
    See also Auschwitz and women
civilization
    contradictions of, 11
Clauberg, Dr. Carl, 118
Clinton, Bill, 104n. 15
closure
    as an illusion, 149
    as dangerous, 149
collective
    guilt, 139n. 13, 141
    responsibility, 139n. 13
    See also memory
concentration camps
    and bureaucracy, 102n. 7
    and incarceration of American
        Japanese, 91, 93, 94, 94nn. 78,
        79
    and mass starvation, 6n. 13
    and secrecy, 107n. 23
    and the murder of Jewish
        scientists, 112n. 35
    and the terrorism of random
        violence, 102nn. 7, 8

as death camps, 6n. 13, 86, 141n.
    20, 143, 144
as historically unique, 15
as the ultimate expression of
    totalitarianism, 103, 104
of Poland, 43
order and control amidst chaos
    and death in, 6
Soviet versus Nazi, 106n. 18
victims of, 139
See also bureaucracy and medical
    experiments
See also under specific names
Coolidge, Calvin, 119
Copernican revolution
    the Holocaust as equivalent to
        the, 146
crematoria, 8, 29, 96. *See also* Krema
culture
    and bestiality, 8
    and mass murder, 9
Cunning of History, The, 128

Dachau, 5, 28n. 72, 140n. 14
    and art, 5n. 9
    and medical experiments, 116,
        117
    and trees, 4, 4n. 6
    as a cemetery, 4
    as the first concentration camp,
        4n. 5
    as a symbol of the Holocaust, 4
    as a tourist site, 4
    beauty of, 4
Damned, The, 146, 147
Dawidowicz, Lucy, 142
    as a critic of functionalism, 86n.
        57. *See also* functionalism and
        intentionalism
Descartes, 128
Destruction of the European Jews, 74
De Witt, General John L., 94
dialectic of enlightenment, the, 124.
    See also modernity and science

dialogue, 127, 152
    between the living and the dead,
      152
Drexler, Anton, 20n. 51
Drowned and the Saved, The, 66

Eagle's Nest, The, 2, 2n. 3
Eichmann, 33–42, 74, 149, 150
    and administration of the
      Holocaust, 33
    and autonomy, 88. *See also*
      bureaucracy
    and Israeli trial, 34, 34n. 3, 35n. 5
    and WWII, 34
    as madman and monster, 35
    as normal, 38, 38n. 10, 39
    as ordinary, 36. *See also* Arendt
    birthplace of, 33
Eichmann experiments, The, 45–53, 59,
    60
    and authority, 52
    and conformity, 55
    and Nazism, 53, 54
    and Judeo-Christian ethics, 50,
      51
    and obeyers versus others, 49n.
      39
    and personality (MMPI), 49
    and responsibility, 51
    and sadism, 50
    and variation, 48n. 36
    and violence, 48n. 35, 49
    and weakness, 51, 51n. 42
    and women, 49n. 38
    as irrelevant, 54n. 49
    as process, 68
    as unethical, 47n. 34.
    See also Milgram and Zimbardo
Einsatzgruppen, 34n. 1, 43
Einstein, Albert, 112n. 35
Eisenhower, Milton, 94
Eleni, 153
Elms, Alan C., 49
Emancipation Theory, 80

Encyclopedia of the Holocaust, 137
Enlightenment, the, 138n. 9
existentialism, 104n. 12

Fascism, 24
    and Italy, 22
    and Mussolini's Blackshirts, 22n.
      59
    and Nazis, 22n. 59
    and Party power, 85
    as ideology, 22n. 60
    definition of, 22nn. 59, 60.
    See also National Socialism and
      Nazism
Fenelon, Fania, 7
Final Solution, The, 2, 83
    as the outcome of bureaucracy,
      128
    and the Wannsee Conference, 34,
      34n. 2.
    See also genocide
Fischer, Ludwig, 133
Franco-Prussian War
    and the treaty of Brest-Litovsk,
      23n. 62
French Revolution, the, 135, 145
    and the meaning of freedom,
      135
    and violence and chaos, 135
    as a glimmer of hope, 135
Freud, Sigmund, 112n. 35, 125n. 71
Frick, 90
Fromm, Erich, 124n. 66, 125n. 71
functionalism, 84, 87, 89
    and cumulative radicalization,
      87, 88
    and de-emphasis of the state, 87
    and dialecticism, 86
    and the origins of the Holocaust,
      86
    and the twisted road to
      Auschwitz, 88, 89
    as non-Hitler-centric, 86.
    See also intentionalism

Galton, Frances, 118n. 49
gas chambers, 16, 29, 104, 118, 119,
    144
    and Zyklon B, 143
    as killing factories, 83
Gebhardt, Karl, 117n. 47
genocide, 12–14, 15n. 36, 33, 34, 77,
    97, 105, 137, 137n. 7, 141, 142
    and America, 14
    and German bureaucracy, 34n. 2
    and Germany, 14
    and Gypsies, 14
    and Native Americans, 14
    and the Bible, 57n. 56
    and the Near East, 24
    comparison of Turkish and
        German, 24n. 66, 141
    state-sponsored, 27
    uniqueness of the Nazi, 67, 68
    universality of, 152.
    See also historiography and
        violence
German Lutheran Church, The, 89
German Red Cross, the, 117n. 47. See
    also medical experiments
Germans
    as U.S. allies, 139, 140
    as victims, 139, 139n. 14
German Workers' Party, 20n. 51. See
    also Socialist German Workers'
    Party
Germany
    and political theory, 84
    as a state? 84, 85
    as people of "Poets and Think-
        ers", 15, 103
    See also perpetrator explanation
Gestapo, 135n. 5, 152
ghetto, ix, 6n. 13, 43, 128n. 79, 152
    diaries, 13
    Łodz, 72n. 19
    the world as a, 66
    Vilna, the, 13
    Warsaw, the, 13n. 32, 133

Goethe, 8, 19n. 48, 105
Göring, Hermann, 35n. 4, 82
gray zone, 12, 56, 58, 67
    good, evil and the, 129n. 82
Great Railway Bazaar, The, 65
Guttman, Lieutenant Hugo, 21
Gypsies, 16n. 38

Habermas, Jürgen, 141n. 18
Heidegger, Martin, 13n. 31, 124n. 65,
    104n. 12
Heller, John, 122
Hess, Rudolph, 35n. 4
Heydrich, Reinhard, 34n. 1, 81n. 43
Hilberg, Raul, 75, 83, 84, 85n. 53, 132–
    34, 151
Hillgruber, Andreas, 141n. 18
Himmler, Heinrich, 6n. 13
Hirohito, 94
historians' debate. See historiography
historical scholarship, 13, 14
    inductive versus deductive, 74
historiography
    and Bitburg, 138–41, 138n. 10,
        139n. 14, 144
    and the historians' debate, 138,
        141, 141nn. 18, 20, 142
    and the Potawatomi, 137, 138
    the tremendous importance of,
        138
history
    and privilege, 144
    as a mirror, 138. See also histori-
        ography
    fear of, 144
    great man theories of, 18
    hurt of, 12
    responsibility to, 135, 136
Hitler, Adolph, 3, 32, 80–82, 80n. 40,
    85nn. 53, 55, 86–88, 89n. 65, 90, 94,
    106–11, 106n. 19, 114, 119, 126n. 75,
    133, 139n. 12, 140, 141n. 20, 142, 152
    and the abolishment of legisla-
        ture, 85

Hitler *(continued)*
    and the Eagle's Nest, 2, 2n. 3
    and the Munich appeasement of
      1938, 3n. 4
    as an icon of evil, 17, 17n. 41
    as an error of history, 19n. 48
    as the most significant 20th
      century revolutionary, 17.
    See also perpetrator explanation
Hobbes, 84n. 49
holokitsch
    the Holocaust as, 132
Horkheimer, Max, 124n. 66, 129n. 82
Höss, Rudolph, 16n. 38

ideology, 102n. 8, 103, 107, 144
    and modernism, 100
    biological, 108. *See also* metaphor
    definition of, 102n. 6
intentionalism
    and an emphasis on the
      Nuremberg laws of blood and
      honor, 88, 89
    and the origins of the Holocaust,
      86
    as Hitler-centric, 86
    birth of, 86.
    See also functionalism
Italian Fascist Party, 22. *See also*
    Fascism

Jaspers, Karl, 13n. 31, 126n. 74
Jewish Museum of New York, the,
    148
Jewishness
    and Judaism.
    and the Reform Jewish Move-
      ment, 25
    as a stranger, 25, 26
    definition of, 25, 77–79, 95. *See*
      also Nuremberg laws of blood
      and honor
Johns Hopkins University, 94
Joseph, Franz, 37n. 9

Journal of Heredity, 119. *See also*
    medical experiments
Judaism, 25
    genetics as the defining criterion
      of, 77
    racial parameters of, 95
Judenrat, 35n. 5, 128n. 79
Junk, Peter, 147, 148

Kafka, Franz, 72, 72nn. 19, 20, 73
Kennedy, John F., 140
Killy, Herr, 80
Kirkpatrick, Jeanne, 102n. 4
Kollwitz, Käthe, 66
Kor, Eva Mozes, 118n. 48
Kramer, Josef, 7
Krema, 96, 97.
    patenting of, 97.
    See also crematoria
Kremer, Dr. Johann, 12
Kristallnacht, 32, 33. *See also* Berlin
Kuhn, Thomas, 113, 113n. 39, 114

Laks, Syzmon, 7
Landau, Sergeant Felix, 12
language
    and the Holocaust, 136, 137,
      137n. 7
    Esperanto as a, 134
Lebensraum, 138n. 9
Leviathan, 84n. 49. *See also Behemoth*
Levi, Primo, 5n. 10, 127, 144
liberation
    of racial status, 80, 80n. 40
Lohengrin
    and the "Wedding March", 31
Lolita, 38
Lösener, Bernhard, 78, 79, 89, 89n.
    65
Luther, 129n. 82
Luxemburg, Rosa, 109n. 27

machine
    the Holocaust as a, 75

Madagascar
    and forced Jewish emigration, 87
Marcuse, Herbert, 124n. 66
marriage, 81, 82
    and privilege, 82
    See also Nuremberg laws of
        blood and honor
Marx, Karl, 32, 109n. 27
mass murder, 67, 136, 137
    administered, 128
    and book burning, 77n. 37
    and choice, 45
    and conformity, 45, 55
    and careerism, 45
    and German Reserve Police
        Battalion 101, 42–45, 51n. 42,
        59
    and killing children, 67
    and ordinary men, 42, 45. *See also*
        banality
    and psychopathy, 66
    and reason, 124
    and reflexivity, 45
    and science, 110
    and Stalin, 23n. 62
    as habit, routine and tradition,
        75, 76, 83
    assertion of purpose for, 151
    as the quintessence of modernity,
        128
    at Józefów, Poland, 42–44, 59
    bureaucrats and, 88
    of the Potawatomi, 138. *See also*
        historiography.
    scientists and physicians as
        instruments of, 114.
    See also bureaucracy, physicians
        and science
Mauthausen, 4n. 8, 29
    and "186 steps", 29
    and the Wall of Lamentations,
        29
    as beautiful, 29
Maximillian I, 5

meaningless, the Holocaust as,
    74
medical experiments, Nazi, 115–18
    and British eugenics, 118n. 49
    and ethics, 115n. 43
    and Jewish physicians, 115n. 42
    and Operation Paperclip, 116n.
        44
    and racist ideology, 115, 115n. 43
        dwarf experiments, 117
        sterilization, 118
        twin experiments, 117, 118,
            118n. 48
    and the National Research Act of
        1974, 122n. 60
    and the SS, 115
    and U.S. eugenics, 118–20
        Tuskegee Study of Untreated
            Syphilis, 120–22, 120n. 55,
            121n. 58, 122nn. 60, 61
    as unscientific, 122n. 61
    of starvation, 12
    survival and rescue, 115, 116
        at high altitude, 116, 116n. 44
        in freezing temperatures, 116
    treatment, 115, 117n. 45
        immunization, 116
        of battle injuries, 116, 117,
            117n. 46
        of burns, 117
        of gun shot wounds, 117.
    See also physicians and science
Mein Kampf, 19, 36, 86. *See also*
    intentionalism
memoirs, 5, 5nn. 10, 11, 7, 7n. 15, 13,
    66, 86n. 57, 104n. 14
    as gray, 10
    as snapshots in black and white,
        10
    violence in, 11
memorial(s), 131–35
    and the influence of Jugendatil
        and Bauhaus styles, 150
    as fascist artifacts, 134

memorials *(continued)*
    critique of, 134
    meaning of, 134, 151
    Miami, 150
    See also under specific names
memory
    and the connection to history
        and future, 136
    and the meaning of time,
        136
    collective, 135, 135n. 5
    fear of, 144
    historical, 144
Mendelsohn, Moses, 32, 33
Mengele, Josef, 9, 9n. 24, 10, 117, 118,
    122n. 61
Merton, Robert K., 111n. 33
metaphor
    and ideology, 108
    gardening, 108, 108n. 26, 114,
        123, 128
    of darkness versus light, 143
    of hell, 146
    of otherworldliness, 146
    versus analogy, 146
Miami, 152
    as nouvelle Jewish, 150
    memorial, 150
Milgram, J. Stanley, 47n. 34, 48n. 35,
    49n. 39, 54, 54n. 49, 56, 59–61, 68,
    68n. 6, 69
    and Eichmann experiments,
        45–53. *See also* Eichmann
        experiments
    and phenomenology, 46
Minsk, 37, 37n. 9
Mischlinge, 79–81, 79n. 39, 80n. 40,
    89n. 65. *See also* Nuremberg laws of
    blood and honor
misogyny
    exceptions to, 90n. 69
modernism
    and ahistoricism, 99, 100
    and science and medicine, 101.
        See also medical experiments

as opposed to tradition, 100
    Los Angeles as the vanguard of,
        99
    Nazi society as the quintessence
        of, 101
modernity, 124, 126
    and process, 97
    and progress, 129
    and substance, 97
    as regressive, 126
    biblical roots of, 129n. 82
    bureaucracy and secularism as
        products of, 129n. 82
    the holocaust potential of, 129
    the Holocaust as a result of,
        127
Moore, Barrington, 68, 69
morality, 70
Mozart, 3, 8
Mr. Sammler's Planet, 41
Munich, 3
    and birth of the Nazi Party, 3
    appeasement of 1938, 3n. 4
music, 31
    and mass murder, 8
    German, 8
Mussolini, 2
My Lai
    and American war crime, 53n. 47

Napalm
    and responsibility for burned
        babies, 69
National Socialism, 33
    and functionalism, 87. *See also*
        functionalism
    as applied biology, 109
    See also Fascism and Nazism
National Socialist German Workers'
    Party, 99. *See also* Nazism
National Socialist Physicians'
    League, 109. *See also* metaphor and
    physicians
Nazism, 3, 13, 13n. 31, 36n. 6, 55n. 51
    and a Jewish conspiracy, 103

and due process, 29, 68, 78, 79, 82
and irrationality, 111n. 35
and pathology, 54, 55
and race laws, 29
and SA, 90, 90n. 67
and terrorism, 102n. 7, 103. See also totalitarianism
and the centrality of Auschwitz, 101
and wickedness, 56
as an irrational social movement, 106n. 20
as banal, 55, 56. See also banality
causes of
fanaticism, 35
psychopathy, 35, 36
sex perversion, 35
xenophobia, 35
as collective insanity, 35
as demonic, 56
as evil, 35
as feudalism, 85n. 55
as genius, 41
as non-atavistic, 102
ideology of, 84, 84n. 51, 85n. 52
modern nature of, 98. See also modernity
neo-, 33.
See also Fascism, metaphor and National Socialism
Neue Osbabrücker Zeitung, 147
Neumann, Franz, 84nn. 49, 50, 85n. 53, 87, 102
New Yorker, The, 35
Night, 66
Night and Fog, 10n. 27
Nolte, Ernst, 141n. 18, 142, 143
Nomberg-Pryztyk, Sara, 9, 9n. 23, 10n. 25
normalcy, 38, 39
of the Holocaust, 26
thesis, 56, 57.
See also Arendt, banality and Eichmann

Nuremberg
trials, 35, 35n. 4, 86, 88, 149
of Nazi physicians, 122nn. 60, 61. See also medical experiments and physicians
Nuremberg laws of blood and honor, 20n. 52, 76–84, 89–92
Nussbaum, Felix, 146–49
and decadent art, 148
obedience, 12, 31, 53
and bureaucracy, 69
and disobedience, 59, 60, 60n. 65
and hierarchy, 68–70
and Judeo-Christian tradition, 58
and personality, 60
and the paradox of sequential action, 68, 70. See also sociology
and women, 69n. 8
as an expression of culture, 60
crimes of, 53n. 47.
See also Eichmann experiments and Milgram
Olsen, Culbert, 94, 95
Oneg Shabbat, 13n. 32. See also ghetto
opera, 31, 32
orchestra
at Auschwitz, 6–9, 7n. 18
ordinary
the Holocaust as, 76. See also banality
Origins of Totalitarianism, The, 101, 104, 105, 105n. 17
Orwell, George, 139n. 14
Oświeçim, 15n. 36. See also Auschwitz
Ozick, Cynthia, 152

pathology thesis, 56, 57, 125
Pearson, Karl, 118n. 49
Penal Colony, The, 73, 73n. 21, 74
perpetrator explanation
and Germans, 18, 19
and Hitler, 17, 24, 140

physicians
    and eugenics doctrines, 110
    and the euthanasia program, 110
    and the gardening metaphor, 108
    and the Hippocratic Oath, 110n.
        30, 112, 122n. 61
    and the Law for the Prevention
        of Genetically Diseased
        Offspring (sterilization law),
        109
    and medicalization, 110
    Aryan, 109
    as strongest supporters of Hitler,
        108, 109
Platek, Felka, 147, 149
Plessy v. Ferguson, 92
poetry
    of survivors, 13
Poland
    and its first free election, 132
    and Lech Wałęsa, 132
    and Tadeusz Mazowiecki, 132
    and the last synagogue, 133
    and the Palace of Culture, 133
    and the Vistula, 134
postmodern
    the world as, 100
power, ix, 66
    and feudalism, 85n. 55. *See also*
        Nazism
    and ideology, 84
    and violence, 85
    in modern societies, 72
    in traditional societies, 71, 72,
        72n. 17
    Nazi centers of, 85
    of the bureaucratic machine, 73
Proctor, Robert, 114n. 40
Prufer, Kurt, 97

race
    and miscegenation, 91, 92
    and the hypo-decent rule, 95, 96
    and the Ku Klux Klan, 93

and the one-drop rule, 92, 93n.
    74, 96
    as a cultural invention, 96
    as a fixed biological category, 96
    definition of U.S., 91, 91n. 71, 95,
        96
    See also Nuremberg laws of
        blood and honor
Racial Hygiene, 114
racism, 12. *See also* anti-Semitism and
    genocide
radical situationalism, 56
railway system. *See* trains
Rapaport, Nathan, 135n. 3
Rassenschande, 81, 82. *See also*
    Nuremberg laws of blood and
    honor
rationality
    and social organization, 71
    bureaucratic, 71, 86. *See also*
        bureaucracy
    instrumental, 97
    iron cage of, 71, 71n. 15. *See also*
        Weber
Ravensbruck, 116–18, 117n. 47. *See
    also* medical experiments
Reagan, Ronald, 102n. 4, 139, 139nn.
    13, 14, 140, 140n. 14, 144. *See also*
        historiography
Redgrave, Vanessa, 7n. 15
Reichsbahn, the (DB), 63–66. *See also*
    trains
reflexivity, 25, 152
    and autobiography, 26n.
        69
    and Holocaust Studies, 28
    as sociological method, 26n. 69
    See also sociology
Rilke, 8
rituals
    bed-making, 5, 6
    roll call, 6n. 14
Röhm, Earnst, 90n. 67
romance, the suffering of, 82

Roosevelt, Franklin, 94
Rubenstein, Richard, 127, 127n. 77, 129, 129n. 82
Ruff, Siegfried, 116n. 44
Russia
    and Polish architecture, 133
    and the Russian Revolution, 141, 142
    as concentration camp liberators, 4n. 5
    as U.S. enemy, 139, 140, 140n. 15
Sachsenhausen, 118. *See also* medical experiments
Sammler, Arthur, 41
San Francisco Chronicle, The
    and anti-Japanese campaign, 93
Sartre, Jean-Paul, 104n. 12
Schacht, 90
Scholem, Gershom, 149
Schrödinger, Erwin, 112n. 35
science
    and applied biology, 112
    and biologism, 123, 123n. 63
    and enlightenment, 123, 124, 124n. 65
    and instrumental reason, 123, 124
    and power and prestige, 113, 114
    and scientism, 123, 123n. 62, 124
    as the quintessence of democracy, 111
    bad, 122n. 61
    German, 111n. 35, 112
    good, 111n. 33, 122n. 61
    impact of the Holocaust on, 145
    Nazi, 111
        as perverted by politicians, 111, 112
        as perverted by scientists, 111–13
    normal, 113, 113n. 39, 114. *See also* Kuhn
    progressive, 112, 112n. 36

Soviet, 111n. 34
    See also medical experiments, metaphor and physicians
secret
    the Holocaust as a, 107, 107n. 23. *See also* totalitarianism
selections, 7, 144
    and children, 9n. 24
    and elderly, 9n. 24
    and women, 9n. 24
    as masturbation, 8
    at death camps, 143
sexism, 81, 81n. 42, 90n. 69. *See also* misogyny
    and medical experiments, 121n. 58
Shawl, The, 136
Shoah, 4n. 8, 63, 131, 143
    as a masterpiece, 74n. 27
shtetl, 152
Simmel, Georg, 25n. 68
    and dominant ideology, 26. *See also* sociology
slave labor
    and BASF tapes, 152
    and Bayer aspirin, 152
    and I. G. Farben, 15n. 36
Sobibór, 143
Socialist German Workers' Party, 20n. 51. *See also* German Workers' Party
sociology
    and chaos, 26
    and Holocaust writing, 26n. 69
    and homology versus analogy, 53n. 48, 138n. 9
    and meditation, 26, 27
    and Simmel's stranger, 26
    and the functional division of labor, 68. *See also* obedience
    and theories of mass society, 106, 106n. 20
    and the role of the other, 39. *See also* Eichmann
    macro, 30, 126

sociology *(continued)*
  messianic, 26
  meso, 30
  micro, 30, 126
  positivistic, 26, 26n. 69
  the birth of, 135n. 4.
  See also reflexivity and Weber
Soviet Gulag, the, 141–44
Spanish Inquisition, The, 77n. 36
SS, 6, 6n. 13, 12, 42, 99, 149
  and the Auschwitz orchestra, 7,
    7n. 18
  and the Reichsbahn, 64, 64n. 2.
    See also trains
  and the SD, 34n. 1
  as insane, 54
  headquarters, 148
Stalin, 105, 106, 106n. 19, 109n. 27
  and realism in art, 134, 135
  See also Arendt and totalitarianism
Sudetenland, 3n. 4
sunflower
  imagery of, 11, 11n. 28
survivors, 1, 5, 5n. 10, 127
  and idyllic childhoods, 136
  and funerals, 136
  and privileged voice, 40, 41
  and privileged writing, 27, 28,
    28n. 73
  and suicide, 6n. 12, 15n. 35
  and the nightmare of trains, 65,
    66. *See also* trains
  memories of, 131
  of death camps, 143
  *See also under specific names and
    memoirs*

tatoos, 16n. 38, 144, 150, 152
theodicy, 129n. 82
  as disingenuous, 151
Tojo, 94
Topf & Sohne, 96, 97. *See also* crematoria, Krema and Prufer
totalitarianism, 40n. 18, 42, 101, 102,
  104n. 12, 105, 140

and arbitrariness, 104
and communism, 102n. 4
and good science, 111n. 33. *See
  also* science
and ideology, 102
and loneliness, 107, 107n. 22
and propaganda, 103
and terrorism, 102, 102n. 7
and the industrial revolution, 107
and the SS, 106
as resulting from,
  anti-Semitism, 102n. 4
  imperialism, 102n. 4
  racism, 102n. 4
as total domination, 104
secrecy as the basis of, 107
See also banality, modernism and
  Nazism
tourist
  memories of a, 131, 132
  of the Holocaust, 1, 1n. 1, 2, 29,
    150
tours
  as strange and disorienting, 132
trains, ix, 10n. 26, 15, 63–66, 144
  as a powerful image of the
    Holocaust, 63
  as civilized transportation, 65
Trapp, Major William "Papa", 42–45,
  43n. 24
Treblinka, 63, 133, 143, 144
Treister, Kenneth, 151
Trial, The, 73
Trotsky, Leon, 109n. 27
Tucholsky, Kurt, 73n. 23

unique
  the Holocaust as, 76, 143
United Nations, the, 102n. 4

victims
  guilty, 106
  innocent, 104, 105, 105n. 16. *See
    also* totalitarianism
  scholarship on, 17

Vietnam War, 26
violence
  mob, 67
  state-sponsored, 24
  See also genocide

Waffen-SS, 6n. 13, 139. *See also* SS
Wagner, 33, 152
  and National Socialism, 32
  as Germany's greatest prophetic
    figure, 32
  the dark boldness of, 31
War Relocation Authority, 94. *See also*
  concentration camps
Warren, Earl, 95, 95n. 80
Warsaw, 132, 133
  as a symbol of the cold war, 133
  Ghetto, 133–35
    as artificial, 133
    memorial, 133, 134
  Pact, 133
  sculpture, 135n. 3
  uprising, 131
Washington, Booker T., 121n. 57
Washington Star, 121. *See also* medical
  experiments
Weber, Max, 71, 71nn. 14–16, 72n. 18,
  75, 97, 127, 127n. 77, 129n. 82
weddings
  the sweetness and näiveté of, 31
Weimar Republic, The, 80
  constitution, 71n. 14
  See also Weber and WWI
Wiesel, Elie, 151
women
  and medical experiments, 117,
    118, 121n. 58

at Auschwitz, 9, 9n. 24, 10, 10n.
  26
WWI, 23, 71n. 14, 141
  and German life, 35, 36
  and hair manufacturing, 143
  and Jewish activism in leftist
    politics, 109n. 27
  and mass death, 24, 24n. 66
  and modernism, 102n. 4
  and the battle of Verdun, 23
  and the Somme, 23
  and the Turks massacre of
    Armenians, 23
  and the Versailles Treaty, 23
  as the "Great War", 23, 24
  memoirs of, 24n. 66
WWII, 18, 71, 81, 91, 93, 141
  and D-Day, 104n. 15
  and Pearl Harbor, 93
  and mass death, 24
  Reagan's characterization of, 140
  See also concentration camps

Yad Vashem, 131–33
  as kitsch, 132
Yahil, Leni, 89
Yom Hashon, 139n. 14

Zamenhoff, Lazarus, 134
Ziereis, Franz "Babyface", 29
Zimbardo, Philip
  and prison experiments, 52n. 45
  See also Eichmann experiments
Zimmer, Wendelin, 147, 148
Zion, 134
Zuckerman, Itsak, 131